The Gold Key and the Green Life

By Elizabeth Sutherland

Lent term (1973)
The seer of Kintail (1974)
Hannah hereafter (1976)
The eye of God (1977)
The weeping tree (1980)
Ravens and black rain (1985)

The prophecies of the Brahan Seer
by Alexander Mackenzie, edited and
introduced by Elizabeth Sutherland (1977)

THE GOLD KEY
AND THE GREEN LIFE

Some fantasies and Celtic tales

by
GEORGE MACDONALD
and
FIONA MACLEOD

Collected and edited by
Elizabeth Sutherland

Constable   London

First published in Great Britain 1986
by Constable and Company Limited
10 Orange Street London WC2H 7EG
ISBN 0 09 467110 9
Copyright © 1986 by Elizabeth Sutherland
Set in Linotron Ehrhardt 10 pt by
Rowland Phototypesetting Limited
Bury St Edmunds, Suffolk
Printed in Great Britain by
St Edmundsbury Press
Bury St Edmunds, Suffolk

For Jeremy –
who first introduced me to modern fantasy fiction

Contents

ACKNOWLEDGEMENTS   9
INTRODUCTION   Elizabeth Sutherland   11

PART ONE
THE GOLD KEY

GEORGE MACDONALD   Elizabeth Sutherland   19
THE ENCHANTED FOREST (*Phantastes*)   George MacDonald   33
THE MAGIC MIRROR (*Phantastes*)   George MacDonald   52
A GHOST STORY (*The Portent*)   George MacDonald   68
THE GOLDEN KEY   George MacDonald   83
THE GRAY WOLF   George MacDonald   109
A TRAGEDY OF BONES (*Lilith*)   George MacDonald   115

PART TWO
THE GREEN LIFE

FIONA MACLEOD   Elizabeth Sutherland   131
THE LAST SUPPER   Fiona Macleod   143
THE WASHER OF THE FORD   Fiona Macleod   151
SILK O' THE KINE   Fiona Macleod   163
ULA AND URLA   Fiona Macleod   169
MIRCATH   Fiona Macleod   175
THE LAUGHTER OF SCATHACH THE QUEEN   Fiona Macleod   179
THE FESTIVAL OF THE BIRDS   Fiona Macleod   184
CATHAL OF THE WOODS   Fiona Macleod   190
THE ANOINTED MAN   Fiona Macleod   215

BIBLIOGRAPHY   220

Acknowledgements

I want to thank Konrad Hopkins, Lecturer at Paisley College of Technology, co-director of Wilfion Books, Publishers, and leading authority in Britain on the life and works of William Sharp/Fiona Macleod for sharing with me so generously his wide knowledge and understanding of the writer.

My thanks also go to Robert Lee Wolff, Rolland Hein and Flavia Alaya for enriching my understanding of George MacDonald and William Sharp.

I would also like to thank the George MacDonald Society and the Librarians at Huntly, Dingwall, Inverness and the Mitchell Library in Glasgow, and Kate Bevan Baker, for so kindly supporting my research.

ELIZABETH SUTHERLAND
1986

Introduction

A long time ago, George MacDonald took me for the first time to 'the Back of the North Wind' by way of the fairy world of the imagination. Half a century later, when I first read the Celtic tales of Fiona Macleod, pen-name and feminine persona of William Sharp, I returned.

MacDonald's fairyland is peopled with tree spirits, goblins and wise old women. His fantasy stories – some for adults, others for children – are like paths meandering by sunlit rivers, under silver moons and by fires of flaming roses, which connect with all the other stories in the mind. In contrast, Sharp's other world is esoteric, sea-girdled, green-wooded, peopled with saints and savages and Celtic gods, all conjured up by images and songs which inch open the doors of psychic consciousness that lead into what Sharp called 'the Green Life'. However, both men were – in the fairy and fantasy parts of their work – mythopoeists whose tales do not date, but like copper coins drop into the deep well of the mind to stir the imagination and inspire the soul.

It seems strange to me that two writers with such power to stir and inspire should not be better known to British readers today. Both were established literary figures in the nineteenth century, publishing numerous works of fiction and poetry, and, in addition, Sharp produced volumes of literary criticism and biography. Yet MacDonald, now best known for his children's stories, is remembered chiefly as the inspirer of C. S. Lewis, and by a devoted group who have organized the London-based George MacDonald Society, but in his native Scotland hardly at all; while Sharp/Macleod, an acknowledged leader of the Celtic Revival in Scotland, is remembered for popularizing the name 'Fiona' and in the name of Wilfion Books (Wilfion, from 'Will' combined with 'Fiona', was the identity of his third personality), a small publishers established to honour him in Paisley, his native town in Scotland.

It is in the United States, where both men made successful tours, that MacDonald and Sharp are most appreciated today. Mac-

Donald's romances *Lilith* and *Phantastes* were reprinted in the Adult Fantasy Library by Ballantine Books, New York, in 1969 and 1970 respectively; Robert Lee Wolff's study of his fiction, *The Golden Key*, was published by Yale University Press in 1961; and Rolland Hein, Professor of English at Wheaton College, Illinois, has written several critical articles on him and a scholarly book called *The Harmony Within*, published in 1982. Furthermore, the *Publishers Weekly*, September 1985, stated that MacDonald's theological novels are undergoing a rebirth in the American Christian press, and several biographies of him are in preparation on both sides of the Atlantic.

Sharp's most recent biographer is the American Professor Flavia Alaya, whose *William Sharp – 'Fiona Macleod'* was published by Harvard University Press in 1970. William Halloran of the University of Wisconsin has been preparing an edition of Sharp's letters as well as a critical study of the Macleod fiction. Konrad Hopkins, co-director of Wilfion Books and also an American, has published articles and a booklet on Sharp, and is preparing a biography of him. And a book called *Doubles* by Karl Miller (Oxford University Press, 1985) devotes pages to discussing the 'double as literary persona created and manipulated by Sharp/Fiona Macleod', in the words of one reviewer, a work that perhaps signals a resurgence of interest in Sharp in Great Britain.

My purpose in bringing the two writers to the attention of a new generation of readers is threefold. First, to acknowledge a personal debt. Without MacDonald I might never have reached that Celtic world of the imagination which has so deeply influenced my own writing, while Sharp reminded me that the Gaelic world of nature is still full of mystery and magic for those who have eyes to see. Secondly, to redress in a small way the relative neglect that has befallen both writers, but particularly Sharp, in the history of literature. Finally, to introduce two delightful men and a selection of their fantasy writings in the hope that the reader will ask for more.

It is interesting to speculate, briefly, on the reasons for their relative neglect. Regarding the bulk of their work, it is generally agreed that neither writer is in the first league. Both wrote too much, too quickly, from the need to earn a living. Literary fashions change, and for modern taste their styles are long-winded and sentimental. Moreover, many of MacDonald's straight novels are written for the most part in broad Scots and require perseverance to read. Sharp's apparent deception over the identity of Fiona Macleod has been an abiding embarrassment to students of literature, and the mystery of Fiona has never been and probably never will be fully understood. He was no transvestite or transexual, nor, I believe, a deliberate deceiver. His feminine persona existed at a spiritual level centred deep in his subconscious mind, or, perhaps, within his soul. While he enjoyed the thrill of secrecy, he was also afraid not only of exposure but of the feminine self which seemed at times to possess him. As will be seen, Fiona Macleod was a formidable personality.

Where both writers excel, and deserve to be remembered, is in the world of fantasy, as mythmakers in the Celtic tradition. With MacDonald, the story, with its underlying allegory and symbolism, is of primary importance. With Sharp, the words themselves, like poetry and incantation, contain the magic. Fiona Macleod, who existed and yet did not exist, is the embodiment of Sharp's mythology.

In addition to the fact that both writers have been largely forgotten by the general reading public, and that both wrote fantasies in the Celtic tradition, there are other intriguing points of similarity between the two men.

Both were born in Scotland, though not in the Gaelic Highlands, and both were strongly influenced by their Celtic ancestry. Both were educated at Scottish universities, MacDonald at Aberdeen and Sharp at Glasgow (but he never took a degree). Both left Scotland in their early twenties to find work in London, MacDonald as a tutor and, for a short time, as a minister, Sharp in a bank. Both married devoted, intelligent women, whose support nurtured not only their literary talent but also their frail health. Both men suffered from bouts of illness, which necessitated their seeking warmer, more salubrious climates. Both men frequently moved house in and around London, the south coast and abroad, and both found Italy to be most congenial in climate and culture. Although MacDonald was born in December 1824 and Sharp some thirty years later, in September 1855, they died within three months of each other, MacDonald in September and Sharp in December 1905. MacDonald's ashes were buried at Bordighera in North Italy, and Sharp's body was laid to rest in a hillside grave near Mount Etna in Sicily.

As children, their lives were very different, however. MacDonald's family was poor materially yet rich in relationships which had a strong acknowledged influence on him for the rest of his life. Sharp came from a wealthy manufacturing family who seemed to have little apparent influence on him, with the exception of his sister Mary, who later acted as Fiona Macleod's secretary. On the other hand, both boys were able to roam freely in the Scottish countryside, MacDonald as a farmer's son in the wooded and well-watered glens and hills of Aberdeenshire, Sharp during long summers spent in the Western Highlands and Islands. Although self-exiled from Scotland for many years of their lives, both looked to the land of the Gael as their spiritual home and returned for visits as often as health and funds permitted.

As family men, too, they were different. Both loved children and reverenced youth, but where MacDonald considered himself fortunate to father eleven children, Sharp and his wife looked upon Fiona Macleod as their only child.

Physically, there were some points of similarity. Both were tall, good-looking and bearded, MacDonald a black-haired, blue-eyed Celt, while Sharp was more Viking in appearance, with blond hair, golden beard (which he sometimes shaved off, leaving himself with only a moustache) and light blue eyes. Although both left Scotland when young, they retained their Scottish accents to the end. In character, both were compassionate to an exceptional degree, fun-loving (but both also suffered from periods of depression) and hospitable. Both had a wide, occasionally overlapping circle of friends, which included John Ruskin, D. G. Rossetti and Ernest Rhys. Although I can find no evidence to indicate they ever met, they would certainly have known of each other.

Spiritually, both were deeply religious men. Sharp rejected his Calvinistic background and became a dedicated pagan in the Celtic sense, a nature worshipper and pantheist, a latter-day Druid. MacDonald, on the other hand, rejected his Calvinistic upbringing and became a non-doctrinaire preacher and theologian, a Christian in the broadest sense of the word. Whereas Sharp, in the persona of Fiona Macleod, demonstrated elements of Christianity in his attitude to Catholicism and St Columba, MacDonald exhibited in his fantasy writing what could be considered as elements of pantheism in his declared belief that God was the Father of all life, to be found in nature as certainly, if not so fully, as in Jesus Christ.

Both men produced about fifty volumes each. Among MacDonald's books were three prose fantasies for adults and eight allegories and collections of fairy tales for children, a few of which remain in print, such as *At the Back of the North Wind, The Princess and the Goblin,* and *The Princess and Curdie* in the single-volume Octopus edition, 1979, while *Phantastes* and *Lilith* are seldom out of print for long. These fantasies are seen today as his most important works. As Fiona Macleod, Sharp wrote three fantasy romances, several collections of short stories (one for children), dramas, poetry, runes and songs, and a short study of the spiritual history of Iona, which is the only one of his works currently in print.

Throughout their lives both men demonstrated a compassionate and practical concern for women and their position in society. MacDonald was particularly involved with their education, while Sharp took an active interest in the women's rights movements of his day. As writers, both men tended to idealize women. MacDonald's mother died when he was eight and his fantasy writings are full of wise women and nurturers who help the narrator in his search for the mother figure, the white lady, pure goddess, to be found only in death. His life may be seen as a long search, an eternal yearning for the life beyond life which sheltered his beloved dead. Sharp's idealized attitude probably originated when, as a sensitive child, he first witnessed and identified with the suffering of his mother in childbirth. Woman and her capacity for endurance and tenderness induced in Sharp a belief that in the next incarnation of the deity, woman would be the saviour of mankind. She is his white lady, glimpsed in ecstatic visions, symbol of the Green Life, of Paradise itself. Sharp's abnormal restlessness, his continual moving from place to place, mirrors his inner search for the Green Life so tantalizingly just out of sight.

Perhaps the most startling similarity between the two men is in their attitude to death. Unafraid, both were obsessed with the life after life, seeing death as essentially beneficent and, as Sharp wrote, 'a vision of life in some divine new birth'. Yet at the end death was to cheat them both. Sharp died at the early age of fifty, leaving a considerable body of work uncompleted, and sadly MacDonald was left stranded in the shadow-land of old age, speechless and withdrawn for the last five or six years of his long life.

As has been seen, the many points of similarity between the lives of the two men are largely coincidental, and though their attitudes are surprisingly alike in some respects, they were shared by other Victorian writers. George and William were not clones nor were they strictly speaking contemporaries. Some may think I have taken an unforgivable liberty in bringing them together in this book. Yet I believe that had they known each other, they would have been friends. As a young man, Sharp would have fitted happily into the MacDonald family gatherings, and MacDonald, who loved the young, would have joyfully welcomed the enthusiastic, sensitive young poet into his home. Their shared Scottishness, their creative talents, their kindly natures, and their Celtic love of the natural world would have surely and graciously bonded them together.

ELIZABETH SUTHERLAND

Part One

THE GOLD KEY

George MacDonald, photographed by Lewis Carroll

George MacDonald

'Countless black carriages drawn by black horses with postilions and all draped in black velvet with nodding plumes.'

This, in 1826, was the two-year-old George MacDonald's first conscious memory of the Duke of Gordon's funeral procession as it passed on its six weeks' journey from London through the little gray town of Huntly on its way to Elgin in the north-east of Scotland. A prophetic image, for death by tuberculosis – the 'constant attendant' as he called it – was to haunt his long eventful life.

When he was only eight, his beautiful Highland mother died of the disease and so in time did his mother-in-law, his father, three brothers, stepsister and four of his own children. Although as a child he led a healthy outdoor existence, he was never strong, plagued throughout his life with pleurisy, bronchitis, asthma, eczema and bleeding from the lungs. A month before his marriage and shortly after he had accepted a call to be minister in Arundel, he haemorrhaged dangerously, and perhaps for the first time came face to face with the fact of his own decease. His wedding gift to his bride was a long poem, *Love Me, Beloved*, which is obsessed with thoughts and visions of death and the importance of loving now so that when dead the lovers may still be together.

'I wis' we were a' deid,' he was to say wistfully as a boy, for in heaven there could be no more separation by death.

Extraordinarily, his son Greville records 'a fact that should not be forgotten that he had scarcely ever any fear of death, and none when it faced him.'

To his own father, George wrote, 'Schiller says "Death cannot be an evil because it is universal." God would not let it be the law of His universe if it were what it looks to us.'

'I think of death,' he wrote in his novel *David Elginbrod*, 'as the first pulse of the new strength shaking itself free from the mouldy remnants of earth-garments, that it may begin in freedom the new life that grows out of the old. The caterpillar dies into the butterfly . . .'

Although throughout his life, the spectre of death lurked close, it kept him waiting at the end. Worn out mentally and physically, MacDonald spent the last five of his eighty-one years silent and withdrawn, waiting with intense patience for the event which, he believed, was birth into more life. All his major fantasies echo this theme.

But death was not the only influence in the life of George MacDonald that was to lead to the poet, theologian and preacher, the essayist and lecturer, novelist, mythmaker and allegorist, author of fifty-two works, being called by G. K. Chesterton 'one of the three or four greatest men of the nineteenth century'.

Most of what we know about him is contained in a full and affectionate biography, *George MacDonald and His Wife*, written by his eldest son, Greville MacDonald, MD, and published by Allen and Unwin in 1924.

Greville tells us that George was born on 10 December 1824 in Huntly, forty miles north-west of Aberdeen and was raised on a small farm some mile and a half from the town square. In 1845, he graduated with prizes in science and chemistry from King's College, Aberdeen, from which university he was later to receive an honorary LL D. After tutoring in London for a couple of years he entered Highbury Theological College and though he did not finish the course, he was ordained in his first and only charge at the Congregational Church, Arundel, in 1850. Three years later, his spiritual integrity and independence of mind forced him to resign, so he moved to Manchester to be near his brother, Charles, and his friends, Alexander John Scott, Principal of Owens College and Henry Septimus Sutton, a religious poet. There he continued to preach, lecture and write until the climate, poverty and ill-health forced him to move south. The rest of his life was spent in various houses in and near London and the south coast with winters abroad mainly in Italy and latterly at Casa Coraggio, Bordighera, a large purpose-built house which he designed and built with the help of contributions from his many friends and admirers.

His skill in public speaking brought him an evening lectureship in Literature at King's College, London, a professorship of English Literature at Bedford College, and a spectacularly successful lecture tour of America. 'Unsoundness' of doctrine prevented him from winning the Chair of Rhetoric and Belles Lettres at Edinburgh University in 1865, but at the express wish of Queen Victoria he received a Civil List pension in 1877.

In 1851 he married Louisa, second of six daughters of James Powell, a wealthy leather merchant and strict Congregationalist. George and Louisa were to have eleven children and a supremely happy marriage. Louisa died in 1902 shortly after their golden wedding and was buried in the Protestant cemetery, Bordighera. George died three years later on 18 December 1905 at Ashtead in Surrey and his ashes were buried beside the body of his wife.

In 1855 and 1857 he published his first books of poetry which were well received, and *Phantastes: A Faerie Romance* followed in 1858. Thereafter his chief works were divided between stories of fairy-fantasy and factual theological novels most of which were intensely Scottish in language, characterization and humour. *Lilith*, his last adult fantasy and his penultimate book, was published in 1895.

His literary reputation, his hospitable nature and likeable personality brought him a host of intimate friends in every walk of life. Although harassed by poverty most of his life, he kept open house for relatives and orphans, students and radicals, writers and theologians together with the humblest of Octavia Hill's poor tenantry from Marylebone – sometimes a hundred at a time – in The Retreat, his Hammersmith home (later to be occupied by William Morris and renamed by him Kelmscott House), and again in Casa Coraggio where his house guests and the British colony abroad mingled with the Italian peasantry on equal footing.

The great of the day counted themselves his friends. Ruskin confided his relationship with Rose La Touche; Lewis Carroll – Uncle Dodgson to his children – gave him the Alice stories to read in manuscript. Lady Noel Byron, widow of the poet, was his generous patron. Mark Twain contemplated collaborating with him on a novel. Other close friends included the Pre-Raphaelites, Robert Browning, Lord Tennyson, the Carlyles, Matthew Arnold, Thackeray and Dickens; and in America, Emerson, Longfellow, R. W. Gilder, J. G. Whittier and Oliver Wendell Holmes. Theologians and social reformers, among them the Christian Socialist the Reverend F. D. Maurice who was eventually to bring him into the Church of England, all found a sympathetic welcome at his board where George was both chief and bard in the Highland sense.

Above all George MacDonald was a Celt.

'Surely it is one of the worst signs of a man to turn his back upon the rock whence he was hewn,' he once wrote in a letter to the *Spectator* concerning his background. That rock was Gaeldom and all that it implied; the clan system that bred fierce loyalty and devotion to freedom and justice within the discipline of the family; the bardic tradition of story-telling, music and romance; the druidic belief in magic, seership and the world of faerie; an intense devotion to the sea, the clan land and the wilderness, and above all an obsession with the world beyond the grave. His writings are full of the symbols of Celtic folklore, ravens and cats, witches and elves, caverns and castles, second sight and ghosts.

His appearance proclaimed his Highland love of finery. Sir William D. Geddes, a fellow student at Aberdeen, remembers 'the radiance of a tartan coat he wore – the most dazzling in dress I ever saw a student wear, but characteristic of the young minstrel'.

Greville records that all his life his 'father's dress was generally more or less a protest against the ugly and unreasonable.' Six foot tall and broad-shouldered, strikingly handsome with astonishing blue eyes, he drew admiring crowds as he strode down a London street in full Highland dress with his plaid fastened to his shoulder with a topaz. He liked to design and adorn his own waistcoats with long rows of gilt buttons. Sometimes he wore a black velvet jacket, sometimes a scarlet cloak over a suit of white serge or flannel. He loved 'the colour, glimmer and star-shine of jewels'. A Chicago journalist wrote of 'his diamond pins, jewelled shirt-studs, massive watch-chain, daintily-shod feet and Christlike countenance' all worn without vanity but with immense enjoyment. He grew a beard, black in youth, white in age, and the sculptor, Alexander Munro, watching him come indoors on a windy day with his 'thick curly hair blowing all about him' modelled a medallion of him on the spot which was later cast in bronze.

Descended from the MacDonalds of Glencoe, his great-grandfather, Gaelic-speaking and Catholic, escaped with his infant son, Charles Edward, from the bloody aftermath of Culloden to take refuge in the caves of Portsoy where he eventually became town piper. Charles Edward was raised a Protestant, earned for himself a partnership in one of the largest bleaching fields in Huntly, opened a thread-spinning factory and a bank. Three of his four sons, including George MacDonald senior, leased the farm of Upper Pirriesmill from the Duke of Gordon, and it was here that the young George, second of six sons, spent most of his childhood.

That farmhouse still stands, plain yet pleasingly proportioned in its ancient sundialed garden. George's attic window still overlooks green and windswept hills. The old bleaching fields, now crossed by the railway, still stretch down to the coiled and wooded River Bogie where the MacDonald boys once played.

Icy-wintered, leafy-summered, the countryside profoundly influenced the sensitive young boy, while farm life instilled in him a lifelong reverence and tenderness for animals. 'Clothes may have been shabby and money scarce,' Greville writes 'but there were cattle in the byre, horses in the stable, wild bees' nests in the stone dykes whose honeycombs eaten like bread were a priceless joy; there were pools for swimming and a boat for boating ... fishing with rod and net ... Kelpies in the dark pots of mountain-burnies, or the still blacker pools of peat cuttings on the moor.' And at night at the hearth there were songs and all the old stories full of magic and mystery.

Probably the strongest influence in George MacDonald's life was his father. Greville records that although his business enterprises were blighted with misfortune, his grandfather 'was as fine a man as might be seen in four parishes, of noble presence, well-built and robust, a "wyse" (wise) man. He was patient and generous; finely humorous; of strong literary tastes and profound religious convictions.'

He was certainly courageous. In 1825 when his left knee joint was found to be tubercular and had to be amputated, he refused the anaesthetizing dram of whisky and to have his face covered. Only when 'the knife transfixed the flesh did he turn his face away and ejaculated a faint sibilant "Whiff".'

During the potato famine his wooden leg and his sense of humour got him out of an awkward situation. The townsfolk accused him of hoarding grain so they built a bonfire in the town square and were about to set fire to his effigy when suddenly he appeared among them. Silencing their angry cries he shouted, 'Bide a wee, lads. Ye've fastened the timmer [timber] leg to the wrang hurdie [hip].' The crowd laughed and later cheered when he showed them his empty barn.

George revered his father. 'How careful my dear father is of everyone,' he once wrote to his wife, and again, 'I think there is scarcely one other manly straightforward man to equal my father.' With his sons he was firm but understanding, generous and sensitive until his death in 1858 when George was to write to Louisa, 'You would almost fancy he had been a kind of chief of the clan ... I am glad my father has got through. I love him more than ever.'

It is arguable that a child's first understanding of God comes from his relationship with his father. If George MacDonald senior was the most important earthly figure in his son's youth, God, his Heavenly Father was undoubtedly the most abiding and controlling influence throughout his long life.

Scottish Calvinism which included the doctrine of salvation for the elect and damnation to everlasting hell for the rest, was the tenet of the Missionar Kirk – the Congregational Church – to which the MacDonald family belonged. George saw Calvinism at its best in his father who trusted totally in a God who was the Good Shepherd of his flock, and at its worst in his formidable paternal grandmother Isabella who was haunted until her death at ninety-two by a belief in the reality of hell and her need to protect her family at all costs from damnation. She was convinced that her eldest son who had fled to America to avoid his debtors was beyond redemption, and that it was sinful for her to continue to love him. The young George, witnessing both his grandmother's agony over her own 'lost sheep' and also his human father's devotion to himself and his brothers, came to an understanding of the love of God that was to be the cornerstone of his life, and at the same time get him into constant theological trouble.

The idea of eternal damnation was as hateful to him as was the belief that any soul in heaven could rejoice while his brothers suffered in hell. If a man could feel such compassion, how much more must a loving God agonize over one soul left in hell. 'I well remember,' he wrote in *Weighed and Wanting*, 'feeling as a child that I did not care for God to love me if he did not love everybody.' It was not that George disbelieved in hell. Rather it was in his concept of hell that he differed from the Congregationalists of his day. To him, hell was not a place of physical torment, but rather of mental and spiritual agony. Nor was it confined to the next world. Hell could be experienced here and now. Life on earth could be seen as hell from which man 'died' into true life. Nor did he see hell as everlasting and outwith the reach of God. He believed with Blake that 'God is within and without, even in the depths of hell,' entirely loving, just and trustworthy, never ceasing to work for the salvation of souls, in this world and the next.

MacDonald also believed that literary and artistic talent came directly from God to be used in the same way as a sermon to evangelize. Thus when he exchanged his pulpit at Arundel for a literary life, he was not abandoning the ministry of the word. Far from it. He was still the preacher, believing that the written word had equal power with speech to inspire good works. With every sentence he wrote, he sought at conscious and unconscious levels to convince readers of his own religious beliefs.

Although the ministry was not George's first choice of career – as a boy he wanted to go to sea – nor yet his second which was to be a doctor had family funds permitted, he was a born preacher. Greville humorously recalls his first boyhood attempt on the farmhouse kitchen table. When the servant flicked at him with a dishcloth 'he turned upon her in righteous anger as he set straight the improvised bands about his neck: "div ye no ken fan ye're speakin' til a meenister, Bell. Ye's no fleg [frighten] awa' the Rev Georgie MacDonald as gin he war a buzzin' flee [fly]. Losh, woman, nest to Dr Chaumers [Chalmers] he's the grandest preacher in a' Scotland."'

George's short ministry in Arundel was successful as far as the poor, the sick and the young were concerned for he was a devoted pastor but 'his flaming words against mammon-worship and cruelty and self-seeking' were resented by the more affluent members of his congregation. He was finding the same narrow outlook among the Congregationalists at Arundel that he had hated in Calvinist Scotland. In 1851 he wrote to his father, 'I firmly believe people have hitherto been a great deal too much taken up with doctrine and far too little with practice ... We are far too anxious to be defined and to have finished well-polished sharp-edged systems, forgetting that the more perfect a theory about the infinite, the surer it is to be wrong ... I am neither Arminian nor Calvinist. To no system would I subscribe.'

His views on Sabbath observance and compulsory church attendance, his hope that animals might have a part in heaven and that the heathen might be given another chance after death, led to accusations from his deacons that his doctrine was unsound and that he was tainted with German liberalism, so they reduced his stipend in the hope that he would resign. A year later in order to heal the breach that now existed among his flock, he left Arundel and the full-time ministry, though he continued to preach when asked to do so.

The accusation of 'Germanism' was not, perhaps, without some foundation. The works of Shakespeare, Milton, Spenser, Bunyan, Blake, Swedenborg, Boehme and William Law all played an important part in influencing the young MacDonald. During his student years he discovered the German mystical and romantic writers and it is obvious that E. T. W. Hoffman whose *Golden Pot* he read and reread with enjoyment, and Friedrich von Hardenberg better known as Novalis, were strong influences on his literary life. He identified more closely with Novalis whose tragic life seemed in so many ways to parallel his own. Both were brought up in strict religious homes, both had tuberculosis – Novalis died of the disease at the age of twenty-nine – and both were much preoccupied with death, goodness and the ubiquity of God. Novalis's theory that all life is connected, that 'animals, plants and stones, stars and breezes are all part of humanity', exactly matched MacDonald's own beliefs and both sought to convey those beliefs within the framework of myth and *Märchen* (fairy-tale). During his own severe illness at the start of his ministry at Arundel, MacDonald translated and printed privately twelve of the *Spiritual Songs* of Novalis. He introduced *Phantastes* with a lengthy quotation from Novalis which describes in detail what he meant by 'fairy tale'.

'... A fairy tale is like a dream-picture without coherence. A collection of wonderful things and events ... The world of the Märchen is the world that is entirely opposite to the world of truth and is yet just as similar to it as is Chaos to the completed created universe ...'

The last chapter of *Phantastes* is headed with an even more significant quotation (also repeated elsewhere in his works) which sums up not only the content of the book but also MacDonald's strong belief: 'Our life is no dream; but it ought to become one, and perhaps will.'

So far it would seem that the three aspects of fatherhood – human, divine and a combination of the two as seen in the Celtic clan system where the chief is both father and king, divinely inaugurated – were the major influences in MacDonald's life. It could also be said that just as George MacDonald senior represented all that was Christian, courageous and generous to his son, so that son became the most affectionate of fathers to his own eleven children. He learned the art of fatherhood from an expert.

Yet in his works of fantasy, the male figure dwindles to insignificance, and woman dominates. Women as nurturers and sages, as fickle and predatory, or pure and perfect, guide and govern the narrator at every turn of the plot. Their prototypes are all to be found at important stages in MacDonald's life.

Dead before she could become less than perfect to her eight-year-old son, his mother, Helen, left three relics which George treasured in a secret drawer of his cabinet. These were a lock of her golden-brown hair, a silver-set seal with the name 'George' engraved on a red stone which had been her wedding gift to her husband, and a letter. This was written by his mother, weak from childbirth and tuberculosis, to her mother-in-law, the formidable Isabella, who – in her domineering way – insisted that the infant George be weaned immediately.

'Do you know I was almost angry on Saturday when your letter came to my dear G. about weaning our dear little Boy – for I was very unwilling to do it – and I always thought I would have been able to give him three months at least. But O! my heart was very sore when I saw that you, my dear husband . . . and indeed all the rest – were so earnest about it – that I was forced to begin that morning. And he has not got anything from me since. But I cannot help my heart being very much grieved for him yet, for he has not forgot it: poor little fellow he is behaving wonderfully well as yet. He cryed desperate a while the first night but he has cryed very little since and I hope the worst is over . . .'

Although George was sent to a wet-nurse and later when Helen died was in the care of a loving aunt until his father remarried a delightful stepmother, and although his father gave his sons the best of care, Greville records, 'He rarely caressed his boys: it was not the fashion in those days to do so; nor could he make up to them for the loss of their mother.' Robert Lee Wolff in his scholarly study of the works of George MacDonald, *The Golden Key*, believes that his abrupt weaning followed by the long illness and death of his mother wounded George for life. It was the mother figure he desperately sought. This bred in him a threefold guilt that he did not love his father enough, that he had been given no cause by his father to feel deprived or rebellious and that try as he might he could not become the perfect son. Therefore, secretly he hated his father.

C. S. Lewis, on the other hand, rejects the Freudian approach taken by Wolff. He sees George's relationship with his father as 'almost perfect' and dismisses any thought of psychological conflict between the two.

The truth lies, perhaps, somewhere between these points of view. Certainly George idealized his mother and her influence on his inner life was profound. Because – for him – she was beautiful and good and dead, then death and the life beyond must be good enough to contain her. George too had to be good not just out of gratitude to his father, but because only by leading a good life did he stand a chance of seeing his beloved mother again, who was to be found not only in heaven but also in the earth itself, that great mother of us all into whose womb all finally return.

Anodos, the hero of *Phantastes*, says from his grave, 'Now that I lay in her bosom, the whole earth, and each of her many births, was as a body to me, at my will. I seemed to feel the great heart of the mother beating into mine, and feeding me with her own life, her own essential being and nature.' But the story does not end there. Anodos rises from his grave in 'a single large primrose' which is plucked by his beloved White Lady and put in her bosom, again the symbol of motherhood. When the flower dies he rises to the clouds where he realizes 'that it is by loving, and not by being loved, that one can come nearest the soul of another'. This is the lesson that Anodos takes back to earth. This was the creed by which MacDonald lived.

Works of fantasy full of dreams and symbolism that come straight from the subconscious mind of the author lay themselves open to psychological interpretation that can be arrogant, belittling and misleading. Modern psychologists have a humbler approach to the mind of man, realizing that deprivation, separation and grief, all of which were experienced by MacDonald, do not necessarily lead to hatred, or guilt, or depression, although he too had periods of doubt and misery. Rather, MacDonald was able to work out his anxieties in his fantasies and at the same time learn from them a high spiritual awareness and greater capacity for love.

If MacDonald's boyhood was wounded by the loss of his mother, his early manhood may have suffered a cut no less painful at the hands of a woman whose name is unknown.

While a student, George took a holiday job, Greville records, 'in a certain castle or mansion in the far North, the locality of which I have failed to trace' but which might have been Thurso Castle or possibly Dunbeath Castle. There he first came into contact with the world of literature outside the bounds of academic scholarship, and the effect on him was profound.

'Now I was in my element,' he wrote as the narrator in *The Portent* who also found work in a library. 'The very outside of a book had a charm to me. It was a kind of sacrament – an outward and visible sign of an inward and spiritual grace; as, indeed, what on God's earth is not? . . . I found a perfect set of our poets . . . I began to nibble at that portion of the collection which belonged to the sixteenth century... many romances of a very marvellous sort... I likewise came upon a whole nest of the German classics... Happening to be a tolerable reader of German, I found in these volumes a mine of wealth inexhaustible.'

Wolff, from his understanding of MacDonald's fiction, suggests that he fell in love with a daughter or member of the household. No doubt she was beautiful and found MacDonald equally attractive, but she had no intention of continuing an affair with the son of a poor farmer. As a result, George's pride in his Celtic blood was as bruised as his pride in his manhood. She was to become the source of all the wicked women, the jilts and flirts and deceivers epitomized by the Alder Maid in *Phantastes*, that appear throughout his fiction, and as MacDonald aged, so too did she to become the cruel mother culminating in *Lilith*, Adam's first wife, whose hatred led her to destroy her own children.

This experience – and it is generally agreed that MacDonald suffered some sort of emotional or spiritual crisis at the castle – was to give MacDonald on the one hand a permanent distrust of the upper classes in general, and at the same time a touching need to belong. Anodos in *Phantastes* and Vane in *Lilith* and Campbell in *The Portent* are all nobly born. On the positive side, his personal rejection gave him a great tenderness for and understanding of the poor and despised in Victorian society.

Apart from the woman in the library (who may not have existed), MacDonald's experience of women was generally good. His indomitable grandmother who taught herself to read at the age of sixty, his devoted aunt, Christina Mackay, his beloved stepmother, Margaret McColl, who, Greville writes, 'took the place of mother in the hearts of both father and boys; indeed my father owed to her everything that the most devoted of mothers can give,' all played their part in shaping the writer and the man. Formidable grandmothers, nurses and wise maternal figures abound in his fantasies, but undoubtedly the woman who played the greatest part in his adult life, who was to be his lover, nurse and friend, was his wife.

He chose well. Louisa illuminated his life. Intelligent with a sense of humour and a strong talent for music and drama, she was also pretty, slim and perfectly proportioned with a tiny waist. One of her sisters wrote of her, 'the house was always dull when she was away: she was the gay influence. Like the twinkle of her wonderful eyes, she brightened all around her; they could always and at once see the ridiculous in everyone and every situation.' She was to need every ounce of her gaiety and humour, for life with eleven children to raise on a pitiful income, with constant illness, separation and house removals, was never easy. Yet the marriage was strong, for Louisa was in sympathy with all George's ideals, his admirer, protector and lover to the end.

A visitor to the family in 1858 gives this vivid pen picture of the family.

'I was delightfully received by a strikingly handsome young man and a most kind lady, who made me feel at once at home. There were five children at that time, all beautifully behaved and going about the house without troubling anyone . . . I was much struck by the way in which they carried on their lives with one another. At a certain time in the afternoon you would, on going upstairs to the drawing room, see on the floor several bundles – each one containing a child! On being spoken to, they said, so happily and peacefully, "We are resting," that the intruder felt she must immediately disappear. No nurse was with them. One word from the father or mother was sufficient to bring instant attention . . . In the evenings, when the children were all in bed, Mr MacDonald would be writing in his study – *Phantastes*, it was – and Mrs MacDonald would go down and sit with her husband, when he would read to her what he had been writing; and I would hear them discussing it on their return to the drawing room. To hear him read Browning's *Saul* with his gracious and wonderful power was a thing I shall never forget. Mrs MacDonald's energy and courage were untiring and her capabilities very unusual.'

Louisa shared with George a great love for acting and charades. It was she who later adapted *Pilgrim's Progress* as a play for the family with George as Mr Greatheart and their eldest daughter, Lilia, brilliant in the part of Christiana. The family financial situation was so critical that Louisa decided to give professional performances which were popular and well-attended, but not all of the family approved. George himself disliked seeing his wife and children – apart from the talented Lilia – take the stage, but he saw it as Louisa's interpretation of God's will, and her way of relieving him from 'the intolerable weariness' of continually writing and lecturing.

From Louisa, George learned how the love and unselfishness of a woman can affect the soul of a man, how the mystery of married love can reflect the mystery of the love of God. One of their few disagreements was over the publication of *Lilith*, a book Louisa detested for its startling imagery. Both agreed to let Greville arbitrate and when he declared it to be enthralling, Louisa gave in, thus fulfilling George's tongue-in-cheek recipe for the perfect marriage. 'I was law, she was grace. But grace often yielded to law, and law sometimes yielded to grace' (*The Seaboard Parish*). His last story, *Far Above Rubies*, about a struggling author and his supportive wife, which appeared in the Christmas edition of *The Sketch* in 1898, is a tender tribute to Louisa. When, close to eighty, slim and pretty to the end, she died, his children dared not tell their father at first. When they did so, he wept bitterly.

All his life MacDonald loved young people and was at his best with children. J. M. Bulloch quotes him as saying, 'He who will be a man and will not be a child, must – he cannot help himself – become a little man, a dwarf.' He believed that 'only God can be perfectly abandonedly simple and devoted . . . It is his childlikeness that makes him our God and Father.'

He never lost his own child-heart and fascination for fairyland. A hypnotic story-teller, he also enjoyed the fun of family life. Greville remembered 'the high tides at Bude when the south-west wind brought furious white-maned sea-horses scrambling over the sea-wall into the haven. My father, happy as his boys in dodging these drenching smotherers, would, with Maurice and Bernard, ages three and two, one under each arm, race across it to the Chapel-rock, and sometimes half up to his knees in the foamy water.' Sir Johnston Forbes-Robertson remembered the children's parties, 'how he used to cover himself with a skin rug and pretend to be a bear, to the great delight of us all!'

His children's fairy allegories have survived. Best known and most often republished are *At the Back of the North Wind* (1871), *The Princess and the Goblin* (1872), and *The Princess and Curdie* (1883), unforgettable stories to those lucky enough to have been brought up on them. Although no child was expected to look behind the fairy adventure and find the message that salvation and goodness go hand-in-hand, and that the only enemy to salvation is selfishness, the feel of the books is right, the taste after all those years is still wholesome.

As a user of words, George MacDonald is not generally considered to be in the first league of poets or novelists. He wrote too quickly and too much from the necessity to feed his family. He preached too obviously and his prose is often long-winded and sentimental. G. K. Chesterton states, 'he wrote nothing empty; but he wrote much that is rather too full.'

It is as a mythmaker that he excels, for in such works the story is all-important. Where action and characterization in straight novels appeal to the senses and the intellect, the landscapes and images of myth reach down to the deep dark pool of the subconscious, which is the source of our own dreams and creativity. To walk in the forests of *Phantastes* or the wastelands of *Lilith* is to enter a world that is as new as childhood and as old as time, as unknown as tomorrow yet as familiar as a fireside, frightening as werewolves and vampires, comforting as a caress. *The Golden Key*, which appeals to adults and children alike, may be read as the adventures of two children in fairyland and understood as the journey made by man and woman through life into death and beyond. The power of MacDonald's myths can liven the circuit of a dormant memory and spark into light a dulled imagination. C. S. Lewis was transformed by them and W. H. Auden recognized in them 'a very considerable literary gift'.

'Corage! God Mend Al!' – his anagram of the name George MacDonald – became the family motto. It is apt in its reflection of the great Celt's creed. Above all, George MacDonald was a courageous man in the face of illness, poverty and death, and in his attempts to moderate Calvinism, enlighten souls and to practise his high ideals. The role of Mr Greatheart which he played so powerfully on Louisa's stage, he fulfilled in life.

E.S.

The Enchanted Forest

George MacDonald called *Phantastes* a Faerie Romance because it is primarily a search for love as symbolized by the beloved mother he lost as a child to death. The hero, Anodos, ('pathless' according to Wolff) may be seen as a self-portrait of the author who is introduced to Fairyland (Phantastes or the world of the imagination) on his twenty-first birthday by a tiny woman who hints that she is his fairy grandmother. She materializes from a secret drawer in Anodos's secretary, the same drawer no doubt in which MacDonald kept the few precious relics of his mother.

Anodos spends twenty-one earth days away, a life- and death-time in Fairyland where he has many adventures each of which represents different stages and difficulties encountered in real life. When he returns he has learned that 'all love will, one day, meet with its return', and that 'good is always coming'. C. S. Lewis wrote that it was the goodness pervading *Phantastes* that was 'to convert, even to baptize' his imagination which in due course created great fantasies such as the Narnia books for children and *The Great Divorce*. It is that same goodness which reaches down into our hearts today.

In the following edited excerpt which I have called *The Enchanted Forest*, Anodos comes into contact with the three types of women who dominate MacDonald's fiction. The Beech Tree represents true woman and true wife, the wise, unselfish nurturer who gives of herself to protect her lover or her child. The White Lady, symbol of purity, goodness and divine love, is brought to life by the incantations of Anodos the poet, but when his love becomes selfish and tainted with lust, he loses her and evokes instead the Alder Maid, symbol of indecency and deceit, who, aping the White Lady, leads him close to spiritual death represented by the gross and heartless Ash.

The landscapes of *Phantastes*, the fairy wise women, the tree spirits and talking creatures, the power of incantation, the magic and the terror are all part of the familiar world of Celtic folklore. The quality of the book, its geniality, innocence and optimism, come straight from the store of MacDonald's own particular gold.

E.S.

The trees, which were far apart where I entered, giving free passage to level rays of the sun, closed rapidly as I advanced, so that ere long their crowded stems barred the sunlight out, forming as it were a thick grating between me and the east. I seemed to be advancing towards a second midnight. In the midst of the intervening twilight, however, before I entered what appeared to be the darkest portion of the forest, I saw a country maiden coming towards me from its very depths. She did not seem to observe me, for she was apparently intent upon a bunch of wild flowers which she carried in her hand. I could hardly see her face; for, though she came right towards me, she never looked up. But when we met, instead of passing, she turned and walked alongside of me for a few yards, still keeping her face downwards, and busied with her flowers. She spoke rapidly, however, all the time, in a low tone, as if talking to herself, but evidently addressing the purport of her words to me. She seemed afraid of being observed by some lurking foe. 'Trust the Oak,' said she; 'trust the Oak, and the Elm, and the great Beech. Take care of the Birch, for though she is honest, she is too young not to be changeable. But shun the Ash and the Alder; for the Ash is an ogre – you will know him by his thick fingers; and the Alder will smother you with her web of hair, if you let her near you at night.' All this was uttered without pause or alteration of tone. Then she turned suddenly and left me, walking still with the same unchanging gait. I could not conjecture what she meant, but satisfied myself with thinking that it would be time enough to find out her meaning when there was need to make use of her warning; and that the occasion would reveal the admonition . . .

Before noon, I fancied I saw a thin blue smoke rising amongst the stems of larger trees in front of me; and soon I came to an open spot of ground in which stood a little cottage, so built that the stems of four great trees formed its corners, while their branches met and intertwined over its roof, heaping a great cloud of leaves over it, up towards the heavens. I wondered at finding a human dwelling in this neighbourhood; and yet it did not look altogether human, though sufficiently so to encourage me to expect some sort of food. Seeing no door, I went round to the other side, and there I found one, wide open. A woman sat beside it, preparing some vegetables for dinner. This was homely and comforting. As I came near, she looked up, and seeing me, showed no surprise, but bent her head again over her work, and said in a low tone:

'Did you see my daughter?'

'I believe I did,' said I. 'Can you give me something to eat, for I am very hungry.'

'With pleasure,' she replied, in the same tone; 'but do not say anything more, till you come into the house, for the Ash is watching us.'

Having said this, she rose and led the way ino the cottage; which, I now saw, was built of the stems of small trees set closely together, and was furnished with rough chairs and tables, from which even the bark had not been removed . . .

Here she placed some bread and some milk before me, with a kindly apology for the homeliness of the fare, with which, however, I was in no humour to quarrel. I now thought it time to try to get some explanation of the strange words both of her daughter and herself.

'What did you mean by speaking so about the Ash?'

She rose and looked out of the little window. My eyes followed her; but as the window was too small to allow anything to be seen from where I was sitting, I rose and looked over her shoulder. I had just time to see, across the open space, on the edge of the denser forest, a single large ash-tree, whose foliage showed bluish, amidst the truer green of the other trees around it; when she pushed me back with an expression of impatience and terror, and then almost shut out the light from the window by setting up a large old book in it.

'In general,' said she, recovering her composure, 'there is no danger in the daytime, for then he is sound asleep; but there is something unusual going on in the woods; there must be some solemnity among the fairies tonight, for all the trees are restless, and although they cannot come awake, they see and hear in their sleep.'

'But what danger is to be dreaded from him?'

Instead of answering the question, she went again to the window and looked out, saying she feared the fairies would be interrupted by foul weather, for a storm was brewing in the west.

'And the sooner it grows dark, the sooner the Ash will be awake,' added she . . .

At this instant, a grey cat rushed in like a demon, and disappeared in a hole in the wall.

'There, I told you!' said the woman.

'But what of the ash-tree?' said I, returning once more to the subject. Here, however, the young woman, whom I had met in the morning, entered. A smile passed between the mother and daughter;

and then the latter began to help her mother in little household duties.

'I should like to stay here till the evening,' I said; 'and then go on my journey, if you will allow me.'

'You are welcome to do as you please; only it might be better to stay all night, than risk the dangers of the wood then. Where are you going?'

'Nay, that I do not know,' I replied; 'but I wish to see all that is to be seen, and therefore I should like to start just at sundown.'

'You are a bold youth, if you have any idea of what you are daring; but a rash one, if you know nothing about it; and, excuse me, you do not seem very well informed about the country and its manners. However, no one comes here but for some reason, either known to himself or to those who have charge of him; so you shall do just as you wish.'

Accordingly I sat down, and feeling rather tired, and disinclined for further talk, I asked leave to look at the old book which still screened the window. The woman brought it to me directly, but not before taking another look towards the forest, and then drawing a white blind over the window. I sat down opposite to it by the table, on which I laid the great old volume, and read. It contained many wondrous tales of Fairy Land, and olden times, and the Knights of King Arthur's table. I read on and on, till the shades of the afternoon began to deepen; for in the midst of the forest it gloomed earlier than in the open country . . .

Here a low hurried cry from my hostess caused me to look up from the book, and I read no more.

'Look there!' she said; 'look at his fingers!'

Just as I had been reading in the book, the setting sun was shining through a cleft in the clouds piled up in the west; and a shadow as of a large distorted hand, with thick knobs and humps on the fingers, so that it was much wider across the fingers than across the undivided part of the hand, passed slowly over the little blind, and then as slowly returned in the opposite direction.

'He is almost awake, mother; and greedier than usual tonight.'

'Hush, child; you need not make him more angry with us than he is; for you do not know how soon something may happen to oblige us to be in the forest after nightfall.'

'But you are in the forest,' said I; 'how is it that you are safe here?'

'He dares not come nearer than he is now,' she replied; 'for any of those four oaks, at the corners of our cottage, would tear him to pieces: they are our friends. But he stands there and makes awful faces at us sometimes, and stretches out his long arms and fingers, and tries to kill us with fright; for, indeed, that is his favourite way of doing. Pray, keep out of his way tonight.' . . .

The woman and I continued the conversation for a few minutes longer . . . But now the daughter returned with the news, that the Ash had just gone away in a south-westerly direction; and, as my course seemed to lie eastward, she hoped I should be in no danger of meeting him if I departed at once . . .

By this time, my hostess was quite anxious that I should be gone. So, with warm thanks for their hospitality, I took my leave, and went my way through the little garden towards the forest . . .

Here and there, whole mighty trees glowed with an emitted phosphorescent light. You could trace the very course of the great roots in the earth by the faint light that came through; and every twig, and every vein on every leaf was a streak of pale fire.

All this time, as I went on through the wood, I was haunted with the feeling that other shapes, more like my own in size and mien, were moving about at a little distance on all sides of me. But as yet I could discern none of them, although the moon was high enough to send a great many of her rays down between the trees, and these rays were unusually bright, and sight-giving, notwithstanding she was only a half-moon . . .

Soon a vague sense of discomfort possessed me. With variations of relief, this gradually increased; as if some evil thing were wandering about in my neighbourhood, sometimes nearer and sometimes further off, but still approaching . . . At length the thought crossed my mind with horror: 'Can it be possible that the Ash is looking for me? or that, in his nightly wanderings, his path is gradually verging towards mine?' I comforted myself, however, by remembering that he had started quite in another direction; one that would lead him, if he kept it, far apart from me; especially as, for the last two or three hours, I had been diligently journeying eastward. I kept on my way, therefore, striving by direct effort of the will against the encroaching fear . . . To add to my distress, the clouds in the west had risen nearly to the top of the skies, and they and the moon were travelling slowly towards each other. Indeed, some of their advanced guard had already met her, and she had begun to wade through a filmy vapour that gradually deepened. At length she was for a moment almost entirely obscured. When she shone out again, with a brilliancy increased by the contrast, I saw plainly on the path before me – from around which at this spot the trees receded, leaving a small space of green sward – the shadow of a large hand, with knotty joints and protuberances here and there. Especially I remarked, even in the midst of my fear, the bulbous points of the finger. I looked hurriedly all round, but could see nothing from which such a shadow should fall ... I looked, and peered, and intensified my vision, all to no purpose. I could see nothing of that kind, not even an ash-tree in the neighbourhood. Still the shadow remained; not steady, but moving to and fro; and once I saw the fingers close, and grind themselves close, like the claws of a wild animal, as if in uncontrollable longing for some anticipated prey. There seemed but one mode left of discovering the substance of this shadow. I went forward boldly, though with an inward shudder which I would not heed, to the spot where the shadow lay, threw myself on the ground, laid my head within the form of the hand, and turned my eyes towards the moon. Good heavens! what did I see? I wonder that ever I arose, and that the very shadow of the hand did not hold me where I lay until fear had frozen my brain. I saw the strangest figure; vague, shadowy, almost transparent, in the central parts, and gradually deepening in substance towards the outside, until it ended in extremities capable of casting such a shadow as fell from the hand through the awful fingers of which I now saw the moon. The hand was uplifted in the attitude of a paw about to strike its prey. But the face, which throbbed with fluctuating and pulsatory visibility – not from changes in the light it reflected, but from changes in its own conditions of reflecting power, the alterations being from within, not from without – it was horrible. I do not know how to describe it. It caused a new sensation. Just as one cannot translate a horrible odour, or a ghastly pain, or a fearful sound, into words, so I cannot describe this new form of awful hideousness. I can only try to describe something that is not it, but seems somewhat parallel to it; or at least is suggested by it. It reminded me of what I had heard of vampires; for the face resembled that of a corpse more than anything else I can think of, especially when I can conceive such a face in motion but not suggesting any life as the source of the motion. The features were rather handsome than otherwise, except the mouth, which had scarcely a curve in it. The lips were of equal thickness; but the thickness was not at all remarkable, even although they looked slightly swollen . . . But the most awful of the features were the eyes. These were alive, yet not with life. They seemed lighted up with an infinite greed. A gnawing voracity, which devoured the devourer, seemed to be the indwelling and propelling power of the whole ghastly apparition. I lay for a few moments simply imbruted with terror; when another cloud, obscuring the moon, delivered me from the immediately paralysing effects of the presence to the vision of the object of horror, while it added the force of imagination to the power of fear within me; inasmuch as, knowing far worse cause for apprehension than before, I remained equally ignorant from what I had to defend myself, or how to take any precautions: he might be upon me in the darkness any moment. I sprang to my feet, and sped I knew not whither, only away from the spectre. I thought no longer of the path, and often narrowly escaped dashing myself against a tree, in my headlong flight of fear.

Great drops of rain began to patter on the leaves. Thunder began to mutter, then growl in the distance. I ran on. The rain fell heavier . . . I sprang forward, stung to yet wilder speed; but had not run many steps before my foot slipped, and, vainly attempting to recover myself, I fell at the foot of one of the large trees. Half-stunned, I yet raised myself, and almost involuntarily looked back. All I saw was the hand within three feet of my face. But, at the same moment, I felt two large soft arms thrown round me from behind; and a voice like a woman's said: 'Do not fear the goblin; he dares not hurt you now.' With that, the hand was suddenly withdrawn as from a fire, and disappeared in the darkness and the rain. Overcome with the mingling of terror and joy, I lay for some time almost insensible. The first thing I remember is the sound of a voice above me, full and low, and strangely reminding me of the sound of a gentle wind amidst the leaves of a great tree. It murmured over and over again: 'I may love him, I may love him; for he is a man, and I am only a beech-tree.' I found I was seated on the ground, leaning against a human form, and supported still by the arms around me, which I knew to be those of a woman who must be rather above the human size, and largely proportioned. I turned my head, but without moving otherwise, for I feared lest the arms should untwine themselves; and clear, somewhat mournful eyes met mine. At least that is how they impressed me; but I could see very little of colour or outline as we sat in the dark and rainy shadow of the tree. The face seemed very lovely, and solemn from its stillness; with the aspect of one who is quite content, but waiting for something. I saw my conjecture from her arms was correct: she was above the human scale throughout, but not greatly.

'Why do you call yourself a beech-tree?' I said.

'Because I am one,' she replied, in the same low, musical, murmuring voice.

'You are a woman,' I returned.

'Do you think so? Am I very like a woman then?'

'You are a very beautiful woman. Is it possible you should not know it?'

'I am very glad you think so. I fancy I feel like a woman sometimes. I do so tonight – and always when the rain drips from my hair. For there is an old prophecy in our woods that one day we shall all be men and women like you. Do you know anything about it in your region? Shall I be very happy when I am a woman? I fear not; for it is always in nights like these that I feel like one. But I long to be a woman for all that.'

I had let her talk on, for her voice was like a solution of all musical sounds. I now told her that I could hardly say whether women were happy or not. I knew one who had not been happy; and for my part, I had often longed for Fairyland, as she now longed for the world of men. But then neither of us had lived long, and perhaps people grew happier as they grew older. Only I doubted it. I could not help sighing. She felt the sigh, for her arms were still round me. She asked me how old I was.

'Twenty-one,' said I.

'Why, you baby!' said she; and kissed me with the sweetest kiss of winds and odours. There was a cool faithfulness in the kiss that revived my heart wonderfully. I felt that I feared the dreadful Ash no more.

'What did the horrible Ash want with me?' I said.

'I am not quite sure, but I think he wants to bury you at the foot of his tree. But he shall not touch you, my child.'

'Are all the ash-trees as dreadful as he?'

'Oh, no. They are all disagreeable selfish creatures – (what horrid men they will make, if it be true!) but this one has a hole in his heart that nobody knows of but one or two; and he is always trying to fill it up, but he cannot. That must be what he wanted you for. I wonder if he will ever be a man. If he is, I hope they will kill kim.'

'How kind of you to save me from him!'

'I will take care that he shall not come near you again. But there are some in the wood more like me, from whom, alas! I cannot protect you. Only if you see any of them very beautiful, try to walk round them.'

'What then?'

'I cannot tell you more. But now I must tie some of my hair about you, and then the Ash will not touch you. Here, cut some off. You men have strange cutting things about you.'

She shook her long hair loose over me, never moving her arms.

'I cannot cut your beautiful hair. It would be a shame.'

'Not cut my hair! It will have grown long enough before any is wanted again in this wild forest. Perhaps it may never be of any use again – not till I am a woman.' And she sighed.

As gently as I could, I cut with a knife a long tress of flowing, dark hair, she hanging her beautiful head over me. When I had finished, she shuddered and breathed deep, as one does when an acute pain, steadfastly endured without sign of suffering, is at length relaxed. She then took the hair and tied it round me, singing a strange sweet song, which I could not understand, but which left in me a feeling like this –

I saw thee ne'er before;
I see thee never more;
But love, and help, and pain, beautiful one,
Have made thee mine, till all my years are done.

I cannot put more of it into words. She closed her arms about me again, and went on singing. The rain in the leaves, and a light wind that had arisen, kept her song company. I was wrapt in a trance of still delight. It told me the secret of the woods, and the flowers, and the birds. At one time I felt as if I was wandering in childhood through sunny spring forests, over carpets of primroses, anemones, and little white starry things – I had almost said, creatures, and finding new wonderful flowers at every turn. At another, I lay half dreaming in the hot summer noon, with a book of old tales beside me, beneath a great beech; or, in autumn, grew sad because I trod on the leaves that had sheltered me, and received their last blessing in the sweet odours of decay; or, in a winter evening, frozen-still, looked up, as I went home to a warm fireside, through the netted boughs and twigs to the cold, snowy moon, with her opal zone around her. At last I had fallen asleep; for I know nothing more that passed, till I found myself lying under a superb beech-tree, in the clear light of the morning, just before sunrise. Around me was a girdle of fresh beech-leaves. Alas! I brought nothing with me out of fairy-land, but memories – memories. The great boughs of the beech hung drooping around me. At my head rose its smooth stem, with its great sweeps of curving surface that swelled like undeveloped limbs. The leaves and branches above kept on the song which had sung me asleep; only now, to my mind, it sounded like a farewell and a speed-well. I sat a long time, unwilling to go; but my unfinished story urged me on. I must act and wander. With the sun well risen, I rose, and put my ams as far as they would reach around the beech-tree, and kissed it, and said goodbye. A trembling went through the leaves; a few of the last drops of the night's rain fell from off them at my feet; and as I walked slowly away, I seemed to hear in a whisper once more the words: 'I may love him, I may love him; for he is a man, and I am only a beech-tree.' . . .

I walked on, in the fresh morning air, as if new-born . . . There was little to distinguish the woods to-day from those of my own land; except that all the wild things, rabbits, birds, squirrels, mice, and the numberless other inhabitants, were very tame; that is, they did not run away from me, but gazed at me as I passed, frequently coming nearer, as if to examine me more closely . . . Now and then, too, a dim human figure would appear and disappear, at some distance, amongst the trees, moving like a sleep-walker. But no one ever came near me.

This day I found plenty of food in the forest – strange nuts and fruits I had never seen before. I hesitated to eat them; but argued that, if I could live on the air of fairy-land, I could live on its food also. I found my reasoning correct, and the result was better than I had hoped; for it not only satisfied my hunger, but operated in such a way upon my senses, that I was brought into far more complete relationship with the things around me. The human forms appeared much more dense and defined; more tangibly visible, if I may say so. I seemed to know better which direction to choose when any doubt arose. I began to feel in some degree what the birds meant in their songs, though I could not express it in words, any more than you can some landscapes . . . Some of the creatures I never heard speak at all, and believe they never do so, except under the impulse of some great excitement. The mice talked; but the hedgehogs seemed very phlegmatic; and though I met a couple of moles above ground several times, they never said a word to each other in my hearing. There were

The Enchanted Forest

no wild beasts in the forest; at least, I did not see one larger than a wild cat. There were plenty of snakes, however, and I do not think they were all harmless; but none ever bit me . . .

But just where the path seemed to end, rose a great rock, quite overgrown with shrubs and creeping plants, some of them in full and splendid blossom: these almost concealed an opening in the rock, into which the path appeared to lead. I entered, thirsting for the shade which it promised. What was my delight to find a rocky cell, all the angles rounded away with rich moss, and every ledge and projection crowded with lovely ferns, the variety of whose forms, and groupings, and shades wrought in me like a poem; for such a harmony could not exist, except they all consented to some one end! A little well of the clearest water filled a mossy hollow in one corner. I drank, and felt as if I knew what the elixir of life must be; then threw myself on a mossy mound that lay like a couch along the inner end. Here I lay in a delicious reverie for some time; during which all lovely forms, and colours, and sounds seemed to use my brain as a common hall, where they could come and go, unbidden and unexcused. I had never imagined that such capacity for simple happiness lay in me, as was now awakened by this assembly of forms and spiritual sensations, which yet were far too vague to admit of being translated into any shape common to my own and another mind. I had lain for an hour, I should suppose, though it may have been far longer, when, the harmonious tumult in my mind having somewhat relaxed, I became aware that my eyes were fixed on a strange, time-worn bas-relief on the rock opposite to me. This, after some pondering, I concluded to represent Pygmalion, as he awaited the quickening of his statue. The sculptor sat more rigid than the figure to which his eyes were turned. That seemed about to step from its pedestal and embrace the man, who waited rather than expected.

'A lovely story,' I said to myself. 'This cave, now, with the bushes cut away from the entrance to let the light in, might be such a place as he would choose, withdrawn from the notice of men, to set up his block of marble, and mould into a visible body the thought already clothed with form in the unseen hall of the sculptor's brain. And, indeed, if I mistake not,' I said, starting up, as a sudden ray of light arrived at that moment through a crevice in the roof, and lighted up a small portion of the rock, bare of vegetation, 'this very rock is marble, white enough and delicate enough for any statue, even if destined to become an ideal woman in the arms of the sculptor.'

I took my knife and removed the moss from a part of the block on which I had been lying; when, to my surprise, I found it more like alabaster than ordinary marble, and soft to the edge of the knife. In fact, it was alabaster. By an inexplicable, though by no means unusual kind of impulse, I went on removing the moss from the surface of the stone; and soon saw that it was polished, or at least smooth, throughout. I continued my labour; and after clearing a space of about a couple of square feet, I observed what caused me to prosecute the work with more interest and care than before. For the ray of sunlight had now reached the spot I had cleared, and under its lustre the alabaster revealed its usual slight transparency when polished, except where my knife had scratched the surface; and I observed that the transparency seemed to have a definite limit, and to end upon an opaque body like the more solid, white marble. I was careful to scratch no more. And first, a vague anticipation gave way to a startling sense of possibility; then, as I proceeded, one revelation after another produced the entrancing conviction, that under the crust of alabaster, lay a dimly visible form in marble, but whether of man or woman I could not yet tell. I worked on as rapidly as the necessary care would permit; and when I had uncovered the whole mass, and, rising from my knees, had retreated a little way, so that the effect of the whole might fall on me, I saw before me with sufficient plainness – though at the same time with considerable indistinctness, arising from the limited amount of light the place admitted, as well as from the nature of the object itself – a block of pure alabaster enclosing the form, apparently in marble, of a reposing woman. She lay on one side, with her hand under her cheek, and her face towards me; but her hair had fallen partly over her face, so that I could not see the expression of the whole. What I did see, appeared to me perfectly lovely; more near the face that had been born with me in my soul, than anything I had seen before in nature or art. The actual outlines of the rest of the form were so indistinct, that the more than semi-opacity of the alabaster seemed insufficient to account for the fact; and I conjectured that a light robe added its obscurity. Numberless histories passed through my mind of change of substance from enchantment and other causes, and of imprisonments such as this before me. I thought of the Prince of the Enchanted City, half marble and half a living man; of Ariel; of Niobe; of the Sleeping Beauty in the Wood; of the bleeding trees; and many other histories. Even my adventure of the preceding evening with the lady of the beech-tree contributed to arouse the wild hope, that by some means life might be given to this form also, and that, breaking from her alabaster tomb, she might glorify my eyes with her presence. 'For,' I argued, 'who can tell but this cave may be the home of Marble, and this, essential Marble – that spirit of marble which, present throughout, makes it capable of being moulded into any form? Then if she should awake! But how to awake her? A kiss awoke the Sleeping Beauty: a kiss cannot reach her through the incrusting alabaster.' I kneeled, however, and kissed the pale coffin; but she slept on. I bethought me of Orpheus, and the following stones; – that trees should follow his music seemed nothing surprising now. Might not a song awake this form, that the glory of motion might for a time displace the loveliness of rest? Sweet sounds can go where kisses may not enter . . .

I sat down on the ground by the 'antenatal tomb,' leaned upon it with my face towards the head of the figure within, and sang – the words and tones coming together, and inseparably connected, as if word and tone formed one thing; or, as if each word could be uttered only in that tone, and was incapable of distinction from it, except in idea, by an acute analysis. I sang something like this: but the words are only a dull representation of a state whose very elevation precluded the possibility of remembrance; and in which I presume the words really employed were as far above these, as that state transcended this wherein I recall it:

> Marble woman, vainly sleeping
> In the very death of dreams!
> Wilt thou – slumber from thee sweeping,
> All but what with vision teems –
> Hear my voice come through the golden
> Mist of memory and hope;
> And with shadowy smile embolden
> Me with primal Death to cope?
>
> Thee the sculptors all pursuing,
> Have embodied but their own;
> Round their visions, form induing,
> Marble vestments thou hast thrown;
> But thyself, in silence winding,
> Thou hast kept eternally;
> Thee they found not, many finding –
> I have found thee: wake for me.

As I sang, I looked earnestly at the face so vaguely revealed before me. I fancied, yet believed it to be but fancy, that through the dim veil of the alabaster, I saw a motion of the head as if caused by a sinking sigh. I gazed more earnestly, and concluded that it was but fancy. Nevertheless I could not help singing again:

>Rest is now filled full of beauty,
>And can give thee up, I ween;
>Come thou forth, for other duty;
>Motion pineth for her queen.
>. . .
>
>Or, if still thou choosest rather
>Marble, be its spell on me;
>Let thy slumber round me gather,
>Let another dream with thee!

Again I paused, and gazed through the stony shroud, as if, by very force of penetrative sight, I would clear every lineament of the lovely face. And now I thought the hand that had lain under the cheek, had slipped a little downward. But then I could not be sure that I had at first observed its position accurately. So I sang again; for the longing had grown into a passionate need of seeing her alive:

>. . . Cold lady of the lovely stone!
>   Awake! or I shall perish here;
>And thou be never more alone,
>   My form and I for ages near.
>
>But words are vain; reject them all –
>   They utter but a feeble part:
>Hear thou the depths from which they call,
>   The voiceless longing of my heart.

There arose a slightly crashing sound. Like a sudden apparition that comes and is gone, a white form, veiled in a light robe of whiteness, burst upwards from the stone, stood, glided forth, and gleamed away towards the woods. For I followed to the mouth of the cave, as soon as the amazement and concentration of delight permitted the nerves of motion again to act; and saw the white form amidst the trees, as it crossed a little glade on the edge of the forest where the sunlight fell full, seeming to gather with intenser radiance on the one object that floated rather than flitted through its lake of beams. I gazed after her in a kind of despair; found, freed, lost! It seemed useless to follow, yet follow I must. I marked the direction she took; and without once looking round to the forsaken cave, I hastened towards the forest . . .

The sunny afternoon died into the loveliest twilight. Great bats began to flit about with their own noiseless flight, seemingly purposeless, because its objects are unseen. The monotonous music of the owl issued from all unexpected quarters in the half-darkness around me. The glow-worm was alight here and there, burning out into the great universe. The night-hawk heightened all the harmony and stillness with his oft-recurring, discordant jar. Numberless unknown sounds came out of the unknown dusk; but all were of twilight-kind, oppressing the heart as with a condensed atmosphere of dreamy undefined love and longing. The odours of night arose, and bathed me in that luxurious mournfulness peculiar to them, as if the plants whence they floated had been watered with bygone tears. Earth drew me towards her bosom; I felt as if I could fall down and kiss her. I forgot I was in Fairy Land, and seemed to be walking in a perfect night of our own old nursing earth. Great stems rose about me, uplifting a thick multitudinous roof above me of branches, and twigs, and leaves – the bird and insect world uplifted over mine, with its own landscapes, its own thickets, and paths, and glades, and dwellings; its own bird-ways and insect-delights. Great boughs crossed my path; great roots based the tree-columns, and mightily clasped the earth, strong to lift and strong to uphold. It seemed an old, old forest, perfect in forest ways and pleasures. And when, in the midst of this ecstasy, I remembered that under some close canopy of leaves, by some giant stem, or in some mossy cave, or beside some leafy well, sat the lady of the marble, whom my songs had called forth into the outer world, waiting (might it not be?) to meet and thank her deliverer in a twilight which would veil her confusion, the whole night became one dream-realm of joy, the central form of which was everywhere present, although unbeheld. Then, remembering how my songs seemed to have called her from the marble, piercing through the pearly shroud of alabaster – 'Why,' thought I, 'should not my voice reach her now, through the ebon night that inwraps her.' My voice burst into song so spontaneously that it seemed involuntarily.

Not a sound
But, echoing in me,
Vibrates all around
With a blind delight,
Till it breaks on thee,
Queen of Night!
. . .

Let no moon
Creep up the heaven to-night.
I in darksome noon
Walking hopefully,
Seek my shrouded light –
Grope for thee!

Darker grow
The borders of the dark!
Through the branches glow,
From the roof above,
Star and diamond-spark,
Light for love.

Scarcely had the last sounds floated away from the hearing of my own ears, when I heard instead a low delicious laugh near me. It was not the laugh of one who would not be heard, but the laugh of one who has just received something long and patiently desired – a laugh that ends in a low musical moan. I started, and, turning sideways, saw a dim white figure seated beside an intertwining thicket of smaller trees and underwood.

'It is my white lady!' I said, and flung myself on the ground beside her; striving, through the gathering darkness, to get a glimpse of the form which had broken its marble prison at my call.

'It is your white lady,' said the sweetest voice, in reply, sending a thrill of speechless delight through a heart which all the love charms of the preceding day and evening had been tempering for this culminating hour. Yet, if I would have confessed it, there was something either in the sound of the voice, although it seemed sweetness itself, or else in this yielding which awaited no gradation of gentle approaches, that did not vibrate harmoniously with the beat of my inward music. And likewise, when, taking her hand in mine, I drew closer to her, looking for the beauty of her face, which, indeed, I found too plenteously, a cold shiver ran through me; but 'it is the marble,' I said to myself, and heeded it not.

She withdrew her hand from mine, and after that would scarce allow me to touch her. It seemed strange, after the fulness of her first greeting, that she could not trust me to come close to her. Though her words were those of a lover, she kept herself withdrawn as if a mile of space interposed between us.

'Why did you run away from me when you woke in the cave?' I said.

'Did I?' she returned. 'That was very unkind of me; but I did not know better.'

'I wish I could see you. The night is very dark.'

'So it is. Come to my grotto. There is light there.'

'Have you another cave, then?'

'Come and see.'

But she did not move until I rose first, and then she was on her feet before I could offer my hand to help her. She came close to my side, and conducted me through the wood. But once or twice, when, involuntarily almost, I was about to put my arm around her as we walked on through the warm gloom, she sprang away several paces, always keeping her face full towards me, and then stood looking at me, slightly stooping, in the attitude of one who fears some half-seen enemy. It was too dark to discern the expression of her face. Then she would return and walk close beside me again, as if nothing had happened. I thought this strange; but, besides that I had almost, as I said before, given up the attempt to account for appearances in fairy land, I judged that it would be very unfair to expect from one who had slept so long and had been so suddenly awakened, a behaviour correspondent to what I might unreflectingly look for. I knew not what she might have been dreaming about. Besides, it was possible that, while her words were free, her sense of touch might be exquisitely delicate.

At length, after walking a long way in the woods, we arrived at another thicket, through the intertexture of which was glimmering a pale rosy light.

'Push aside the branches,' she said, 'and make room for us to enter.'

I did as she told me.

'Go in,' she said; 'I will follow you.'

I did as she desired, and found myself in a little cave, not very unlike the marble cave. It was festooned and draperied with all kinds of green that cling to shady rocks. In the furthest corner, half-hidden in leaves, through which it glowed, mingling lovely shadows between them, burned a bright rosy flame on a little earthen lamp. The lady glided round by the wall from behind me, still keeping her face towards me, and seated herself in the furthest corner, with her back to the lamp, which she hid completely from my view. I then saw indeed a form of perfect loveliness before me. Almost it seemed as if the light of the rose-lamp shone through her (for it could not be reflected from her); such a delicate shade of pink seemed to shadow what in itself must be a marbly whiteness of hue. I discovered afterwards, however, that there was one thing in it I did not like; which was, that the white part of the eye was tinged with the same slight roseate hue as the rest of the form. It is strange that I cannot recall her features; but they, as well as her somewhat girlish figure, left on me simply and only the impression of intense loveliness. I lay down at her feet, and gazed up into her face as I lay.

She began, and told me a strange tale, which, likewise, I cannot recollect; but which, at every turn and every pause, somehow or other fixed my eyes and thoughts upon her extreme beauty; seeming always to culminate in something that had a relation, revealed or hidden, but always operative, with her own loveliness. I lay entranced. It was a tale which brings back a feeling as of snows and tempests; torrents and water-spirits; lovers parted for long, and meeting at last; with a gorgeous summer night to close up the whole. I listened till she and I were blended with the tale; till she and I were the whole history. And we had met at last in this same cave of greenery, while the summer night hung round us heavy with love, and the odours that crept through the silence from the sleeping woods were the only signs of an outer world that invaded our solitude. What followed I cannot clearly remember. The succeeding horror almost obliterated it. I woke as a grey dawn stole into the cave. The damsel had disappeared; but in the shrubbery at the mouth of the cave, stood a strange horrible object. It looked like an open coffin set up on one end; only that the part for the head and neck was defined from the shoulder-part. In fact it was a rough representation of the human frame, only hollow, as if made of decaying bark torn from a tree. It had arms, which were only slightly seamed, down from the shoulder-blade by the elbow, as if the bark had healed again from the cut of a knife. But the arms moved, and the hands and fingers were tearing asunder a long silky tress of hair. The thing turned round – it had for a face and front those of my enchantress, but now of a pale greenish hue in the light of the morning, and with dead lustreless eyes. In the horror of the moment, another fear invaded me. I put my hand to my waist, and found indeed that my girdle of beech-leaves was gone. Hair again in her hands, she was tearing it fiercely. Once more as she turned, she laughed a low laugh, but now full of scorn and derision; and then she said, as if to a companion with whom she had been talking while I slept, 'There he is; you can take him now.' I lay still, petrified with dismay and fear; for I now saw another figure beside her; which, although vague and indistinct, I yet recognized but too well. It was the Ash-tree. My beauty was the Maid of the Alder! and she was giving me, spoiled of my only availing defence, into the hands of my awful foe. The Ash bent his Gorgon-head, and entered the cave. I could not stir. He drew near me. His ghoul-eyes and his ghastly face fascinated me. He came stooping, with the hideous hand outstretched, like a beast of prey. I had given myself up to a death of unfathomable horror, when, suddenly, and just as he was on the point of seizing me, the dull, heavy blow of an axe echoed through the wood, followed by others in quick repetition. The Ash shuddered and groaned, withdrew the outstretched hand, retreated backwards to the mouth of the cave, then turned and disappeared amongst the trees. The other walking Death looked at me once, with a careless dislike on her beautifully moulded features; then, heedless any more to conceal her hollow deformity, turned her frightful back and likewise vanished amid the green obscurity without. I lay and wept. The Maid of the Alder-tree had befooled me – nearly slain me – in spite of all the warnings I had received from those who knew my danger.

The Magic Mirror

'All mirrors are magic mirrors,' Anodos ponders as he approaches the shimmering Palace of Fairyland reflected in moonlight, itself a reflection of the sun.

This second edited excerpt from *Phantastes* is a complete story which Anodos discovers in the Palace library. 'While I read it,' Anodos explains, 'I was Cosmo and his history was mine. Yet, all the time, I seemed to have a kind of double consciousness and the story a double meaning . . . wherein two souls loving each other and longing to come nearer, do, after all, but behold each other as in a glass darkly.'

This timeless story is about lovers who prefer the image of the beloved to the reality, and cling blindly to the reflection. It is also about the difference between unselfish sexual love that can lead to a deeper understanding of divine love, and destructive passion which can only lead to spiritual death. At the point in the story where Cosmo's innocent love degenerates into jealousy, MacDonald interjects into the text, the paradox, 'who lives, he dies; who dies, he is alive'. Cosmo has a decision to make, either to free his lady by smashing the mirror thereby allowing her the freedom to choose to come to him; or selfishly to keep her for himself, spellbound against her will. He makes the wrong choice.

The story which owes much to the influence of Hoffman and Novalis may appear to be out of place in *Phantastes*, as its physical setting in Prague seems to have little connection with the fairy world of the imagination, yet the subject reflects the major theme that runs through the book, the quest for ideal love. Cosmo's tragedy reflects Anodos's own experience when his lust loses him his White Lady to her evil reflection, the Alder Maid, and thereby almost loses him his life.

E.S.

Cosmo von Wehrstahl was a student at the University of Prague. Though of a noble family, he was poor, and prided himself upon the independence that poverty gives; for what will not a man pride himself upon, when he cannot get rid of it? . . .

His lodging consisted of one large low-ceiled room, singularly bare of furniture; for besides a couple of wooden chairs, a couch which served for dreaming on both by day and night, and a great press of black oak, there was very little in the room that could be called furniture. But curious instruments were heaped in the corners; and in one stood a skeleton, half-leaning against the wall, half-supported by a string about its neck. One of its hands, all of fingers, rested on the heavy pommel of a great sword that stood beside it. Various weapons were scattered about over the floor. The walls were utterly bare of adornment; for the few strange things, such as a large dried bat with wings dispread, the skin of a porcupine, and a stuffed sea-mouse, could hardly be reckoned as such. But although his fancy delighted in vagaries like these, he indulged his imagination with far different fare . . . He used to lie on his hard couch, and read a tale or a poem, till the book dropped from his hand; but he dreamed on, he knew not whether awake or asleep, until the opposite roof grew upon his sense, and turned golden in the sunrise. Then he arose too; and the impulses of vigorous youth kept him ever active, either in study or in sport, until again the close of the day left him free; and the world of night, which had lain drowned in the cataract of the day, rose up in his soul, with all its stars, and dim-seen phantom shapes.

One afternoon, towards dusk, he was wandering dreamily in one of the principal streets, when a fellow-student roused him by a slap on the shoulder, and asked him to accompany him into a little back alley to look at some old armour which he had taken a fancy to possess. Cosmo was considered an authority in every matter pertaining to arms, ancient or modern . . . He accompanied him willingly. They entered a narrow alley, and thence a dirty little court, where a low arched door admitted them into a heterogeneous assemblage of everything musty, and dusty, and old, that could well be imagined. His verdict on the armour was satisfactory, and his companion at once concluded the purchase. As they were leaving the place, Cosmo's eye was attracted by an old mirror of an elliptical shape, which leaned against the wall, covered with dust. Around it was some curious carving, which he could see but very indistinctly by the glimmering light which the owner of the shop carried in his hand. It was this carving that attracted his attention; at least so it appeared to him. He left the place, however, with his friend, taking no further notice of it. They walked together to the main street, where they parted and took opposite directions.

No sooner was Cosmo left alone, than the thought of the curious old mirror returned to him. A strong desire to see it more plainly arose within him, and he directed his steps once more towards the shop. The owner opened the door when he knocked, as if he had expected him. He was a little, old, withered man, with a hooked nose, and burning eyes constantly in a slow restless motion, and looking here and there as if after something that eluded them. Pretending to examine several other articles, Cosmo at last approached the mirror, and requested to have it taken down.

'Take it down yourself, master; I cannot reach it,' said the old man.

Cosmo took it down carefully, when he saw that the carving was indeed delicate and costly, being both of admirable design and execution; containing withal many devices which seemed to embody some meaning to which he had no clue. This, naturally, in one of his tastes and temperament, increased the interest he felt in the old mirror; so much, indeed, that he now longed to possess it, in order to study its frame at his leisure. He pretended, however, to want it only for use; and saying he feared the plate could be of little service, as it was rather old, he brushed away a little of the dust from its face, expecting to see a dull reflection within. His surprise was great when he found the reflection brilliant, revealing a glass not only uninjured by age, but wondrously clear and perfect (should the whole correspond to this part) even for one newly from the hands of the maker. He asked carelessly what the owner wanted for the thing. The old man replied by mentioning a sum of money far beyond the reach of poor Cosmo, who proceeded to replace the mirror where it had stood before.

'You think the price too high?' said the old man.

'I do not know that it is too much for you to ask,' replied Cosmo; 'but it is far too much for me to give.'

The old man held up his light towards Cosmo's face. 'I like your look,' said he.

Cosmo could not return the compliment. In fact, now he looked closely at him for the first time, he felt a kind of repugnance to him, mingled with a strange feeling of doubt whether a man or a woman stood before him.

'What is your name?' he continued.

'Cosmo von Wehrstahl.'

'Ah, ah! I thought as much. I see your father in you. I knew your father very well, young sir. I dare say in some odd corners of my house, you might find some old things with his crest and cipher upon them still. Well, I like you: you shall have the mirror at the fourth part of what I asked for it; but upon one condition.'

'What is that?' said Cosmo; for, although the price was still a great deal for him to give, he could just manage it; and the desire to possess the mirror had increased to an altogether unaccountable degree, since it had seemed beyond his reach.

'That if you should ever want to get rid of it again, you will let me have the first offer.'

'Certainly,' replied Cosmo, with a smile; adding, 'a moderate condition indeed.'

'On your honour?' insisted the seller.

'On my honour,' said the buyer; and the bargain was concluded.

'I will carry it home for you,' said the old man, as Cosmo took it in his hands.

'No, no; I will carry it myself,' said he; for he had a peculiar dislike to revealing his residence to any one, and more especially to this person, to whom he felt every moment a greater antipathy.

'Just as you please,' said the old creature, and muttered to himself as he held his light at the door to show him out of the court: 'Sold for the sixth time! I wonder what will be the upshot of it this time. I should think my lady had enough of it by now!'

Cosmo carried his prize carefully home . . . He reached his lodging in safety, and leaned his purchase against the wall, rather relieved, strong as he was, to be rid of its weight; then, lighting his pipe, threw himself on the couch, and was soon lapt in the folds of one of his haunting dreams.

He returned home earlier than usual the next day, and fixed the mirror to the wall, over the hearth, at one end of his long room. He then carefully wiped away the dust from its face, and, clear as the water of a sunny spring, the mirror shone out from beneath the envious covering . . . He gazed vacantly for a few moments into the depth of the reflected room. But ere long he said, half aloud: 'What a strange thing a mirror is! and what a wondrous affinity exists between it and a man's imagination! For this room of mine, as I behold it in the glass, is the same, and yet not the same. It is not the mere representation of the room I live in, but it looks just as if I were reading about it in a story I like. All its commonness has disappeared. The mirror has lifted it out of the region of fact into the realm of art; and the very representing of it to me has clothed with interest that which was otherwise hard and bare ... That skeleton, now – I almost fear it, standing there so still, with eyes only for the unseen, like a watchtower looking across all the waste of this busy world into the quiet regions of rest beyond. And yet I know every bone and every joint in it as well as my own fist. And that old battle-axe looks as if any moment it might be caught up by a mailed hand, and, borne forth by the mighty arm, go crashing through casque, and skull, and brain, invading the Unknown with yet another bewildered ghost. I should like to live in *that* room if I could only get into it.'

Scarcely had the half-moulded words floated from him, as he stood gazing into the mirror, when, striking him as with a flash of amazement that fixed him in his posture, noiseless and unannounced, glided suddenly through the door into the reflected room, with stately motion, yet reluctant and faltering step, the graceful form of a woman, clothed all in white. Her back only was visible as she walked slowly up to the couch in the further end of the room, on which she laid herself wearily, turning towards him a face of unutterable loveliness, in which suffering, and dislike, and a sense of compulsion, strangely mingled with the beauty. He stood without the power of motion for some moments, with his eyes irrecoverably fixed upon her; and even after he was conscious of the ability to move, he could not summon up courage to turn and look on her, face to face, in the veritable chamber in which he stood. At length, with a sudden effort, in which the exercise of the will was so pure, that it seemed involuntary, he turned his face to the couch. It was vacant. In bewilderment, mingled with terror, he turned again to the mirror: there, on the reflected couch, lay the exquisite lady-form. She lay with closed eyes, whence two large tears were just welling from beneath the veiling lids; still as death, save for the convulsive motion of her bosom.

Cosmo himself could not have described what he felt. His emotions were of a kind that destroyed consciousness, and could never be clearly recalled. He could not help standing yet by the mirror, and keeping his eyes fixed on the lady, though he was painfully aware of his rudeness, and feared every moment that she would open hers, and meet his fixed regard. But he was, ere long, a little relieved; for, after a while, her eyelids slowly rose, and her eyes remained uncovered, but unemployed for a time; and when, at length, they began to wander about the room, as if languidly seeking to make some acquaintance with her environment, they were never directed towards him: it seemed nothing but what was in the mirror could affect her vision; and, therefore, if she saw him at all, it could only be his back, which, of necessity, was turned towards her in the glass. The two figures in the mirror could not meet face to face, except he turned and looked at her, present in his room; and, as she was not there, he concluded that if he were to turn towards the part in his room corresponding to that in which she lay, his reflection would either be invisible to her altogether, or at least it must appear to her to gaze vacantly towards her, and no meeting of the eyes would produce the impression of spiritual proximity. By and by her eyes fell upon the skeleton, and he saw her shudder and close them. She did not open them again; but signs of repugnance continued evident on her countenance. Cosmo would have removed the obnoxious thing at once, but he feared to discompose her yet more by the assertion of his presence, which the act would involve. So he stood and watched her. The eyelids yet shrouded the eyes, as a costly case the jewels within; the troubled expression gradually faded from the countenance, leaving only a faint sorrow behind; the features settled into an unchanging expression of rest; and by these signs, and the slow regular motion of her breathing, Cosmo knew that she slept. He could now gaze on her without embarrassment. He saw that her figure, dressed in the simplest robe of white, was worthy of her face; and so harmonious, that either the delicately-moulded foot, or any finger of the equally delicate hand, was an index to the whole. As she lay, her whole form manifested the relaxation of perfect repose. He gazed till he was weary, and at last seated himself near the new-found shrine, and mechanically took up a book, like one who watches by a sick bed. But his eyes gathered no thoughts from the page before him . . .

How long he sat he knew not; but at length he roused himself, rose, and, trembling in every portion of his frame, looked again into the mirror. She was gone. The mirror reflected faithfully what his room presented, and nothing more . . . When the first pangs of his disappointment had passed, Cosmo began to comfort himself with the hope that she might return, perhaps the next evening, at the same hour. Resolving that if she did, she should not at least be scared by the hateful skeleton, he removed that and several other articles of questionable appearance into a recess by the side of the hearth, whence they could not possibly cast any reflection into the mirror;

and having made his poor room as tidy as he could, sought the solace of the open sky and of a night wind that had begun to blow; for he could not rest where he was. When he returned, somewhat composed, he could hardly prevail with himself to lie down on his bed; for he could not help feeling as if she had lain upon it; and for him to lie there now would be something like sacrilege. However, weariness prevailed; and laying himself on the couch, dressed as he was, he slept till day.

With a beating heart, beating till he could hardly breathe, he stood in dumb hope before the mirror, on the following evening . . . And just as the room vibrated with the strokes of the neighbouring church bell, announcing the hour of six, in glided the pale beauty, and again laid herself on the couch. Poor Cosmo nearly lost his senses with delight. She was there once more! Her eyes sought the corner where the skeleton had stood, and a faint gleam of satisfaction crossed her face, apparently at seeing it empty. She looked suffering still, but there was less of discomfort expressed in her countenance than there had been the night before. She took more notice of the things about her, and seemed to gaze with some curiosity on the strange apparatus standing here and there in her room. At length, however, drowsiness seemed to overtake her, and again she fell asleep. Resolved not to lose sight of her this time, Cosmo watched the sleeping form. Her slumber was so deep and absorbing, that a fascinating repose seemed to pass contagiously from her to him, as he gazed upon her; and he started as if awaking from a dream, when the lady moved, and, without opening her eyes, rose, and passed from the room with the gait of a somnambulist.

Cosmo was now in a state of extravagant delight. Most men have a secret treasure somewhere. The miser has his golden hoard; the virtuoso his pet ring; the student his rare book; the poet his favourite haunt; the lover his secret drawer; but Cosmo had a mirror with a lovely lady in it. And now that he knew by the skeleton, that she was affected by the things around her, he had a new object in life: he would turn the bare chamber in the mirror into a room such as no lady need disdain to call her own. This he could effect only by furnishing and adorning his. And Cosmo was poor. Yet he possessed accomplishments that could be turned to account; although, hitherto, he had preferred living on his slender allowance, to increasing his means by what his pride considered unworthy of his rank. He was the best swordsman in the University; and now he offered to give lessons in fencing and similar exercises, to such as chose to pay him well for the trouble. His proposal was heard with surprise by the students; but it was eagerly accepted by many . . . So that very soon he had a good deal of money at his command. The first thing he did was to remove his apparatus and oddities into a closet in the room. Then he placed his bed and a few other necessaries on each side of the hearth, and parted them from the rest of the room by two screens of Indian fabric. Then he put an elegant couch for the lady to lie upon, in the corner where his bed had formerly stood; and, by degrees, every day adding some article of luxury, converted it, at length, into a rich boudoir.

Every night, about the same time, the lady entered. The first time she saw the new couch, she started with a half-smile; then her face grew very sad, the tears came to her eyes, and she laid herself upon the couch, and pressed her face into the silken cushions, as if to hide from everything. She took notice of each addition and each change as the work proceeded; and a look of acknowledgement, as if she knew that some one was ministering to her, and was grateful for it, mingled with the constant look of suffering . . .

Meantime, how fared Cosmo? As might be expected in one of his temperament, his interest had blossomed into love, and his love – shall I call it *ripened*, or – *withered* into passion? But, alas! he loved a shadow. He could not come near her, could not speak to her, could not hear a sound from those sweet lips, to which his longing eyes would cling like bees to their honey-founts. Ever and anon, he sang to himself:

'I shall die for love of the maiden;'

and ever he looked again, and died not; though his heart seemed ready to break with intensity of life and longing. And the more he did for her, the more he loved her; and he hoped that, although she never appeared to see him, yet she was pleased to think that one unknown would give his life to her . . .

Who lives, he dies; who dies, he is alive.

One evening, as he stood gazing on his treasure, he thought he saw a faint expression of self-consciousness on her countenance, as if she surmised that passionate eyes were fixed upon her. This grew; till at last the red blood rose over her neck, and cheek, and brow. Cosmo's longing to approach her became almost delirious. This night she was dressed in an evening costume, resplendent with diamonds. This could add nothing to her beauty, but it presented it in a new aspect; enabled her loveliness to make a new manifestation of itself in a new embodiment... Diamonds glittered from amidst her hair, half-hidden in its luxuriance like stars through dark rain-clouds; and the bracelets on her white arms flashed all the colours of a rainbow of lightnings, as she lifted her snowy hands to cover her burning face. But her beauty shone down all its adornment. 'If I might have but one of her feet to kiss,' thought Cosmo, 'I should be content.' Alas! he deceived himself, for passion is never content. Nor did he know that there are *two* ways out of her enchanted house. But, suddenly, as if the pang had been driven into his heart from without, revealing itself first in pain, and afterwards in definite form, the thought darted into his mind, 'She has a lover somewhere. Remembered words of his bring the colour on her face now. I am nowhere to her. She lives in another world all day, and all night, after she leaves me. Why does she come and make me love her, till I, a strong man, am too faint to look upon her more?' He looked again, and her face was pale as a lily. A sorrowful compassion seemed to rebuke the glitter of the restless jewels, and the slow tears rose in her eyes. She left her room sooner this evening than was her wont... The next evening, for the first time since she began to come, she came not.

And now Cosmo was in wretched plight. Since the thought of a rival had occurred to him, he could not rest for a moment. More than ever he longed to see the lady face to face... Meantime he waited with unspeakable anxiety for the next night, hoping she would return: but she did not appear. And now he fell really ill. Rallied by his fellow-students on his wretched looks, he ceased to attend the lectures. His engagements were neglected. He cared for nothing. The sky, with the great sun in it, was to him a heartless, burning desert. The men and women in the streets were mere puppets, without motives in themselves, or interest to him. He saw them all as on the ever-changing field of a *camera obscura*. She – she alone and altogether – was his universe, his well of life, his incarnate good. For six evenings she came not...

Reasoning with himself, that it must be by some enchantment connected with the mirror, that the form of the lady was to be seen in it, he determined to attempt to turn to account what he had hitherto studied principally from curiosity. 'For,' said he to himself, 'if a spell can force her presence in that glass (and she came unwillingly at first), may not a stronger spell, such as I know, especially with the aid of her half-presence in the mirror, if ever she appears again, compel her living form to come to me here? If I do her wrong, let love be my excuse. I want only to know my doom from her own lips.' He never doubted, all the time, that she was a real earthly woman; or, rather, that there was a woman, who, somehow or other, threw this reflection of her form into the magic mirror.

He opened his secret drawer, took out his books of magic, lighted his lamp, and read and made notes from midnight till three in the morning, for three successive nights. Then he replaced his books; and the next night went out in quest of the materials necessary for the conjuration. These were not easy to find; for, in love-charms and all incantations of this nature, ingredients are employed scarcely fit to be mentioned, and for the thought even of which, in connection with her, he could only excuse himself on the score of his bitter need. At length he succeeded in procuring all he required; and on the seventh evening from that on which she had last appeared, he found himself prepared for the exercise of unlawful and tyrannical power.

He cleared the centre of the room; stooped and drew a circle of red on the floor, around the spot where he stood; wrote in the four quarters mystical signs, and numbers which were all powers of seven or nine; examined the whole ring carefully, to see that no smallest break had occurred in the circumference; and then rose from his bending posture. As he rose, the church clock struck seven; and, just as she had appeared the first time, reluctant, slow, and stately, glided in the lady. Cosmo trembled; and when, turning, she revealed a countenance worn and wan, as with sickness or inward trouble, he grew faint, and felt as if he dared not proceed. But as he gazed on the face and form, which now possessed his whole soul, to the exclusion of all other joys and griefs, the longing to speak to her, to know that she heard him, to hear from her one word in return, became so unendurable, that he suddenly and hastily resumed his preparations. Stepping carefully from the circle, he put a small brazier into its centre. He then set fire to its contents of charcoal, and while it burned up, opened his window and seated himself, waiting, beside it . . . Soon the charcoal glowed. Cosmo sprinkled upon it the incense and other substances which he had compounded, and, stepping within the circle, turned his face from the brazier and towards the mirror. Then, fixing his eyes upon the face of the lady, he began with a trembling voice to repeat a powerful incantation. He had not gone far, before the lady grew pale; and then, like a returning wave, the blood washed all its banks with its crimson tide, and she hid her face in her hands. Then he passed to a conjuration stronger yet. The lady rose and walked uneasily to and fro in her room. Another spell; and she seemed seeking with her eyes for some object on which they wished to rest. At length it seemed as if she suddenly espied him; for her eyes fixed themselves full and wide upon his, and she drew gradually, and somewhat unwillingly, close to her side of the mirror, just as if his eyes had fascinated her. Cosmo had never seen her so near before. Now at least, eyes met eyes; but he could not quite understand the expression of hers. They were full of tender entreaty, but there was something more that he could not interpret. Though his heart seemed to labour in his throat, he would allow no delight or agitation to turn him from his task. Looking still in her face, he passed on to the mightiest charm he knew. Suddenly the lady turned and walked out of the door of her reflected chamber. A moment after, she entered his room with veritable presence; and, forgetting all his precautions, he sprang from the charmed circle, and knelt before her. There she stood, the living lady of his passionate visions, alone beside him, in a thundery twilight, and the glow of a magic fire.

'Why,' said the lady, with a trembling voice, 'didst thou bring a poor maiden through the rainy streets alone?'

'Because I am dying for love of thee; but I only brought thee from the mirror there.'

'Ah, the mirror!' and she looked up at it, and shuddered. 'Alas! I am but a slave, while that mirror exists. But do not think it was the power of thy spells that drew me; it was thy longing desire to see me, that beat at the door of my heart, till I was forced to yield.'

'Canst thou love me then?' said Cosmo, in a voice calm as death, but almost inarticulate with emotion.

'I do not know,' she replied sadly; 'that I cannot tell, so long as I am bewildered with enchantments. It were indeed a joy too great, to lay my head on thy bosom and weep to death; for I think thou lovest me, though I do not know; – but –'

Cosmo rose from his knees.

'I love thee as – nay, I know not what – for since I have loved thee, there is nothing else.'

He seized her hand: she withdrew it.

'No, better not; I am in thy power, and therefore I may not.'

She burst into tears, and, kneeling before him in her turn, said –

'Cosmo, if thou lovest me, set me free, even from thyself: break the mirror.'

'And shall I see thyself instead?'

'That I cannot tell. I will not deceive thee; we may never meet again.'

A fierce struggle arose in Cosmo's bosom. Now she was in his power. She did not dislike him at least; and he could see her when he would. To break the mirror would be to destroy his very life, to banish out of his universe the only glory it possessed. The whole world would be but a prison, if he annihilated the one window that looked into the paradise of love. Not yet pure in love, he hesitated.

With a wail of sorrow, the lady rose to her feet. 'Ah! he loves me not; he loves me not even as I love him; and alas! I care more for his love than even for the freedom I ask.'

'I will not wait to be willing,' cried Cosmo; and sprang to the corner where the great sword stood.

Meantime it had grown very dark; only the embers cast a red glow through the room. He seized the sword by the steel scabbard, and stood before the mirror; but as he heaved a great blow at it with the heavy pommel, the blade slipped half-way out of the scabbard, and the pommel struck the wall above the mirror. At that moment, a terrible clap of thunder seemed to burst in the very room beside them; and ere Cosmo could repeat the blow, he fell senseless on the hearth. When he came to himself, he found that the lady and the mirror had both disappeared. He was seized with a brain fever, which kept him to his couch for weeks.

When he recovered his reason, he began to think what could have become of the mirror . . . He concluded that, either by supernatural agency, he having exposed himself to the vengeance of the demons in leaving the circle of safety, or in some other mode, the mirror had probably found its way back to its former owner; and, horrible to think of, might have been by this time once more disposed of, delivering up the lady into the power of another man; who, if he used his power no worse than he himself had done, might yet give Cosmo abundant cause to curse the selfish indecision which prevented him from shattering the mirror at once. Indeed, to think that she whom he loved, and who had prayed to him for freedom, should be still at the mercy, in some degree, of the possessor of the mirror, and was at least exposed to his constant observation, was in itself enough to madden a chary lover.

Anxiety to be well retarded his recovery; but at length he was able to creep abroad. He first made his way to the old broker's, pretending to be in search of something else. A laughing sneer on the creature's face convinced him that he knew all about it; but he could not see it amongst his furniture, or get any information out of him as to what had become of it. He expressed the utmost surprise at hearing it had been stolen; a surprise which Cosmo saw at once to be counterfeited; while, at the same time, he fancied that the old wretch was not at all anxious to have it mistaken for genuine. Full of distress, which he concealed as well as he could, he made many searches, but with no avail. Of course he could ask no questions; but he kept his ears awake for any remotest hint that might set him in a direction of search. He never went out without a short heavy hammer of steel about him, that he might shatter the mirror the moment he was made happy by the sight of his lost treasure, if ever that blessed moment should arrive . . .

One night, he mingled with a crowd that filled the rooms of one of the most distinguished mansions in the city; for he accepted every invitation, that he might lose no chance, however poor, of obtaining some information that might expedite his discovery. Here he wandered about, listening to every stray word that he could catch, in the hope of a revelation. As he approached some ladies who were talking quietly in a corner, one said to another: 'Have you heard of the strange illness of the Princess von Hohenweiss?'

'Yes; she has been ill for more than a year now. It is very sad for so fine a creature to have such a terrible malady. She was better for some weeks lately, but within the last few days, the same attacks have returned, apparently accompanied with more suffering than ever. It is altogether an inexplicable story.'

'Is there a story connected with her illness?'

'I have only heard imperfect reports of it; but it is said that she gave offence some eighteen months ago to an old woman who had held an office of trust in the family, and who, after some incoherent threats, disappeared. This peculiar affection followed soon after. But the strangest part of the story is its association with the loss of an antique mirror, which stood in her dressing-room, and of which she constantly made use.'

Here the speaker's voice sank to a whisper; and Cosmo, although his very soul sat listening in his ears, could hear no more. He trembled too much to dare to address the ladies, even if it had been advisable to expose himself to their curiosity. The name of the Princess was well known to him, but he had never seen her; except indeed it was she, which now he hardly doubted, who had knelt before him on that dreadful night. Fearful of attracting attention, for, from the weak state of his health, he could not recover an appearance of calmness, he made his way to the open air, and reached his lodgings; glad in this, that he at least knew where she lived, although he never dreamed of approaching her openly, even if he should be happy enough to free her from her hateful bondage. He hoped, too, that as he had unexpectedly learned so much, the other and far more important part might be revealed to him ere long.

'Have you seen Steinwald lately?'

'No, I have not seen him for some time. He is almost a match for me at the rapier, and I suppose he thinks he needs no more lessons.'

'I wonder what has become of him. I want to see him very much. Let me see: the last time I saw him, he was coming out of that old broker's den, to which, if you remember, you accompanied me once, to look at some armour. That is fully three weeks ago.'

This hint was enough for Cosmo. Von Steinwald was a man of influence in the court, well known for his reckless habits and fierce passions. The very possibility that the mirror should be in his possession was hell itself to Cosmo. But violent or hasty measures of any sort were most unlikely to succeed. All that he wanted was an opportunity of breaking the fatal glass; and to obtain this, he must bide his time. He revolved many plans in his mind, but without being able to fix upon any.

At length, one evening, as he was passing the house of Von Steinwald, he saw the windows more than usually brilliant. He watched for a while and seeing that company began to arrive, hastened home, and dressed as richly as he could, in the hope of mingling with the guests unquestioned; in effecting which, there could be no difficulty for a man of his carriage.

In a lofty, silent chamber, in another part of the city, lay a form more like marble than a living woman. The loveliness of death seemed frozen upon her face, for her lips were rigid, and her eyelids closed. Her long white hands were crossed over her breast, and no breathing disturbed their repose. Beside the dead, men speak in whispers, as if the deepest rest of all could be broken by the sound of a living voice. Just so, though the soul was evidently beyond the reach of all intimations from the senses, the two ladies, who sat beside her, spoke in the gentlest tones of subdued sorrow.

'She has lain so for an hour.'

'This cannot last long, I fear.'

'How much thinner she has grown within the last few weeks! If she would only speak, and explain what she suffers, it would be better for her. I think she has visions in her trances, but nothing can induce her to refer to them when she is awake.'

'Does she ever speak in these trances?'

'I have never heard her; but they say she walks sometimes, and once put the whole household in a terrible fright by disappearing for a whole hour, and returning drenched with rain, and almost dead with exhaustion and fright. But even then she would give no account of what had happened.'

A scarce audible murmur from the yet motionless lips of the lady here startled her attendants. After several ineffectual attempts at articulation, the word '*Cosmo!*' burst from her. Then she lay still as before; but only for a moment. With a wild cry, she sprang from the couch erect on the floor, flung her arms above her head, with clasped and straining hands, and, her wide eyes flashing with light, called aloud, with a voice exultant as that of a spirit bursting from a sepulchre, 'I am free! I am free! I thank thee!' Then she flung herself on the couch, and sobbed; then rose, and paced wildly up and down the room, with gestures of mingled delight and anxiety. Then turning to her motionless attendants – 'Quick, Lisa, my cloak and hood!' Then lower – 'I must go to him. Make haste, Lisa! You may come with me, if you will.'

In another moment they were in the street, hurrying along towards one of the bridges over the Moldau. The moon was near the zenith, and the streets were almost empty. The Princess soon outstripped her attendant, and was half-way over the bridge, before the other reached it.

'Are you free, lady? The mirror is broken: are you free?'

The words were spoken close beside her, as she hurried on. She turned; and there, leaning on the parapet in a recess of the bridge, stood Cosmo, in a splendid dress, but with a white and quivering face.

'Cosmo! – I am free – and thy servant for ever. I was coming to you now.'

'And I to you, for Death made me bold; but I could get no further. Have I atoned at all? Do I love you a little – truly?'

'Ah, I know now that you love me, my Cosmo; but what do you say about death?'

He did not reply. His hand was pressed against his side. She looked more closely: the blood was welling from between the fingers. She flung her arms around him with a faint bitter wail.

When Lisa came up, she found her mistress kneeling above a wan dead face, which smiled on in the spectral moonbeams.

A Ghost Story

The Portent, from which novel the following edited excerpt is taken, originally appeared serialized in the *Cornhill Magazine* of 1860 together with Thackeray's *Lovel the Widower*, and Trollope's *Framley Parsonage*. This eerie ghost story about 'second sight' and 'second hearing' differs from MacDonald's other novels in that it has no apparent allegory or religious message. 'If you see anything in it, take it and I am glad you have it; but I wrote it for the tale,' he told his wife. Wolff sees it as straddling the borderline between his fairy allegories and his Scottish novels.

The following story comes at the beginning of the book and stands as a complete ghost tale on its own, a Celtic mystery set in awesome Highland scenery. In the remainder of the book, the hero-narrator, Campbell, moves to England to work as a tutor in a library where he meets the beautiful sleep-walking Lady Alice who is to become his 'fere' or chosen mate. *The Portent* contains much that would seem to be autobiographical. Campbell, like MacDonald, loved to roam in the hills, was obsessed by – but unafraid of – the dead, travelled south to become a tutor, worked in a library which was to become the setting for romance. Although the theme and opening chapters are essentially Celtic, the influence of the German romantic writers such as Hoffman and Novalis, whose works Campbell finds in the English library, and whose writings MacDonald found in some northern library, predominates in the book.

E.S.

My father belonged to the wide-spread family of the Campbells, and possessed a small landed property in the north of Argyll. But although of long descent and high connection, he was no richer than many a farmer of a few hundred acres. For, with the exception of a narrow belt of arable land at its foot, a bare hill formed almost the whole of his possessions. The sheep ate over it, and no doubt found it good; I bounded and climbed all over it, and thought it a kingdom . . .

There was one spot upon the hill, half-way between the valley and the moorland, which was my favourite haunt. This part of the hill was covered with great blocks of stone, of all shapes and sizes – here crowded together, like the slain where the battle had been fiercest; there parting asunder from spaces of delicate green – of softest grass. In the centre of one of these green spots, on a steep part of the hill, were three huge rocks – two projecting out of the hill, rather than standing up from it, and one, likewise projecting from the hill, but lying across the tops of the two, so as to form a little cave, the back of which was the side of the hill. This was my refuge, my home within a home, my study – and, in the hot noons, often my sleeping chamber, and my house of dreams . . . I would lie till nothing but the stars and the dim outlines of hills against the sky was to be seen, and then rise and go home, as sure of my path as if I had been descending a dark staircase in my father's house.

On the opposite side the valley, another hill lay parallel to mine; and behind it, at some miles' distance, a great mountain. As often as, in my hermit's cave, I lifted my eyes from the volume I was reading, I saw this mountain before me. Very different was its character from that of the hill on which I was seated. It was a mighty thing, a chieftain of the race, seamed and scarred, featured with chasms and precipices and overleaning rocks, themselves huge as hills; here blackened with shade, there overspread with glory; interlaced with the silvery lines of falling streams, which, hurrying from heaven to earth, cared not how they went, so it were downwards. Fearful stories were told of the gulfs, sullen waters, and dizzy heights upon that terror-haunted mountain. In storms the wind roared like thunder in its caverns and along the jagged sides of its cliffs, but at other times that uplifted land – uplifted, yet secret and full of dismay – lay silent as a cloud on the horizon.

I had a certain peculiarity of constitution, which I have some reason to believe I inherit. It seems to have its root in an unusual delicacy of hearing which often conveys to me sounds inaudible to those about me. This I have had many opportunities of proving. It has likewise, however, brought me sounds which I could never trace back to their origin; though they may have arisen from some natural operation which I had not perseverance or mental acuteness sufficient to discover. From this, or, it may be, from some deeper cause with which this is connected, arose a certain kind of fearfulness associated with the sense of hearing, of which I have never heard a corresponding instance. Full as my mind was of the wild and sometimes fearful tales of a Highland nursery, fear never entered my mind by the eyes; nor, when I brooded over tales of terror, and fancied new and yet more frightful embodiments of horror, did I shudder at any imaginable spectacle, or tremble lest the fancy should become fact, and from behind the whin-bush or the elder-hedge should glide forth the tall swaying form of the Boneless. When alone in bed, I used to lie awake, and look out into the room, peopling it with the forms of all the persons who had died within the scope of my memory and acquaintance. These fancied forms were vividly present to my imagination. I pictured them pale, with dark circles around their hollow eyes, visible by a light which glimmered within them; not the light of life, but a pale, greenish phosphorescence, generated by the decay of the brain inside. Their garments were white and trailing, but torn and soiled, as by trying often in vain to get up out of the buried coffin. But so far from being terrified by these imaginings, I used to delight in them; and in the long winter evenings, when I did not happen to have any book that interested me sufficiently, I used even to look forward with expectation to the hour when, laying myself straight upon my back, as if my bed were my coffin, I could call up from underground all who had passed away, and see how they fared, yea, what progress they had made towards final dissolution of form; – but all the time, with my fingers pushed hard into my ears, lest the faintest sound should invade the silent citadel of my soul. If inadvertently I removed one of my fingers, the agony of terror I instantly experienced is indescribable. I can compare it to nothing but the rushing in upon my brain of a whole churchyard of spectres. The very possibility of hearing a sound, in such a mood, and at such a time, was almost enough to paralyse me. So I could scare myself in broad daylight, on the open hill-side, by imagining unintelligible sounds; and my imagination was both original and fertile in the invention of such. But my mind was too active to be often subjected to such influences ... As I grew older, I almost outgrew them. Yet sometimes one awful dread would seize me – that, perhaps, the prophetic power manifest in the gift of second sight, which, according to the testimony of my old nurse, had belonged to several of my ancestors, had been in my case transformed in kind without losing its nature, transferring its abode from the sight to the hearing, whence resulted its keenness, and my fear and suffering.

A Ghost Story

One summer evening, I had lingered longer than usual in my rocky retreat: I had lain half dreaming in the mouth of my cave, till the shadows of evening had fallen, and the gloaming had deepened half-way towards the night. But the night had no more terrors for me than the day . . . When I lifted my head, only a star here and there caught my eye; but, looking intently into the depths of blue-gray, I saw that they were crowded with twinkles. The mountain rose before me a large mass of gloom; but its several peaks stood out against the sky with a clear, pure, sharp outline, and looked nearer to me than the bulk from which they rose heavenwards. One star trembled and throbbed upon the very tip of the loftiest, the central peak, which seemed the spire of a mighty temple where the light was worshipped – crowned, therefore, in the darkness, with the emblem of the day. I was lying, as I have said, with this fancy still in my thought, when suddenly I heard, clear, though faint and far away, the sound as of the iron-shod hoofs of a horse, in furious gallop along an uneven rocky surface. It was more like a distinct echo than an original sound. It seemed to come from the face of the mountain, where no horse, I knew, could go at that speed, even if its rider courted certain destruction. There was a peculiarity, too, in the sound – a certain tinkle, or clank, which I fancied myself able, by auricular analysis, to distinguish from the body of the sound. Supposing the sound to be caused by the feet of a horse, the peculiarity was just such as would result from one of the shoes being loose. A terror – strange even to my experience – seized me, and I hastened home. The sounds gradually died away as I descended the hill. Could they have been an echo from some precipice of the mountain? I knew of no road lying so that, if a horse were galloping upon it, the sounds would be reflected from the mountain to me.

The next day, in one of my rambles, I found myself near the cottage of my old foster-mother, who was distantly related to us, and was a trusted servant in the family at the time I was born. On the death of my mother, which took place almost immediately after my birth, she had taken the entire charge of me, and had brought me up, though with difficulty; for she used to tell me, I should never be either *folk* or *fairy*. For some years she had lived alone in a cottage, at the bottom of a deep green circular hollow, upon which, in walking over a heathy table-land, one came with a sudden surprise. I was her frequent visitor. She was a tall, thin, aged woman, with eager eyes, and well-defined, clear-cut features. Her voice was harsh, but with an undertone of great tenderness. She was scrupulously careful in her attire, which was rather above her station. Altogether, she had much the bearing of a gentlewoman. Her devotion to me was quite motherly. Never having had any family of her own, although she had been the wife of one of my father's shepherds, she expended the whole maternity of her nature upon me. She was always my first resource in any perplexity, for I was sure of all the help she could give me. And as she had much influence with my father, who was rather severe in his notions, I had had occasion to beg her interference. No necessity of this sort, however, had led to my visit on the present occasion.

I ran down the side of the basin, and entered the little cottage. Nurse was seated on a chair by the wall, with her usual knitting, a stocking, in one hand; but her hands were motionless, and her eyes wide open and fixed. I knew that the neighbours stood rather in awe of her, on the ground that she had the second sight; but, although she often told us frightful enough stories, she had never alluded to such a gift as being in her possession. Now I concluded at once that she was *seeing*. I was confirmed in this conclusion when, seeming to come to herself suddenly, she covered her head with her plaid, and sobbed audibly, in spite of her efforts to command herself. But I did not dare to ask her any questions, nor did she attempt any excuse for her behaviour. After a few moments, she unveiled herself, rose, and welcomed me with her usual kindness; then got me some refreshment, and began to question me about matters at home. After a pause, she said suddenly: 'When are you going to get your commission, Duncan, do you know?' I replied that I had heard nothing of it; that I did not think my father had influence or money enough to procure me one, and that I feared I should have no such good chance of distinguishing myself. She did not answer, but nodded her head three times, slowly and with compressed lips – apparently as much as to say, 'I know better.'

Just as I was leaving her, it occurred to me to mention that I had heard an odd sound the night before. She turned towards me, and looked at me fixedly. 'What was it like, Duncan, my dear?'

'Like a horse galloping with a loose shoe,' I replied.

'Duncan, Duncan, my darling!' she said, in a low, trembling voice, but with passionate earnestness, 'you did not hear it? Tell me that you did not hear it! You only want to frighten poor old nurse: some one has been telling you the story!'

It was my turn to be frightened now; for the matter became at once associated with my fears as to the possible nature of my auricular peculiarities. I assured her that nothing was farther from my intention than to frighten her; that, on the contrary, she had rather alarmed me; and I begged her to explain. But she sat down white and trembling, and did not speak. Presently, however, she rose again, and saying, 'I have known it happen sometimes without anything very bad following,' began to put away the basin and plate I had been using, as if she would compel herself to be calm before me. I renewed my entreaties for an explanation, but without avail. She begged me to be content for a few days, as she was quite unable to tell the story at present. She promised, however, of her own accord, that before I left home she would tell me all she knew.

The next day a letter arrived announcing the death of a distant relation, through whose influence my father had had a lingering hope of obtaining an appointment for me. There was nothing left but to look out for a situation as tutor.

I was now almost nineteen. I had completed the usual curriculum of study at one of the Scotch universities; and, possessed of a fair knowledge of mathematics and physics, and what I considered rather more than a good foundation for classical and metaphysical acquirement, I resolved to apply for the first suitable situation that offered. But I was spared the trouble. A certain Lord Hilton, an English nobleman, residing in one of the midland counties, having heard that one of my father's sons was desirous of such a situation, wrote to him, offering me the post of tutor to his two boys, of the ages of ten and twelve . . . I was to receive a hundred pounds a year, and to hold in the family the position of a gentleman, which might mean anything or nothing, according to the disposition of the heads of the family. Preparations for my departure were immediately commenced.

I set out one evening for the cottage of my old nurse, to bid her goodbye for many months, probably years. I was to leave the next day for Edinburgh, on my way to London, whence I had to repair by coach to my new abode – almost to me like the land beyond the grave, so little did I know about it, and so wide was the separation between it and my home. The evening was sultry when I began my walk, and before I arrived at its end, the clouds rising from all quarters of the horizon, and especially gathering around the peaks of the mountain, betokened the near approach of a thunderstorm. This was a great delight to me. Gladly would I take leave of my home with the memory of a last night of tumultuous magnificence; followed, probably, by a day of weeping rain, well suited to the mood of my own heart in bidding farewell to the best of parents and the dearest of homes . . .

'I am come to bid you good-bye, Margaret; and to hear the story which you promised to tell me before I left home: I go to-morrow.'

'Do you go so soon, my darling? Well, it will be an awful night to tell it in; but, as I promised, I suppose I must.'

At the moment, two or three great drops of rain, the first of the storm, fell down the wide chimney, exploding in the clear turf-fire.

'Yes, indeed you must,' I replied.

After a short pause, she commenced. Of course she spoke in Gaelic; and I translate from my recollection of the Gaelic; but rather from the impression left upon my mind, than from any recollection of the words. She drew her chair near the fire, which we had reason to fear would soon be put out by the falling rain, and began.

'How old the story is, I do not know. It has come down through many generations. My grandmother told it to me as I tell it to you; and her mother and my mother sat beside, never interrupting, but nodding their heads at every turn. Almost it ought to begin like the fairy tales, *Once upon a time*, – it took place so long ago; but it is too dreadful and too true to tell like a fairy tale. – There were two brothers, sons of the chief of our clan, but as different in appearance and disposition as two men could be. The elder was fair-haired and strong, much given to hunting and fishing; fighting too, upon occasion, I daresay, when they made a foray upon the Saxon, to get back a mouthful of their own. But he was gentleness itself to every one about him, and the very soul of honour in all his doings. The younger was very dark in complexion, and tall and slender compared to his brother. He was very fond of book-learning, which, they say, was an uncommon taste in those times. He did not care for any sports or bodily exercises but one; and that, too, was unusual in these parts. It was horsemanship. He was a fierce rider, and as much at home in the saddle as in his study-chair. You may think that, so long ago, there was not much fit room for riding hereabouts; but, fit or not fit, he rode. From his reading and riding, the neighbours looked doubtfully upon him, and whispered about the black art. He usually bestrode a great powerful black horse, without a white hair on him; and people said it was either the devil himself, or a demon-horse from the devil's own stud. What favoured this notion was, that, in or out of the stable, the brute would let no other than his master go near him. Indeed, no one would venture, after he had killed two men, and grievously maimed a third, tearing him with his teeth and hoofs like a wild beast. But to his master he was obedient as a hound, and would even tremble in his presence sometimes.

'The youth's temper corresponded to his habits. He was both gloomy and passionate. Prone to anger, he had never been known to forgive. Debarred from anything on which he had set his heart, he would have gone mad with longing if he had not gone mad with rage. His soul was like the night around us now, dark, and sultry, and silent, but lighted up by the red levin of wrath, and torn by the bellowings of thunder-passion. He must have his will: hell might have his soul. Imagine, then, the rage and malice in his heart, when he suddenly became aware that an orphan girl, distantly related to them, who had lived with them for nearly two years, and whom he had loved for almost all that period, was loved by his elder brother, and loved him in return. He flung his right hand above his head, swore a terrible oath that if he might not, his brother should not, rushed out of the house, and galloped off among the hills.

'The orphan was a beautiful girl, tall, pale, and slender, with plentiful dark hair, which, when released from the snood, rippled down below her knees. Her appearance formed a strong contrast with that of her favoured lover, while there was some resemblance between her and the younger brother. This fact seemed, to his fierce selfishness, ground for a prior claim . . .

'At the moment when he learned their mutual attachment, probably through a domestic, the lady was on her way to meet her lover as he returned from the day's sport. The appointed place was on the edge of a deep, rocky ravine, down in whose dark bosom brawled and foamed a little mountain torrent. You know the place, Duncan, my dear, I dare say.'

(Here she gave me a minute description of the spot, with directions how to find it.)

'Whether any one saw what I am about to relate, or whether it was put together afterwards, I cannot tell. The story is like an old tree – so old that it has lost the marks of its growth. But this is how my grandmother told it to me. – An evil chance led him in the right direction. The lovers, startled by the sound of the approaching horse, parted in opposite directions along a narrow mountain-path on the edge of the ravine. Into this path he struck at a point near where the lovers had met, but to opposite sides of which they had now receded; so that he was between them on the path. Turning his horse up the course of the stream, he soon came in sight of his brother on the ledge before him. With a suppressed scream of rage, he rode headlong at him, and ere he had time to make the least defence, hurled him over the precipice. The helplessness of the strong man was uttered in one single despairing cry as he shot into the abyss. Then all was still. The sound of his fall could not reach the edge of the gulf. Divining in a moment that the lady, whose name was Elsie, must have fled in the opposite direction, he reined his steed on his haunches. He could touch the precipice with his bridle-hand half outstretched; his sword-hand half outstretched would have dropped a stone to the bottom of the ravine. There was no room to wheel. One desperate practicability alone remained. Turning his horse's head towards the edge, he compelled him, by means of the powerful bit, to rear till he stood almost erect; and so, his body swaying over the gulf, with quivering and straining muscles, to turn on his hind-legs. Having completed the half-circle, he let him drop, and urged him furiously in the opposite direction. It must have been by the devil's own care that he was able to continue his gallop along that ledge of rock.

'He soon caught sight of the maiden. She was leaning, half fainting, against the precipice. She had heard her lover's last cry, and although it had conveyed no suggestion of his voice to her ear, she trembled from head to foot, and her limbs would bear her no farther. He checked his speed, rode gently up to her, lifted her unresisting, laid her across the shoulders of his horse, and, riding carefully till he reached a more open path, dashed again wildly along the mountain-side. The lady's long hair was shaken loose, and dropped trailing on the ground. The horse trampled upon it, and stumbled, half dragging her from the saddle-bow. He caught her, lifted her up, and looked at her face. She was dead. I suppose he went mad. He laid her again across the saddle before him, and rode on, reckless whither. Horse, and man, and maiden were found the next day, lying at the foot of a cliff, dashed to pieces. It was observed that a hind-shoe of the horse was loose and broken. Whether this had been the cause of his fall, could not be told; but ever when he races, as race he will, till the day of doom, along that mountain-side, his gallop is mingled with the clank of the loose and broken shoe. For, like the sin, the punishment is awful: he shall carry about for ages the phantom-body of the girl, knowing that her soul is away, sitting with the soul of his brother,

A Ghost Story

down in the deep ravine, or scaling with him the topmost crags of the towering mountain-peaks. There are some who, from time to time, see the doomed man careering along the face of the mountain, with the lady hanging across the steed; and they say it always betokens a storm, such as this which is now raving around us.'

I had not noticed till now, so absorbed had I been in her tale, that the storm had risen to a very ecstasy of fury.

'They say, likewise, that the lady's hair is still growing; for, every time they see her, it is longer than before; and that now such is its length and the headlong speed of the horse, that it floats and streams out behind, like one of those curved clouds, like a comet's tail, far up in the sky; only the cloud is white, and the hair dark as night. And they say it will go on growing till the Last Day, when the horse will falter and her hair will gather in; and the horse will fall, and the hair will twist, and twine, and wreathe itself like a mist of threads about him, and blind him to everything but her. Then the body will rise up within it, face to face with him, animated by a fiend, who, twining *her* arms around him, will drag him down to the bottomless pit.'

I may mention something which now occurred, and which had a strange effect on my old nurse. It illustrates the assertion that we see around us only what is within us: marvellous things enough will show themselves to the marvellous mood. – During a short lull in the storm, just as she had finished her story, we heard the sound of iron-shod hoofs approaching the cottage. There was no bridle-way into the glen. A knock came to the door, and, on opening it, we saw an old man seated on a horse, with a long, slenderly-filled sack lying across the saddle before him. He said he had lost the path in the storm, and, seeing the light, had scrambled down to inquire his way. I perceived at once, from the scared and mysterious look of the old woman's eyes, that she was persuaded that this appearance had more than a little to do with the awful rider, the terrific storm, and myself who had heard the sound of the phantom-hoofs. As he ascended the hill, she looked after him, with wide and pale but unshrinking eyes; then turning in, shut and locked the door behind her, as by a natural instinct. After two or three of her significant nods, accompanied by the compression of her lips, she said:

'He need not think to take me in, wizard as he is, with his disguises. I can see him through them all. Duncan, my dear, when you suspect anything, do not be too incredulous. This human demon is of course a wizard still, and knows how to make himself, as well as anything he touches, take a quite different appearance from the real one; only every appearance must bear some resemblance, however distant, to the natural form. That man you saw at the door, was the phantom of which I have been telling you. What he is after now, of course, I cannot tell; but you must keep a bold heart, and a firm and wary foot, as you go home tonight.'

I showed some surprise, I do not doubt; and, perhaps, some fear as well; but I only said, 'How do you know him, Margaret?'

'I can hardly tell you,' she replied; 'but I do know him. I think he hates me. Often, of a wild night, when there is moonlight enough by fits, I see him tearing round this little valley, just on the top edge – all round; the lady's hair and the horse's mane and tail driving far behind, and mingling, vaporous, with the stormy clouds. About he goes, in wild careering gallop; now lost as the moon goes in, then visible far round when she looks out again – an airy, pale-gray spectre, which few eyes but mine could see; for, as far as I am aware, no one of the family but myself has ever possessed the double gift of seeing and hearing both. In this case I hear no sound, except now and then a clank from the broken shoe. – But I did not mean to tell you that I had ever seen him. I am not a bit afraid of him. He cannot do more than he may. His power is limited; else ill enough would he work, the miscreant.'

'But,' said I, 'what has all this, terrible as it is, to do with the fright you took at my telling you that I had heard the sound of the broken shoe? Surely you are not afraid of only a storm?'

'No, my boy; I fear no storm. But the fact is, that that sound is seldom heard, and never, as far as I know, by any of the blood of that wicked man, without betokening some ill to one of the family, and most probably to the one who hears it – but I am not quite sure about that. Only some evil it does portend, although a long time may elapse before it shows itself; and I have a hope it may mean some one else than you.'

'Do not wish that,' I replied. 'I know no one better able to bear it than I am; and I hope, whatever it may be, that I only shall have to meet it. It must surely be something serious to be so foretold – it can hardly be connected with my disappointment in being compelled to be a pedagogue instead of a soldier.'

'Do not trouble yourself about that, Duncan,' replied she. 'A solider you must be. The same day you told me of the clank of the broken horseshoe, I saw you return wounded from battle, and fall

A Ghost Story

fainting from your horse in the street of a great city, – only fainting, thank God. But I have particular reasons for being uneasy at *your* hearing that boding sound. – Can you tell me the day and hour of your birth?'

'No,' I replied. 'It seems very odd when I think of it, but I really do not know even the day.'

'Nor any one else; which is stranger still,' she answered.

'How does that happen, nurse?'

'We were in terrible anxiety about your mother at the time. So ill was she, after you were just born, in a strange, unaccountable way, that you lay almost neglected for more than an hour. In the very act of giving birth to you, she seemed to the rest around her to be out of her mind, so wildly did she talk; but I knew better. I knew that she was fighting some evil power; and what power it was, I knew full well; for twice, during her pains, I heard the click of the horseshoe. But no one could help her. After her delivery, she lay as if in a trance, neither dead, nor at rest, but as if frozen to ice, and conscious of it all the while. Once more I heard the terrible sound of iron: and, at the moment, your mother started from her trance, screaming. "My child! my child!" We suddenly became aware that no one had attended to the child, and rushed to the place where he lay wrapped in a blanket. Uncovering him, we found him black in the face, and spotted with dark spots upon the throat. I thought he was dead; but, with great and almost hopeless pains, we succeeded in making him breathe, and he gradually recovered. But his mother continued dreadfully exhausted. It seemed as if she had spent her life for her child's defence and birth. That was you, Duncan, my dear.

'I was in constant attendance upon her. About a week after your birth, as near as I can guess, just in the gloaming, I heard yet again the awful clank – only once. Nothing followed till about midnight. Your mother slept, and you lay asleep beside her. I sat by the bedside. A horror fell upon me suddenly, though I neither saw nor heard anything. Your mother started from her sleep with a cry, which sounded as if it came from far away, out of a dream, and did not belong to this world. My blood curdled with fear. She sat up in bed, with wide staring eyes, and half-open rigid lips, and, feeble as she was, thrust her arms straight out before her with great force, her hands open and lifted up, with the palms outwards. The whole action was of one violently repelling another. She began to talk wildly as she had done before you were born, but, though I seemed to hear and understand it all at the time, I could not recall a word of it afterwards . . . I tried to comfort and encourage her. All the time, I was in a state of indescribable cold and suffering, whether more bodily or mental I could not tell. But at length I heard yet again the clank of the shoe. A sudden peace seemed to fall upon my mind – or was it a warm, odorous wind that filled the room? Your mother dropped her arms, and turned feebly towards her baby. She saw that he slept a blessed sleep. She smiled like a glorified spirit, and fell back exhausted on the pillow. I went to the other side of the room to get a cordial. When I returned to the bedside, I saw at once that she was dead. Her face smiled still, with an expression of the uttermost bliss.'

Nurse ceased, trembling as overcome by the recollection; and I was too much moved and awed to speak. At length, resuming the conversation, she said: 'You see it is no wonder, Duncan, my dear, if, after all this, I should find, when I wanted to fix the date of your birth, that I could not determine the day or the hour when it took place. All was confusion in my poor brain. But it was strange that no one else could, any more than I. One thing only I can tell you about it. As I carried you across the room to lay you down, for I assisted at your birth, I happened to look up to the window. Then I saw what I did not forget, although I did not think of it again till many days after, – a bright star was shining on the very tip of the thin crescent moon.'

'Oh, then,' said I, 'it is possible to determine the day and the very hour when my birth took place.'

'See the good of book-learning!' replied she. 'When you work it out, just let me know, my dear, that I may remember it.'

'That I will.'

A silence of some moments followed. Margaret resumed:

'I am afraid you will laugh at my foolish fancies, Duncan; but in thinking over all these things, as you may suppose I often do, lying awake in my lonely bed, the notion sometimes comes to me: What if my Duncan be the youth whom his wicked brother hurled into the ravine, come again in a new body, to live out his life on the earth, cut short by his brother's hatred? If so, his persecution of you, and of your mother for your sake, is easy to understand. And if so, you will never never be able to rest till you find your fere, wherever she may have been born on the face of the earth. For born she must be, long ere now, for you to find. I misdoubt me much, however, if you will find her without great conflict and suffering between, for the Powers of Darkness will be against you; though I have good hope that you will

A Ghost Story

overcome at last. – You must forgive the fancies of a foolish old woman, my dear.' . . .

Few more words were spoken on either side, but after receiving renewed exhortations to carefulness on my way home, I said goodbye to dear old nurse, considerably comforted, I must confess, that I was not doomed to be a tutor all my days; for I never questioned the truth of that vision and its consequent prophecy.

I went out into the midst of the storm, into the alternating throbs of blackness and radiance; now the possessor of no more room than what my body filled, and now isolated in world-wide space. And the thunder seemed to follow me, bellowing after me as I went.

Absorbed in the story I had heard, I took my way, as I thought, homewards. The whole country was well known to me. I should have said, before that night, that I could have gone home blindfold. Whether the lightning bewildered me and made me take a false turn, I cannot tell; for the hardest thing to understand, in intellectual as well as normal mistakes, is – how we came to go wrong. But after wandering for some time, plunged in meditation, and with no warning whatever of the presence of inimical powers, a brilliant lightning-flash showed me that at least I was not near home. The light was prolonged for a second or two by a slight electric pulsation; and by that I distinguished a wide space of blackness on the ground in front of me. Once more wrapped in the folds of a thick darkness, I dared not move. Suddenly it occurred to me what the blackness was, and whither I had wandered. It was a huge quarry, of great depth, long disused, and half filled with water. I knew the place perfectly. A few more steps would have carried me over the brink. I stood still, waiting for the next flash, that I might be quite sure of the way I was about to take before I ventured to move. While I stood, I fancied I heard a single hollow plunge in the black water far below. When the lightning came, I turned, and took my path in another direction.

After walking for some time across the heath, I fell. The fall became a roll, and down a steep declivity I went, over and over, arriving at the bottom uninjured.

Another flash soon showed me where I was – in the hollow valley, within a couple of hundred yards from nurse's cottage. I made my way towards it. There was no light in it, except the feeblest glow from the embers of her peat fire. 'She is in bed,' I said to myself, 'and I will not disturb her.' . . .

By this time the storm had lulled. The moon had been up for some time, but had been quite concealed by tempestuous clouds. Now, however, these had begun to break up; and, while I stood looking into the cottage, they scattered away from the face of the moon, and . . . I found my way home without any further difficulty, and went to bed, where I soon fell asleep, thoroughly wearied, more by the mental excitement I had been experiencing, than by the amount of bodily exercise I had gone through.

My sleep was tormented with awful dreams; yet, strange to say, I awoke in the morning refreshed and fearless. The sun was shining through the chinks in my shutters, which had been closed because of the storm, and was making streaks and bands of golden brilliancy upon the wall. I had dressed and completed my preparations long before I heard the steps of the servant who came to call me.

What a wonderful thing waking is! The time of the ghostly moonshine passes by, and the great positive sunlight comes. A man who dreams, and knows that he is dreaming, thinks he knows what waking is; but knows it so little, that he mistakes, one after another, many a vague and dim change in his dream for an awaking. When the true waking comes at last, he is filled and overflowed with the power of its reality. So, likewise, one who, in the darkness, lies waiting for the light about to be struck, and trying to conceive, with all the force of his imagination, what the light will be like, is yet, when the reality flames up before him, seized as by a new and unexpected thing, different from and beyond all his imagining. He feels as if the darkness were cast to an infinite distance behind him. So shall it be with us when we wake from this dream of life into the truer life beyond, and find all our present notions of being, thrown back as into a dim, vapoury region of dreamland, where yet we thought we knew, and whence we looked forward into the present. This must be what Novalis means when he says: 'Our life is not a dream; but it may become a dream, and perhaps ought to become one.'

And so I look back upon the strange history of my past; sometimes asking myself – 'Can it be that all this has really happened to the same *me*, who am now thinking about it in doubt and wonderment.'

The Golden Key

Included among MacDonald's collection of children's tales, *Dealings with the Fairies*, 1867, *The Golden Key* is that special delight, an allegory which appeals equally to children and adults, though, obviously at different levels. The child will read it as the adventures of two children with a golden key who travel through fairyland in search of the lock. At a deeper level it may be seen as the journey of a man and wife through life into death and beyond.

The tale is full of symbolism and significance which like a puzzle takes time to unravel, and which perhaps should not be analysed too closely for fear of destroying its mystery. Certainly, the story should be read first before any interpretation so that its beauty and goodness and truth can be allowed to stir the imagination to come to its own conclusions.

Many poets and scholars, including R. L. Wolff, Rolland Hein, C. S. Lewis and W. H. Auden, have made their own interpretations of the allegory and all are worth studying. Briefly, the gold key may be said to represent the gift of love to be found to a greater or lesser degree in all men. (Wolff also sees it as symbolizing the male phallus which is why Mossy finds it rather than Tangle, and the analogy is worth following throughout the story.) The quest is for the keyhole, the completion of love, human and divine, to be found in 'the land from whence the shadows fall'. The wise and beautiful grandmother, symbol of mother earth and a familiar figure in MacDonald's fantasies, prepares the children for their journey through life. Her feathered fishes who crave to be eaten so that they may attain a higher life form as guardian angels, remind Christians of Holy Communion, the sacrament that provides sustenance for the soul on its journey through life.

Time passes at a different rate in fairyland. Mossy and Tangle enjoy their youth in the enchanted forest where the birds and beasts, like human aquaintances, are either generous or mean. Together the couple ascend precipices and travel the long dark tunnel which could be said to represent the trials of marriage and middle age. With difficulty they descend to the great plains of age where they are haunted by beautiful shadows that seem to reflect a better world and make them long for 'the land from whence the shadows fall'. The two are separated when Tangle dies first, but life after death continues for her. Without the key, that special talent for loving, the journey is longer and harder for Tangle. She meets the three Old Men of the Sea, the Earth and Fire – an evolutionary paradox – who, the older they are, the younger they appear. Thus the Old Man of the Sea, the youngest in evolutionary terms, is seen as a man in his prime, the Earth appears as a brilliant youth, and Fire, the oldest, is represented by a child, the Christ-child, MacDonald's clearest image of God the Father, who gives Tangle a serpent – Celtic symbol of wisdom – which leads her towards her goal.

Mossy dies seven years later but his talent for loving gives him the Christ-like ability to walk on water so that he quickly reaches the first of the two sapphire keyholes, perfection of human love, and finds Tangle greatly changed but recognizable as his beloved. Together they find the second keyhole and the door which leads them up the rainbow to 'the land from whence the shadows fall', heaven and perfect love.

E.S.

There was a boy who used to sit in the twilight and listen to his great-aunt's stories.

She told him that if he could reach the place where the end of the rainbow stands he would find there a golden key.

'And what is the key for?' the boy would ask. 'What is it the key of? What will it open?'

'That nobody knows,' his aunt would reply. 'He has to find that out.'

'I suppose, being gold,' the boy once said, thoughtfully, 'that I could get a good deal of money for it if I sold it.'

'Better never find it than sell it,' returned his aunt.

And then the boy went to bed and dreamed about the golden key.

Now all that his great-aunt told the boy about the golden key would have been nonsense, had it not been that their little house stood on the borders of Fairyland. For it is perfectly well known that out of Fairyland nobody ever can find where the rainbow stands. The creature takes such good care of its golden key, always flitting from

The Golden Key

place to place, lest any one should find it! But in Fairyland it is quite different. Things that look real in this country look very thin indeed in Fairyland, while some of the things that here cannot stand still for a moment, will not move there. So it was not in the least absurd of the old lady to tell her nephew such things about the golden key.

'Did you ever know anybody find it?' he asked, one evening.
'Yes. Your father, I believe, found it.'
'And what did he do with it, can you tell me?'
'He never told me.'
'What was it like?'
'He never showed it to me.'
'How does a new key come there always?'
'I don't know. There it is.'
'Perhaps it is the rainbow's egg.'
'Perhaps it is. You will be a happy boy if you find the nest.'
'Perhaps it comes tumbling down the rainbow from the sky.'
'Perhaps it does.'

One evening, in summer, he went into his own room, and stood at the lattice-window, and gazed into the forest which fringed the outskirts of Fairyland. It came close up to his great-aunt's garden, and, indeed, sent some straggling trees into it. The forest lay to the east, and the sun, which was setting behind the cottage, looked straight into the dark wood with his level red eye. The trees were all old, and had few branches below, so that the sun could see a great way into the forest; and the boy, being keen-sighted, could see almost as far as the sun. The trunks stood like rows of red columns in the shine of the red sun, and he could see down aisle after aisle in the vanishing distance. And as he gazed into the forest he began to feel as if the trees were all waiting for him, and had something they could not go on with till he came to them. But he was hungry, and wanted his supper. So he lingered.

Suddenly, far among the trees, as far as the sun could shine, he saw a glorious thing. It was the end of a rainbow, large and brilliant. He could count all the seven colours, and could see shade after shade beyond the violet; while before the red stood a colour more gorgeous and mysterious still. It was a colour he had never seen before. Only the spring of the rainbow-arch was visible. He could see nothing of it above the trees.

'The golden key!' he said to himself, and darted out of the house, and into the wood.

He had not gone far before the sun set. But the rainbow only glowed the brighter. For the rainbow of Fairyland is not dependent upon the sun as ours is. The trees welcomed him. The bushes made way for him. The rainbow grew larger and brighter; and at length he found himself within two trees of it.

It was a grand sight, burning away there in silence, with its gorgeous, its lovely, its delicate colours, each distinct, all combining. He could now see a great deal more of it. It rose high into the blue heavens, but bent so little that he could not tell how high the crown of the arch must reach. It was still only a small portion of a huge bow.

He stood gazing at it till he forgot himself with delight – even forgot the key which he had come to seek. And as he stood it grew more wonderful still. For in each of the colours, which was as large as the column of a church, he could faintly see beautiful forms slowly ascending as if by the steps of a winding stair. The forms appeared irregularly – now one, now many, now several, now none – men and women and children – all different, all beautiful.

He drew nearer to the rainbow. It vanished. He started back a step in dismay. It was there again, as beautiful as ever. So he contented himself with standing as near it as he might, and watching the forms that ascended the glorious colours towards the unknown height of the arch, which did not end abruptly, but faded away in the blue air, so gradually that he could not say where it ceased.

When the thought of the golden key returned, the boy very wisely proceeded to mark out in his mind the space covered by the foundation of the rainbow, in order that he might know where to search, should the rainbow disappear. It was based chiefly upon a bed of moss.

Meantime it had grown quite dark in the wood. The rainbow alone was visible by its own light. But the moment the moon rose the rainbow vanished. Nor could any change of place restore the vision to the boy's eyes. So he threw himself down upon the mossy bed, to wait till the sunlight would give him a chance of finding the key. There he fell fast asleep.

When he woke in the morning the sun was looking straight into his eyes. He turned away from it, and the same moment saw a brilliant little thing lying on the moss within a foot of his face. It was the golden key. The pipe of it was of plain gold, as bright as gold could be. The handle was curiously wrought and set with sapphires. In a terror of delight he put out his hand and took it, and had it.

He lay for a while, turning it over and over, and feeding his eyes upon its beauty. Then he jumped to his feet, remembering that the pretty thing was of no use to him yet. Where was the lock to which the key belonged? It must be somewhere, for how could anybody be so silly as make a key for which there was no lock? Where should he go to look for it? He gazed about him, up into the air, down to the earth, but saw no keyhole in the clouds, in the grass, or in the trees.

Just as he began to grow disconsolate, however, he saw something glimmering in the wood. It was a mere glimmer that he saw, but he took it for a glimmer of rainbow, and went towards it. – And now I will go back to the borders of the forest.

Not far from the house where the boy had lived, there was another house, the owner of which was a merchant, who was much away from home. He had lost his wife some years before, and had only one child, a little girl, whom he left to the charge of two servants, who were very idle and careless. So she was neglected and left untidy, and was sometimes ill-used besides.

Now it is well known that the little creatures commonly called fairies, though there are many different kinds of fairies in Fairyland, have an exceeding dislike to untidiness. Indeed, they are quite spiteful to slovenly people. Being used to all the lovely ways of the trees and flowers, and to the neatness of the birds and all woodland creatures, it makes them feel miserable, even in their deep woods and on their grassy carpets, to think that within the same moonlight lies a dirty, uncomfortable, slovenly house. And this makes them angry with the people that live in it, and they would gladly drive them out of the world if they could. They want the whole earth nice and clean. So they pinch the maids black and blue, and play them all manner of uncomfortable tricks.

But this house was quite a shame, and the fairies in the forest could not endure it. They tried everything on the maids without effect, and at last resolved upon making a clean riddance, beginning with the child. They ought to have known that it was not her fault, but they have little principle and much mischief in them, and they thought that if they got rid of her the maids would be sure to be turned away.

So one evening, the poor little girl having been put to bed early, before the sun was down, the servants went off to the village, locking the door behind them. The child did not know she was alone, and lay contentedly looking out of her window towards the forest, of which, however, she could not see much, because of the ivy and other creeping plants which had straggled across her window. All at once she saw an ape making faces at her out of the mirror, and the heads carved upon a great old wardrobe grinning fearfully. Then two old spider-legged chairs came forward into the middle of the room, and began to dance a queer, old-fashioned dance. This set her laughing, and she forgot the ape and the grinning heads. So the fairies saw they had made a mistake, and sent the chairs back to their places. But they knew that she had been reading the story of Silverhair all day. So the next moment she heard the voices of the three bears upon the stair, big voice, middle voice, and little voice, and she heard their soft, heavy tread, as if they had had stockings over their boots, coming nearer and nearer to the door of her room, till she could bear it no longer. She did just as Silverhair did, and as the fairies wanted her to do: she darted to the window, pulled it open, got upon the ivy, and so scrambled to the ground. She then fled to the forest as fast as she could run.

Now, although she did not know it, this was the very best way she could have gone; for nothing is ever so mischievous in its own place as it is out of it; and, besides, these mischievous creatures were only the children of Fairyland, as it were, and there are many other beings there as well; and if a wanderer gets in among them, the good ones will always help him more than the evil ones will be able to hurt him.

The sun was now set, and the darkness coming on, but the child thought of no danger but the bears behind her. If she had looked round, however, she would have seen that she was followed by a very different creature from a bear. It was a curious creature, made like a fish, but covered, instead of scales, with feathers of all colours, sparkling like those of a humming-bird. It had fins, not wings, and swam through the air as a fish does through the water. Its head was like the head of a small owl.

After running a long way, and as the last of the light was disappearing, she passed under a tree with drooping branches. It dropped its branches to the ground all about her, and caught her as in a trap. She struggled to get out, but the branches pressed her closer and closer to the trunk. She was in great terror and distress, when the air-fish, swimming into the thicket of branches, began tearing them with its beak. They loosened their hold at once, and the creature went on attacking them, till at length they let the child go. Then the air-fish came from behind her, and swam on in front, glittering and sparkling all lovely colours; and she followed.

It led her gently along till all at once it swam in at a cottage-door. The child followed still. There was a bright fire in the middle of the floor, upon which stood a pot without a lid, full of water that boiled and bubbled furiously. The air-fish swam straight to the pot and into the boiling water, where it lay quiet. A beautiful woman rose from the opposite side of the fire and came to meet the girl. She took her up in her arms, and said, –

'Ah, you are come at last! I have been looking for you a long time.'

She sat down with her on her lap, and there the girl sat staring at her. She had never seen anything so beautiful. She was tall and strong, with white arms and neck, and a delicate flush on her face. The child could not tell what was the colour of her hair, but could not help thinking it had a tinge of dark green. She had not one ornament upon her, but she looked as if she had just put off quantities of diamonds and emeralds. Yet here she was in the simplest, poorest little cottage, where she was evidently at home. She was dressed in shining green.

The girl looked at the lady, and the lady looked at the girl.

'What is your name?' asked the lady.

'The servants always called me Tangle.'

'Ah, that was because your hair was so untidy. But that was their fault, the naughty women! Still it is a pretty name, and I will call you Tangle too. You must not mind my asking you questions, for you may ask me the same questions, every one of them, and any others that you like. How old are you?'

'Ten,' answered Tangle.

'You don't look like it,' said the lady.

'How old are you, please?' returned Tangle.

'Thousands of years old,' answered the lady.

'You don't look like it,' said Tangle.

'Don't I? I think I do. Don't you see how beautiful I am?'

And her great blue eyes looked down on the little Tangle, as if all the stars in the sky were melted in them to make their brightness.

'Ah! but,' said Tangle, 'when people live long they grow old. At least I always thought so.'

'I have no time to grow old,' said the lady. 'I am too busy for that. It is very idle to grow old. – But I cannot have my little girl so untidy. Do you know I can't find a clean spot on your face to kiss?'

'Perhaps,' suggested Tangle, feeling ashamed, but not too much so to say a word for herself – 'perhaps that is because the tree made me cry so.'

'My poor darling!' said the lady, looking now as if the moon were melted in her eyes, and kissing her little face, dirty as it was, 'the naughty tree must suffer for making a girl cry.'

'And what is your name, please?' asked Tangle.

'Grandmother,' answered the lady.

'Is it really?'

'Yes, indeed. I never tell stories, even in fun.'

'How good of you!'

'I couldn't if I tried. It would come true if I said it, and then I should be punished enough.'

And she smiled like the sun through a summer-shower.

'But now,' she went on, 'I must get you washed and dressed, and then we shall have some supper.'

'Oh! I had supper long ago,' said Tangle.

'Yes, indeed you had,' answered the lady – 'three years ago. You don't know that it is three years since you ran away from the bears. You are thirteen and more now.'

Tangle could only stare. She felt quite sure it was true.

'You will not be afraid of anything I do with you – will you?' said the lady.

'I will try very hard not to be; but I can't be certain, you know,' replied Tangle.

'I like your saying so, and I shall be quite satisfied,' answered the lady.

She took off the girl's night-gown, rose with her in her arms, and going to the wall of the cottage, opened a door. Then Tangle saw a deep tank, the sides of which were filled with green plants, which had flowers of all colours. There was a roof over it like the roof of the cottage. It was filled with beautiful clear water, in which swam a multitude of such fishes as the one that had led her to the cottage. It was the light their colours gave that showed the place in which they were.

The lady spoke some words Tangle could not understand, and threw her into the tank.

The fishes came crowding about her. Two or three of them got under her head and kept it up. The rest of them rubbed themselves all over her, and with their wet feathers washed her quite clean. Then the lady, who had been looking on all the time, spoke again;

whereupon some thirty or forty of the fishes rose out of the water underneath Tangle, and so bore her up to the arms the lady held out to take her. She carried her back to the fire, and, having dried her well, opened a chest, and taking out the finest linen garments, smelling of grass and lavender, put them upon her, and over all a green dress, just like her own, shining like hers, and soft like hers, and going into just such lovely folds from the waist, where it was tied with a brown cord, to her bare feet.

'Won't you give me a pair of shoes too, grandmother?' said Tangle.

'No, my dear; no shoes. Look here. I wear no shoes.'

So saying she lifted her dress a little, and there were the loveliest white feet, but no shoes. Then Tangle was content to go without shoes too. And the lady sat down with her again, and combed her hair, and brushed it, and then left it to dry while she got the supper.

First she got bread out of one hole in the wall; then milk out of another; then several kinds of fruit out of a third; and then she went to the pot on the fire, and took out the fish, now nicely cooked, and, as soon as she had pulled off its feathered skin, ready to be eaten.

'But,' exclaimed Tangle. And she stared at the fish, and could say no more.

'I know what you mean,' returned the lady. 'You do not like to eat the messenger that brought you home. But it is the kindest return you can make. The creature was afraid to go until it saw me put the pot on, and heard me promise it should be boiled the moment it returned with you. Then it darted out of the door at once. You saw it go into the pot of itself the moment it entered, did you not?'

'I did,' answered Tangle, 'and I thought it very strange; but then I saw you, and forgot all about the fish.'

'In Fairyland,' resumed the lady, as they sat down to the table, 'the ambition of the animals is to be eaten by the people; for that is their highest end in that condition. But they are not therefore destroyed. Out of that pot comes something more than the dead fish, you will see.'

Tangle now remarked that the lid was on the pot. But the lady took no further notice of it till they had eaten the fish, which Tangle found nicer than any fish she had ever tasted before. It was as white as snow, and as delicate as cream. And the moment she had swallowed a mouthful of it, a change she could not describe began to take place in her. She heard a murmuring all about her, which became more and more articulate, and at length, as she went on eating, grew intelligible. By the time she had finished her share, the sounds of all the animals in the forest came crowding through the door to her ears; for the door still stood wide open, though it was pitch-dark outside; and they were no longer sounds only; they were speech, and speech that she could understand. She could tell what the insects in the cottage were saying to each other too. She had even a suspicion that the trees and flowers all about the cottage were holding midnight communications with each other; but what they said she could not hear.

As soon as the fish was eaten, the lady went to the fire and took the lid off the pot. A lovely little creature in human shape, with large white wings, rose out of it, and flew round and round the roof of the cottage; then dropped, fluttering, and nestled in the lap of the lady. She spoke to it some strange words, carried it to the door, and threw it out into the darkness. Tangle heard the flapping of its wings die away in the distance.

'Now have we done the fish any harm?' she said, returning.

'No,' answered Tangle, 'I do not think we have. I should not mind eating one every day.'

'They must wait their time, like you and me too, my little Tangle.'

And she smiled a smile which the sadness in it made more lovely.

'But,' she continued, 'I think we may have one for supper tomorrow.'

So saying she went to the door of the tank, and spoke; and now Tangle understood her perfectly.

'I want one of you,' she said, – 'the wisest.'

Thereupon the fishes got together in the middle of the tank, with their heads forming a circle above the water, and their tails a larger circle beneath it. They were holding a council, in which their relative wisdom should be determined. At length one of them flew up into the lady's hand, looking lively and ready.

'You know where the rainbow stands?' she asked.

'Yes, mother, quite well,' answered the fish.

'Bring home a young man you will find there, who does not know where to go.'

The fish was out of the door in a moment. Then the lady told Tangle it was time to go to bed; and, opening another door in the side of the cottage, showed her a little arbour, cool and green, with a bed of purple heath growing in it, upon which she threw a large wrapper made of the feathered skins of the wise fishes, shining gorgeous in the firelight. Tangle was soon lost in the strangest, loveliest dreams. And the beautiful lady was in every one of her dreams.

In the morning she woke to the rustling of leaves over her head, and the sound of running water. But, to her surprise, she could find no door – nothing but the moss-grown wall of the cottage. So she crept through an opening in the arbour, and stood in the forest. Then she bathed in a stream that ran merrily through the trees, and felt happier; for having once been in her grandmother's pond, she must be clean and tidy ever after; and, having put on her green dress, felt like a lady.

She spent that day in the wood, listening to the birds and beasts and creeping things. She understood all that they said, though she could not repeat a word of it; and every kind had a different language, while there was a common though more limited understanding between all the inhabitants of the forest. She saw nothing of the beautiful lady, but she felt that she was near her all the time; and she took care not to go out of sight of the cottage. It was round, like a snow-hut or a wigwam; and she could see neither door nor window in it. The fact was, it had no windows; and though it was full of doors, they all opened from the inside, and could not even be seen from the outside.

She was standing at the foot of a tree in the twilight, listening to a quarrel between a mole and a squirrel, in which the mole told the squirrel that the tail was the best of him, and the squirrel called the mole Spade-fists, when, the darkness having deepened around her, she became aware of something shining in her face, and looking round, saw that the door of the cottage was open, and the red light of the fire flowing from it like a river through the darkness. She left Mole and Squirrel to settle matters as they might, and darted off to the cottage. Entering, she found the pot boiling on the fire, and the grand, lovely lady sitting on the other side of it.

'I've been watching you all day,' said the lady. 'You shall have something to eat by-and-by, but we must wait till our supper comes home.'

She took Tangle on her knee, and began to sing to her – such songs as made her wish she could listen to them for ever. But at length in rushed the shining fish, and snuggled down in the pot. It was followed by a youth who had outgrown his worn garments. His face was ruddy with health, and in his hand he carried a little jewel, which sparkled in the firelight.

The first words the lady said were, –

'What is that in your hand, Mossy?'

Now Mossy was the name his companions had given him, because he had a favourite stone covered with moss, on which he used to sit whole days reading; and they said the moss had begun to grow upon him too.

Mossy held out his hand. The moment the lady saw that it was the golden key, she rose from her chair, kissed Mossy on the forehead, made him sit down on her seat, and stood before him like a servant. Mossy could not bear this, and rose at once. But the lady begged him, with tears in her beautiful eyes, to sit, and let her wait on him.

'But you are a great, splendid, beautiful lady,' said Mossy.

'Yes, I am. But I work all day long – that is my pleasure; and you will have to leave me so soon!'

'How do you know that, if you please, madam?' asked Mossy.

'Because you have got the golden key.'

'But I don't know what it is for. I can't find the keyhole. Will you tell me what to do?'

'You must look for the keyhole. That is your work. I cannot help you. I can only tell you that if you look for it you will find it.'

'What kind of box will it open? What is there inside?'

'I do not know. I dream about it, but I know nothing.'

'Must I go at once?'

'You may stop here tonight, and have some of my supper. But you must go in the morning. All I can do for you is to give you clothes. Here is a girl called Tangle, whom you must take with you.'

'That *will* be nice,' said Mossy.

'No, no!' said Tangle. 'I don't want to leave you, please, grandmother.'

'You must go with him, Tangle. I am sorry to lose you, but it will be the best thing for you. Even the fishes, you see, have to go into the pot, and then out into the dark. If you fall in with the Old Man of the Sea, mind you ask him whether he has not got some more fishes ready for me. My tank is getting thin.'

So saying, she took the fish from the pot, and put the lid on as before. They sat down and ate the fish, and then the winged creature rose from the pot, circled the roof, and settled on the lady's lap. She talked to it, carried it to the door, and threw it out into the dark. They heard the flap of its wings die away in the distance.

The lady then showed Mossy into just such another chamber as that of Tangle; and in the morning he found a suit of clothes laid beside him. He looked very handsome in them. But the wearer of Grandmother's clothes never thinks about how he or she looks, but thinks always how handsome other people are.

Tangle was very unwilling to go.

'Why should I leave you? I don't know the young man,' she said to the lady.

'I am never allowed to keep my children long. You need not go with him except you please, but you must go some day; and I should like you to go with him, for he has the golden key. No girl need be afraid to go with a youth that has the golden key. You will take care of her, Mossy, will you not?'

'That I will,' said Mossy.

And Tangle cast a glance at him, and thought she should like to go with him.

'And,' said the lady, 'if you should lose each other as you go through the – the – I never can remember the name of that country, – do not be afraid, but go on and on.'

She kissed Tangle on the mouth and Mossy on the forehead, led them to the door, and waved her hand eastward. Mossy and Tangle took each other's hand and walked away into the depth of the forest. In his right hand Mossy held the golden key.

They wandered thus a long way, with endless amusement from the talk of the animals. They soon learned enough of their language to ask them necessary questions. The squirrels were always friendly, and gave them nuts out of their own hoards; but the bees were selfish and rude, justifying themselves on the ground that Tangle and Mossy were not subjects of their queen, and charity must begin at home, though indeed they had not one drone in their poorhouse at the time. Even the blinking moles would fetch them an earth-nut or a truffle now and then, talking as if their mouths, as well as their eyes and ears, were full of cotton wool, or their own velvety fur. By the time they got out of the forest they were very fond of each other, and Tangle was not in the least sorry that her grandmother had sent her away with Mossy.

At length the trees grew smaller, and stood farther apart, and the ground began to rise, and it got more and more steep, till the trees were all left behind, and the two were climbing a narrow path with rocks on each side. Suddenly they came upon a rude doorway, by which they entered a narrow gallery cut in the rock. It grew darker and darker, till it was pitch-dark, and they had to feel their way. At length the light began to return, and at last they came out upon a narrow path on the face of a lofty precipice. This path went winding down the rock to a wide plain, circular in shape, and surrounded on all sides by mountains. Those opposite to them were a great way off, and towered to an awful height, shooting up sharp, blue, ice-enamelled pinnacles. An utter silence reigned where they stood. Not even the sound of water reached them.

Looking down, they could not tell whether the valley below was a grassy plain or a great still lake. They had never seen any space look like it. The way to it was difficult and dangerous, but down the narrow path they went, and reached the bottom in safety. They found it composed of smooth, light-coloured sandstone, undulating in parts, but mostly level. It was no wonder to them now that they had not been able to tell what it was, for this surface was everywhere crowded with shadows. It was a sea of shadows. The mass was chiefly made up of the shadows of leaves innumerable, of all lovely and imaginative forms, waving to and fro, floating and quivering in the breath of a breeze whose motion was unfelt, whose sound was unheard. No forests clothed the mountain-sides, no trees were anywhere to be seen, and yet the shadows of the leaves, branches, and stems of all various trees covered the valley as far as their eyes could reach. They soon spied the shadows of flowers mingled with those of the leaves, and now and then the shadow of a bird with open beak, and throat distended with song. At times would appear the forms of strange, graceful creatures, running up and down the shadow-boles and along the branches, to disappear in the wind-tossed foliage. As they walked they waded knee-deep in the lovely lake. For the shadows were not merely lying on the surface of the ground, but heaped up above it like substantial forms of darkness, as if they had been cast upon a thousand different planes of the air. Tangle and Mossy often lifted their heads and gazed upwards to descry whence the shadows came; but they could see nothing more than a bright mist spread above them, higher than the tops of the mountains, which stood clear against it. No forests, no leaves, no birds were visible.

After a while, they reached more open spaces, where the shadows were thinner; and came even to portions over which shadows only flitted, leaving them clear for such as might follow. Now a wonderful form, half bird-like half human, would float across on outspread sailing pinions. Anon an exquisite shadow group of gambolling children would be followed by the loveliest female form, and that again by the grand stride of a Titanic shape, each disappearing in the surrounding press of shadowy foliage. Sometimes a profile of unspeakable beauty or grandeur would appear for a moment and vanish. Sometimes they seemed lovers that passed linked arm in arm, sometimes father and son, sometimes brothers in loving contest, sometimes sisters entwined in gracefullest community of complex form. Sometimes wild horses would tear across, free, or bestrode by noble shadows of ruling men. But some of the things which pleased them most they never knew how to describe.

About the middle of the plain they sat down to rest in the heart of a heap of shadows. After sitting for a while, each, looking up, saw the other in tears: they were each longing after the country whence the shadows fell.

'We *must* find the country from which the shadows come,' said Mossy.

'We must, dear Mossy,' responded Tangle. 'What if your golden key should be the key to *it?*'

'Ah! that would be grand,' returned Mossy. – 'But we must rest here for a little, and then we shall be able to cross the plain before night.'

So he lay down on the ground, and about him on every side, and over his head, was the constant play of the wonderful shadows. He could look through them, and see the one behind the other, till they mixed in a mass of darkness. Tangle, too, lay admiring, and wondering, and longing after the country whence the shadows came. When they were rested they rose and pursued their journey.

How long they were in crossing this plain I cannot tell; but before night Mossy's hair was streaked with grey, and Tangle had got wrinkles on her forehead.

As evening drew on, the shadows fell deeper and rose higher. At length they reached a place where they rose above their heads, and made all dark around them. Then they took hold of each other's hand, and walked on in silence and in some dismay. They felt the gathering darkness, and something strangely solemn besides, and the beauty of the shadows ceased to delight them. All at once Tangle found that she had not a hold of Mossy's hand, though when she lost it she could not tell.

'Mossy, Mossy!' she cried aloud in terror.

But no Mossy replied.

A moment after, the shadows sank to her feet, and down under her feet, and the mountains rose before her. She turned towards the gloomy region she had left, and called once more upon Mossy. There the gloom lay tossing and heaving, a dark, stormy, foamless sea of shadows, but no Mossy rose out of it, or came climbing up the hill on which she stood. She threw herself down and wept in despair.

Suddenly she remembered that the beautiful lady had told them, if they lost each other in a country of which she could not remember the name, they were not to be afraid, but to go straight on.

'And besides,' she said to herself, 'Mossy has the golden key, and so no harm will come to him, I do believe.'

She rose from the ground, and went on.

Before long she arrived at a precipice, in the face of which a stair was cut. When she had ascended half-way, the stair ceased, and the path led straight into the mountain. She was afraid to enter, and turning again towards the stair, grew giddy at sight of the depth beneath her, and was forced to throw herself down in the mouth of the cave.

When she opened her eyes, she saw a beautiful little creature with wings standing beside her, waiting.

'I know you,' said Tangle. 'You are my fish.'

'Yes. But I am a fish no longer. I am an aëranth now.'

'What is that?' asked Tangle.

'What you see I am,' answered the shape. 'And I am come to lead you through the mountain.'

'Oh! thank you, dear fish – aëranth, I mean,' returned Tangle, rising.

Thereupon the aëranth took to his wings, and flew on through the long, narrow passage, reminding Tangle very much of the way he had swum on before her when he was a fish. And the moment his white wings moved, they began to throw off a continuous shower of sparks of all colours, which lighted up the passage before them. – All at once he vanished, and Tangle heard a low, sweet sound, quite different from the rush and crackle of his wings. Before her was an open arch, and through it came light, mixed with the sound of sea-waves.

She hurried out, and fell, tired and happy, upon the yellow sand of the shore. There she lay, half asleep with weariness and rest, listening to the low plash and retreat of the tiny waves, which seemed ever enticing the land to leave off being land, and become sea. And as she lay, her eyes were fixed upon the foot of a great rainbow standing far

The Golden Key

away against the sky on the other side of the sea. At length she fell fast asleep.

When she awoke, she saw an old man with long white hair down to his shoulders, leaning upon a stick covered with green buds, and so bending over her.

'What do you want here, beautiful woman?' he said.

'Am I beautiful? I am so glad!' answered Tangle, rising. 'My grandmother is beautiful.'

'Yes. But what do you want?' he repeated, kindly.

'I think I want you. Are not you the Old Man of the Sea?'

'I am.'

'Then grandmother says, have you any more fishes ready for her?'

'We will go and see, my dear,' answered the old man, speaking yet more kindly than before. 'And I can do something for you, can I not?'

'Yes – show me the way up to the country from which the shadows fall,' said Tangle.

For there she hoped to find Mossy again.

'Ah! indeed, that would be worth doing,' said the old man. 'But I cannot, for I do not know the way myself. But I will send you to the Old Man of the Earth. Perhaps he can tell you. He is much older than I am.'

Leaning on his staff, he conducted her along the shore to a steep rock, that looked like a petrified ship turned upside down. The door of it was the rudder of a great vessel, ages ago at the bottom of the sea. Immediately within the door was a stair in the rock, down which the old man went, and Tangle followed. At the bottom the old man had his house, and there he lived.

As soon as she entered it, Tangle heard a strange noise, unlike anything she had ever heard before. She soon found that it was the fishes talking. She tried to understand what they said; but their speech was so old-fashioned, and rude, and undefined, that she could not make much of it.

'I will go and see about those fishes for my daughter,' said the Old Man of the Sea.

And moving a slide in the wall of his house, he first looked out, and then tapped upon a thick piece of crystal that filled the round opening. Tangle came up behind him, and peeping through the window into the heart of the great deep green ocean, saw the most curious creatures, some very ugly, all very odd, and with especially queer mouths, swimming about everywhere, above and below, but all coming towards the window in answer to the tap of the Old Man of the Sea. Only a few could get their mouths against the glass; but those who were floating miles away yet turned their heads towards it. The Old Man looked through the whole flock carefully for some minutes, and then turning to Tangle, said, –

'I am sorry I have not got one ready yet. I want more time than she does. But I will send some as soon as I can.'

He then shut the slide.

Presently a great noise arose in the sea. The old man opened the slide again, and tapped on the glass, whereupon the fishes were all as still as sleep.

'They were only talking about you,' he said. 'And they do speak such nonsense! – Tomorrow,' he continued, 'I must show you the way to the Old Man of the Earth. He lives a long way from here.'

'Do let me go at once,' said Tangle.

'No. That is not possible. You must come this way first.'

He led her to a hole in the wall, which she had not observed before. It was covered with the green leaves and white blossoms of a creeping plant.

'Only white-blossoming plants can grow under the sea,' said the old man. 'In there you will find a bath, in which you must lie till I call you.'

Tangle went in, and found a smaller room or cave, in the further corner of which was a great basin hollowed out of a rock, and half-full of the clearest sea-water. Little streams were constantly running into it from cracks in the wall of the cavern. It was polished quite smooth inside, and had a carpet of yellow sand in the bottom of it. Large green leaves and white flowers of various plants crowded up and over it, draping and covering it almost entirely.

No sooner was she undressed and lying in the bath, than she began to feel as if the water were sinking into her, and she were receiving all the good of sleep without undergoing its forgetfulness. She felt the good coming all the time. And she grew happier and more hopeful than she had been since she lost Mossy. But she could not help thinking how very sad it was for a poor old man to live there all alone, and have to take care of a whole seaful of stupid and riotous fishes.

After about an hour, as she thought, she heard his voice calling her, and rose out of the bath. All the fatigue and aching of her long journey had vanished. She was as whole, and strong, and well as if she had slept for seven days.

Returning to the opening that led into the other part of the house, she started back with amazement, for through it she saw the form of a grand man, with a majestic and beautiful face, waiting for her.

'Come,' he said; 'I see you are ready.'

She entered with reverence.

'Where is the Old Man of the Sea?' she asked, humbly.

'There is no one here but me,' he answered, smiling. 'Some people call me the Old Man of the Sea. Others have another name for me, and are terribly frightened when they meet me taking a walk by the shore. Therefore I avoid being seen by them, for they are so afraid, that they never see what I really am. You see me now. – But I must show you the way to the Old Man of the Earth.'

He led her into the cave where the bath was, and there she saw, in the opposite corner, a second opening in the rock.

'Go down that stair, and it will bring you to him,' said the Old Man of the Sea.

With humble thanks Tangle took her leave. She went down the winding-stair, till she began to fear there was no end to it. Still down and down it went, rough and broken, with springs of water bursting out of the rocks and running down the steps beside her. It was quite dark about her, and yet she could see. For after being in that bath, people's eyes always give out a light they can see by. There were no creeping things in the way. All was safe and pleasant though so dark and damp and deep.

At last there was not one step more, and she found herself in a glimmering cave. On a stone in the middle of it sat a figure with its back towards her – the figure of an old man bent double with age. From behind she could see his white beard spread out on the rocky floor in front of him. He did not move as she entered, so she passed round that she might stand before him and speak to him. The moment she looked in his face, she saw that he was a youth of marvellous beauty. He sat entranced with the delight of what he beheld in a mirror of something like silver, which lay on the floor at his feet, and which from behind she had taken for his white beard. He sat on, heedless of her presence, pale with the joy of his vision. She stood and watched him. At length, all trembling, she spoke. But her voice made no sound. Yet the youth lifted up his head. He showed no surprise, however, at seeing her – only smiled a welcome.

'Are you the Old Man of the Earth?' Tangle had said.

And the youth answered, and Tangle heard him, though not with her ears:–

'I am. What can I do for you?'

'Tell me the way to the country whence the shadows fall.'

'Ah! that I do not know. I only dream about it myself. I see its shadows sometimes in my mirror: the way to it I do not know. But I think the Old Man of the Fire must know. He is much older than I am. He is the oldest man of all.'

'Where does he live?'

'I will show you the way to his place. I never saw him myself.'

So saying, the young man rose, and then stood for a while gazing at Tangle.

'I wish I could see that country too,' he said. 'But I must mind my work.'

He led her to the side of the cave, and told her to lay her ear against the wall.

'What do you hear?' he asked.

'I hear,' answered Tangle, 'the sound of a great water running inside the rock.'

'That river runs down to the dwelling of the oldest man of all – the Old Man of the Fire. I wish I could go to see him. But I must mind my work. That river is the only way to him.'

Then the Old Man of the Earth stooped over the floor of the cave, raised a huge stone from it, and left it leaning. It disclosed a great hole that went plumb-down.

'That is the way,' he said.

'But there are no stairs.'

'You must throw yourself in. There is no other way.'

She turned and looked him full in the face – stood so for a whole minute, as she thought: it was a whole year – then threw herself headlong into the hole.

When she came to herself, she found herself gliding down fast and deep. Her head was under water, but that did not signify, for, when she thought about it, she could not remember that she had breathed once since her bath in the cave of the Old Man of the Sea. When she lifted up her head a sudden and fierce heat struck her, and she sank it again instantly, and went sweeping on.

Gradually the stream grew shallower. At length she could hardly keep her head under. Then the water could carry her no farther. She rose from the channel, and went step for step down the burning descent. The water ceased altogether. The heat was terrible. She felt scorched to the bone, but it did not touch her strength. It grew hotter and hotter. She said, 'I can bear it no longer.' Yet she went on.

At the long last, the stair ended at a rude archway in an all but glowing rock. Through this archway Tangle fell exhausted into a cool mossy cave. The floor and walls were covered with moss – green, soft, and damp. A little stream spouted from a rent in the rock and fell into a basin of moss. She plunged her face into it and drank. Then she lifted her head and looked around. Then she rose and looked again. She saw no one in the cave. But the moment she stood upright she had a marvellous sense that she was in the secret of the earth and all its ways. Everything she had seen, or learned from books; all that her grandmother had said or sung to her; all the talk of the beasts, birds, and fishes; all that had happened to her on her journey with Mossy, and since then in the heart of the earth with the Old man and the Older man – all was plain: she understood it all, and saw that everything meant the same thing, though she could not have put it into words again.

The next moment she descried, in a corner of the cave, a little naked child, sitting on the moss. He was playing with balls of various colours and sizes, which he disposed in strange figures upon the floor beside him. And now Tangle felt that there was something in her knowledge which was not in her understanding. For she knew there must be an infinite meaning in the change and sequence and individual forms of the figures into which the child arranged the balls, as well as in the varied harmonies of their colours, but what it all meant she could not tell.* He went on busily, tirelessly, playing his solitary game, without looking up, or seeming to know that there was a stranger in his deep-withdrawn cell. Diligently as a lace-maker shifts her bobbins, he shifted and arranged his balls. Flashes of meaning would now pass from them to Tangle, and now again all would be not merely obscure, but utterly dark. She stood looking for a long time, for there was fascination in the sight; and the longer she looked the more an indescribable vague intelligence went on rousing itself in her mind. For seven years she had stood there watching the naked child with his coloured balls, and it seemed to her like seven hours, when all at once the shape the balls took, she knew not why, reminded her of the Valley of Shadows, and she spoke:–

* I think I must be indebted to Novalis for these geometrical figures.

'Where is the Old Man of the Fire?' she said.

'Here I am,' answered the child, rising and leaving his balls on the moss. 'What can I do for you?'

There was such an awfulness of absolute repose on the face of the child that Tangle stood dumb before him. He had no smile, but the love in his large gray eyes was deep as the centre. And with the repose there lay on his face a shimmer as of moonlight, which seemed as if any moment it might break into such a ravishing smile as would cause the beholder to weep himself to death. But the smile never came, and the moonlight lay there unbroken. For the heart of the child was too deep for any smile to reach from it to his face.

'Are you the oldest man of all?' Tangle at length, although filled with awe, ventured to ask.

'Yes, I am. I am very, very old. I am able to help you, I know. I can help everybody.'

And the child drew near and looked up in her face so that she burst into tears.

'Can you tell me the way to the country the shadows fall from?' she sobbed.

'Yes. I know the way quite well. I go there myself sometimes. But you could not go my way; you are not old enough. I will show you how you can go.'

'Do not send me out into the great heat again,' prayed Tangle.

'I will not,' answered the child.

And he reached up, and put his little cool hand on her heart.

'Now,' he said, 'you can go. The fire will not burn you. Come.'

He led her from the cave, and following him through another archway, she found herself in a vast desert of sand and rock. The sky of it was of rock, lowering over them like solid thunderclouds; and the whole place was so hot that she saw, in bright rivulets, the yellow gold and white silver and red copper trickling molten from the rocks. But the heat never came near her.

When they had gone some distance, the child turned up a great stone, and took something like an egg from under it. He next drew a long curved line in the sand with his finger, and laid the egg in it. He then spoke something Tangle could not understand. The egg broke, a small snake came out, and, lying in the line in the sand, grew and grew till he filled it. The moment he was thus full-grown, he began to glide away, undulating like a sea-wave.

The Golden Key

'Follow that serpent,' said the child. 'He will lead you the right way.'

Tangle followed the serpent. But she could not go far without looking back at the marvellous Child. He stood alone in the midst of the glowing desert, beside a fountain of red flame that had burst forth at his feet, his naked whiteness glimmering a pale rosy red in the torrid fire. There he stood, looking after her, till, from the lengthening distance, she could see him no more. The serpent went straight on, turning neither to the right nor left.

Meantime Mossy had got out of the lake of shadows, and, following his mournful, lonely way, had reached the sea-shore. It was a dark, stormy evening. The sun had set. The wind was blowing from the sea. The waves had surrounded the rock within which lay the Old Man's house. A deep water rolled between it and the shore, upon which a majestic figure was walking alone.

Mossy went up to him and said –

'Will you tell me where to find the Old Man of the Sea?'

'I am the Old Man of the Sea,' the figure answered.

'I see a strong kingly man of middle age,' returned Mossy.

Then the Old Man looked at him more intently, and said –

'Your sight, young man, is better than that of most who take this way. The night is stormy: come to my house and tell me what I can do for you.'

Mossy followed him. The waves flew from before the footsteps of the Old Man of the Sea, and Mossy followed upon dry sand.

When they had reached the cave, they sat down and gazed at each other.

Now Mossy was an old man by this time. He looked much older than the Old Man of the Sea, and his feet were very weary.

After looking at him for a moment, the Old Man took him by the hand and led him into his inner cave. There he helped him to undress, and laid him in the bath. And he saw that one of his hands Mossy did not open.

'What have you in that hand?' he asked.

Mossy opened his hand, and there lay the golden key.

'Ah!' said the Old Man, 'that accounts for your knowing me. And I know the way you have to go.'

'I want to find the country whence the shadows fall,' said Mossy.

'I dare say you do. So do I. But meantime, one thing is certain. – What is that key for, do you think?'

'For a keyhole somewhere. But I don't know why I keep it. I never could find the keyhole. And I have lived a good while, I believe,' said Mossy, sadly. 'I'm not sure that I'm not old. I know my feet ache.'

'Do they?' said the Old Man, as if he really meant to ask the question; and Mossy, who was still lying in the bath, watched his feet for a moment before he replied,

'No, they do not,' he answered. 'Perhaps I am not old either.'

'Get up and look at yourself in the water.'

He rose and looked at himself in the water, and there was not a gray hair on his head or a wrinkle on his skin.

'You have tasted of death now,' said the Old Man. 'Is it good?'

'It is good,' said Mossy. 'It is better than life.'

'No,' said the Old Man: 'it is only more life. – Your feet will make no holes in the water now.'

'What do you mean?'

'I will show you that presently.'

They returned to the outer cave, and sat and talked together for a long time. At length the Old Man of the Sea rose, and said to Mossy –

'Follow me.'

He led him up the stair again, and opened another door. They stood on the level of the raging sea, looking towards the east. Across the waste of waters, against the bosom of a fierce black cloud, stood the foot of a rainbow, glowing in the dark.

'This indeed is my way,' said Mossy, as soon as he saw the rainbow, and stepped out upon the sea. His feet made no holes in the water. He fought the wind, and clomb the waves, and went on towards the rainbow.

The storm died away. A lovely day and a lovelier night followed. A cool wind blew over the wide plain of the quiet ocean. And still Mossy journeyed eastward. But the rainbow had vanished with the storm.

Day after day he held on, and he thought he had no guide. He did not see how a shining fish under the waters directed his steps. He crossed the sea, and came to a great precipice of rock, up which he could discover but one path. Nor did this lead him farther than half-way up the rock, where it ended on a platform. Here he stood and pondered. – It could not be that the way stopped here, else what was the path for? It was a rough path, not very plain, yet certainly a path. – He examined the face of the rock. It was smooth as glass. But as his eyes kept roving hopelessly over it, something glittered, and he caught sight of a row of small sapphires. They bordered a little hole in the rock.

'The keyhole!' he cried.

He tried the key. It fitted. It turned. A great clang and clash, as of iron bolts on huge brazen caldrons, echoed thunderously within. He drew out the key. The rock in front of him began to fall. He retreated from it as far as the breadth of the platform would allow. A great slab fell at his feet. In front was still the solid rock, with this one slab fallen forward out of it. But the moment he stepped upon it, a second fell, just short of the edge of the first, making the next step of a stair, which thus kept dropping itself before him as he ascended into the heart of the precipice. It led him into a hall fit for such an approach – irregular and rude in formation, but floor, sides, pillars, and vaulted roof, all one mass of shining stones of every colour that light can show. In the centre stood seven columns, ranged from red to violet. And on the pedestal of one of them sat a woman, motionless, with her face bowed upon her knees. Seven years had she sat there waiting. She lifted her head as Mossy drew near. It was Tangle. Her hair had grown to her feet, and was rippled like the windless sea on broad sands. Her face was beautiful, like her grandmother's, and as still and peaceful as that of the Old Man of the Fire. Her form was tall and noble. Yet Mossy knew her at once.

'How beautiful you are, Tangle!' he said, in delight and astonishment.

'Am I?' she returned. 'Oh, I have waited for you so long! But you, you are like the Old Man of the Sea. No. You are like the Old Man of the Earth. No, no. You are like the oldest man of all. You are like them all. And yet you are my own old Mossy! How did you come here? What did you do after I lost you? Did you find the keyhole? Have you got the key still?'

She had a hundred questions to ask him, and he a hundred more to ask her. They told each other all their adventures, and were so happy as man and woman could be. For they were younger and better, and stronger and wiser, than they had ever been before.

It began to grow dark. And they wanted more than ever to reach the country whence the shadows fall. So they looked about them for a way out of the cave. The door by which Mossy entered had closed again, and there was half a mile of rock between them and the sea. Neither could Tangle find the opening in the floor by which the serpent had led her thither. They searched till it grew so dark that they could see nothing, and gave it up.

After a while, however, the cave began to glimmer again. The light came from the moon, but it did not look like moonlight, for it gleamed through those seven pillars in the middle, and filled the place with all colours. And now Mossy saw that there was a pillar beside the red one, which he had not observed before. And it was of the same new colour that he had seen in the rainbow when he saw it first in the fairy forest. And on it he saw a sparkle of blue. It was the sapphires round the keyhole.

He took his key. It turned in the lock to the sounds of Æolian music. A door opened upon slow hinges, and disclosed a winding stair within. The key vanished from his fingers. Tangle went up. Mossy followed. The door closed behind them. They climbed out of the earth; and, still climbing, rose above it. They were in the rainbow. Far abroad, over ocean and land, they could see through its transparent walls the earth beneath their feet. Stairs beside stairs wound up together, and beautiful beings of all ages climbed along with them.

They knew that they were going up to the country whence the shadows fall.

And by this time I think they must have got there.

The Gray Wolf

One of the swiftest, shortest and least obtainable of MacDonald's tales, *The Gray Wolf*, may be found in the tenth and final volume of *Works of Fancy and Imagination*, 1871. More sad than horrific, the story tells of the student-narrator's encounter in storm-bound Shetland with a werewolf who combines in her character two of MacDonald's typical women, angel-maid and demon-predator. The tragedy is that the girl understands her nature and hates herself for her voracious appetite, yet cannot change. The oddity is that although the atmosphere is redolent with compassion, MacDonald makes no attempt in the story to overcome the enchantment, but rather leaves the werewolf to her tragic destiny.

E.S.

One evening-twilight in spring, a young English student, who had wandered northwards as far as the outlying fragments of Scotland called the Orkney and Shetland islands, found himself on a small island of the latter group, caught in a storm of wind and hail, which had come on suddenly. It was in vain to look about for any shelter; for not only did the storm entirely obscure the landscape, but there was nothing around him save a desert moss.

At length, however, as he walked on for mere walking's sake, he found himself on the verge of a cliff, and saw, over the brow of it, a few feet below him, a ledge of rock, where he might find some shelter from the blast, which blew from behind. Letting himself down by his hands, he alighted upon something that crunched beneath his tread, and found the bones of many small animals scattered about in front of a little cave in the rock, offering the refuge he sought. He went in, and sat upon a stone. The storm increased in violence, and as the darkness grew he became uneasy, for he did not relish the thought of spending the night in the cave. He had parted from his companions on the opposite side of the island, and it added to his uneasiness that they must be full of apprehension about him. At last there came a lull in the storm, and the same instant he heard a footfall, stealthy and light as that of a wild beast, upon the bones at the mouth of the cave. He started up in some fear, though the least thought might have satisfied him that there could be no very dangerous animals upon the island. Before he had time to think, however, the face of a woman appeared in the opening. Eagerly the wanderer spoke. She started at the sound of his voice. He could not see her well, because she was turned towards the darkness of the cave.

'Will you tell me how to find my way across the moor to Shielness?' he asked.

'You cannot find it to-night,' she answered, in a sweet tone, and with a smile that bewitched him, revealing the whitest of teeth.

'What am I to do, then?' he asked.

'My mother will give you shelter, but that is all she has to offer.'

'And that is far more than I expected a minute ago,' he replied. 'I shall be most grateful.'

She turned in silence and left the cave. The youth followed.

She was barefooted, and her pretty brown feet went catlike over the sharp stones, as she led the way down a rocky path to the shore. Her garments were scanty and torn, and her hair blew tangled in the wind. She seemed about five and twenty, lithe and small. Her long fingers kept clutching and pulling nervously at her skirts as she went. Her face was very gray in complexion, and very worn, but delicately formed, and smooth-skinned. Her thin nostrils were tremulous as eyelids, and her lips, whose curves were faultless, had no colour to give sign of indwelling blood. What her eyes were like he could not see, for she had never lifted the delicate films of her eyelids.

At the foot of the cliff they came upon a little hut leaning against it, and having for its inner apartment a natural hollow within it. Smoke was spreading over the face of the rock, and the grateful odour of food gave hope to the hungry student. His guide opened the door of the cottage; he followed her in, and saw a woman bending over a fire in the middle of the floor. On the fire lay a large fish broiling. The daughter spoke a few words, and the mother turned and welcomed the stranger. She had an old and very wrinkled, but honest face, and looked troubled. She dusted the only chair in the cottage, and placed it for him by the side of the fire, opposite the one window, whence he saw a little patch of yellow sand over which the spent waves spread themselves out listlessly. Under this window there was a bench, upon which the daughter threw herself in an unusual posture, resting her chin upon her hand. A moment after the youth caught the first glimpse of her blue eyes. They were fixed upon him with a strange look of greed, amounting to craving, but as if aware that they belied or betrayed her, she dropped them instantly. The moment she veiled them, her face, notwithstanding its colourless complexion, was almost beautiful.

When the fish was ready, the old woman wiped the deal table, steadied it upon the uneven floor, and covered it with a piece of fine table-linen. She then laid the fish on a wooden platter, and invited the guest to help himself. Seeing no other provision, he pulled from his pocket a hunting knife, and divided a portion from the fish, offering it to the mother first.

'Come, my lamb,' said the old woman; and the daughter approached the table. But her nostrils and mouth quivered with disgust.

The next moment she turned and hurried from the hut.

'She doesn't like fish,' said the old woman, 'and I haven't anything else to give her.'

'She does not seem in good health,' he rejoined.

The woman answered only with a sigh, and they ate their fish with the help of a little rye-bread. As they finished their supper, the youth heard the sound as of the pattering of a dog's feet upon the sand close to the door; but ere he had time to look out of the window, the door opened and the young woman entered. She looked better, perhaps from having just washed her face. She drew a stool to the corner of the fire opposite him. But as she sat down, to his bewilderment, and even horror, the student spied a single drop of blood on her white skin within her torn dress. The woman brought out a jar of whisky, put a rusty old kettle on the fire, and took her place in front of it. As soon as the water boiled, she proceeded to make some toddy in a wooden bowl.

Meantime the youth could not take his eyes off the young woman, so that at length he found himself fascinated, or rather bewitched. She kept her eyes for the most part veiled with the loveliest eyelids fringed with darkest lashes, and he gazed entranced; for the red glow of the little oil-lamp covered all the strangeness of her complexion. But as soon as he met a stolen glance out of those eyes unveiled, his soul shuddered within him. Lovely face and craving eyes alternated fascination and repulsion.

The mother placed the bowl in his hands. He drank sparingly, and passed it to the girl. She lifted it to her lips, and as she tasted – only tasted it – looked at him. He thought the drink must have been drugged and have affected his brain. Her hair smoothed itself back, and drew her forehead backwards with it; while the lower part of her face projected towards the bowl, revealing, ere she sipped, her dazzling teeth in strange prominence. But the same moment the vision vanished; she returned the vessel to her mother, and rising, hurried out of the cottage.

Then the old woman pointed to a bed of heather in one corner with a murmured apology; and the student, wearied both with the fatigues of the day and the strangeness of the night, threw himself upon it, wrapped in his cloak. The moment he lay down, the storm began afresh, and the wind blew so keenly through the crannies of the hut, that it was only by drawing his cloak over his head that he could protect himself from its currents. Unable to sleep, he lay listening to the uproar which grew in violence, till the spray was dashing against the window. At length the door opened, and the young woman came in, made up the fire, drew the bench before it, and lay down in the same strange posture, with her chin propped on her hand and elbow, and her face turned towards the youth. He moved a little; she dropped her head, and lay on her face, with her arms crossed beneath her forehead. The mother had disappeared.

Drowsiness crept over him. A movement of the bench roused him, and he fancied he saw some four-footed creature as tall as a large dog trot quietly out of the door. He was sure he felt a rush of cold wind. Gazing fixedly through the darkness, he thought he saw the eyes of the damsel encountering his, but a glow from the falling together of the remnants of the fire, revealed clearly enough that the bench was vacant. Wondering what could have made her go out in such a storm, he fell fast asleep.

In the middle of the night he felt a pain in his shoulder, came broad awake, and saw the gleaming eyes and grinning teeth of some animal close to his face. Its claws were in his shoulder, and its mouth in the act of seeking his throat. Before it had fixed its fangs, however, he had its throat in one hand, and sought his knife with the other. A terrible struggle followed; but regardless of the tearing claws, he found and opened his knife. He had made one futile stab, and was drawing it for a surer, when, with a spring of the whole body, and one wildly-contorted effort, the creature twisted its neck from his hold, and with something betwixt a scream and a howl, darted from him. Again he heard the door open; again the wind blew in upon him, and it continued blowing; a sheet of spray dashed across the floor, and over his face. He sprung from his couch and bounded to the door.

It was a wild night – dark, but for the flash of whiteness from the waves as they broke within a few yards of the cottage; the wind was raving, and the rain pouring down the air. A gruesome sound as of mingled weeping and howling came from somewhere in the dark. He turned again into the hut and closed the door, but could find no way of securing it.

The lamp was nearly out, and he could not be certain whether the form of the young woman was upon the bench or not. Overcoming a strong repugnance; he approached it, and put out his hands – there was nothing there. He sat down and waited for the daylight: he dared not sleep any more.

When the day dawned at length, he went out yet again, and looked around. The morning was dim and gusty and gray. The wind had fallen, but the waves were tossing wildly. He wandered up and down the little strand, longing for more light.

At length he heard a movement in the cottage. By and by the voice of the old woman called to him from the door.

'You're up early, sir. I doubt you didn't sleep well.'

'Not very well,' he answered. 'But where is your daughter?'

'She's not awake yet,' said the mother. 'I'm afraid I have but a poor breakfast for you. But you'll take a dram and a bit of fish. It's all I've got.'

Unwilling to hurt her, though hardly in good appetite, he sat down at the table. While they were eating, the daughter came in, but turned her face away and went to the further end of the hut. When she came forward after a minute or two, the youth saw that her hair was drenched, and her face whiter than before. She looked ill and faint, and when she raised her eyes, all their fierceness had vanished, and sadness had taken its place. Her neck was now covered with a cotton handkerchief. She was modestly attentive to him, and no longer shunned his gaze. He was gradually yielding to the temptation of braving another night in the hut, and seeing what would follow, when the old woman spoke.

'The weather will be broken all day, sir,' she said. 'You had better be going, or your friends will leave without you.'

Ere he could answer, he saw such a beseeching glance on the face of the girl, that he hesitated, confused. Glancing at the mother, he saw the flash of wrath in her face. She rose and approached her daughter, with her hand lifted to strike her. The young woman stooped her head with a cry. He darted round the table to interpose between them. But the mother had caught hold of her; the handkerchief had fallen from her neck; and the youth saw five blue bruises on her lovely throat – the marks of the four fingers and the thumb of a left hand. With a cry of horror he darted from the house, but as he reached the door he turned. His hostess was lying motionless on the floor, and a huge gray wolf came bounding after him.

There was no weapon at hand; and if there had been, his inborn chivalry would never have allowed him to harm a woman even under the guise of a wolf. Instinctively, he set himself firm, leaning a little forward, with half outstretched arms, and hands curved ready to clutch again at the throat upon which he had left those pitiful marks. But the creature as she sprung eluded his grasp, and just as he expected to feel her fangs, he found a woman weeping on his bosom, with her arms around his neck. The next instant, the gray wolf broke from him, and bounded howling up the cliff. Recovering himself as he best might, the youth followed, for it was the only way to the moor above, across which he must now make his way to find his companions.

All at once he heard the sound of a crunching of bones – not as if a creature was eating them, but as if they were ground by the teeth of rage and disappointment: looking up, he saw close above him the mouth of the little cavern in which he had taken refuge the day before. Summoning all his resolution, he passed it slowly and softly. From within came the sounds of a mingled moaning and growling.

Having reached the top, he ran at full speed for some distance across the moor before venturing to look behind him. When at length he did so, he saw, against the sky, the girl standing on the edge of the cliff, wringing her hands. One solitary wail crossed the space between. She made no attempt to follow him, and he reached the opposite shore in safety.

A Tragedy of Bones

Phantastes, Greville MacDonald writes, was his father's 'first imaginative message'. *Lilith* which appeared in 1896 was his last. Written six years earlier in the white heat of inspiration, it was redrafted some six times before publication, and not well received by his vast readership who preferred his straight novels. Complex in thought, horrific in imagery and crowded with symbolism, *Lilith* is as compulsive to read as MacDonald found it to write.

Like *Phantastes*, the story is a journey through life into death and beyond, but where in the earlier fantasy the theme is the pursuit of love, *Lilith* is more complicated, concerned with the nature of evil and salvation and the belief that goodness can only be achieved by total negation of self to the will of God.

The hero-narrator, Mr Vane, whose name suggests vanity, is taken into the seven dimensions (three of reality, four of the imagination) of Fairyland by a shape-shifting talking raven who is to be his guide and teacher throughout the book. Mr Raven appears as a bird – the Celtic symbol of prophecy – as a librarian, as a sexton, but is in fact Adam. As a sexton, he takes Mr Vane to Eve's great charnel house where, as Adam, he and Eve feed him 'the perfect meal' of bread and wine (Communion) and show him his couch next to that of his father where they suggest he 'sleeps'. (By voluntarily accepting to sleep, Vane would thereby demonstrate his utter dependence on God.) Vane is not yet ready to surrender his individuality, and the subsequent chapters follow his adventures in and out of Fairyland until he is ready to sleep and wake into that life which is usually thought of as death.

Lilith in Jewish mythology is Adam's first wife who leaves him to rule over hell as a blood-sucking, seducing angel who steals and kills children. The personification of selfishness, she appears in each one of Vane's adventures disguised as a white leech or a bat, a spotted leopard or a beautiful white lady flawed by a dark stain on her side. The vivid edited excerpt that follows is Vane's vision of hell ruled over by Lilith whom he does not as yet recognize. It demonstrates

MacDonald's theory that the damned still have a chance of redemption and his belief that evil is corrective, that it 'can be good for you', that evil is necessary to the triumph of good, that in the end evil being wholly destructive must of necessity destroy itself.

Even Lilith who for so long has refused to surrender to sleep, who kills her daughter Lona for fear she will steal her individuality, the ultimate selfish act, is redeemed by the love and goodness of that daughter.

In *Lilith*, MacDonald's three types of women are polarized into the triple-headed goddess. Eve is true mother, true wife, who nurtures all men, the great Mother Earth. Lilith is the personification of evil, the vampire slut, the ultimate Alder Maid. Lona, her daughter, epitomizes pure unselfish love, ideal and divine.

Over the years, *Lilith* has roused in readers strong feelings of admiration or dislike. From the point of view of craftsmanship the structure is flawed, but as allegory and as a statement of belief, the book succeeds. Greville MacDonald who considered it to be his father's finest work called it 'the Revelation of St George'.

E.S.

I rose to resume my journey, and walked many a desert mile. How I longed for a mountain, or even a tall rock, from whose summit I might see across the dismal plain or the dried-up channels to some bordering hope! . . .

About noon I came to a few tamarisk and juniper trees, and then to a few stunted firs . . .

I went deeper into the wood . . .

The trees were now large, and stood in regular, almost geometric, fashion, with roomy spaces between. There was little undergrowth, and I could see a long way in every direction. The forest was like a great church, solemn and silent and empty, for I met nothing on two feet or four that day. Now and then, it is true, some swift thing, and again some slow thing, would cross the space on which my eye happened that moment to settle; but it was always at some distance, and only enhanced the sense of wideness and vacancy. I heard a few birds, and saw plenty of butterflies, some of marvellously gorgeous colouring and combinations of colour, some of a pure and dazzling whiteness.

Coming to a spot where the pines stood farther apart and gave

A Tragedy of Bones

room for flowering shrubs, and hoping it a sign of some dwelling near, I took the direction where yet more and more roses grew, for I was hungry after the voice and face of my kind – after any live soul, indeed, human or not, which I might in some measure understand. What a hell of horror, I thought, to wander alone, a bare existence never going out of itself, never widening its life in another life, but, bound with the cords of its poor peculiarities, lying an eternal prisoner in the dungeon of its own being! I began to learn that it was impossible to live for oneself even, save in the presence of others – then, alas, fearfully possible! evil was only through good! selfishness but a parasite on the tree of life! In my own world I had the habit of solitary song; here not a crooning murmur ever parted my lips! There I sang without thinking; here I thought without singing! there I had never had a bosom-friend; here the affection of an idiot would be divinely welcome! 'If only I had a dog to love!' I sighed – and regarded with wonder my past self, which preferred the company of book or pen to that of man or woman; which, if the author of a tale I was enjoying appeared, would wish him away that I might return to his story. I had chosen the dead rather than the living, the thing thought rather than the thing thinking! 'Any man,' I said now, 'is more than the greatest of books!' I had not cared for my live brothers and sisters, and now I was left without even the dead to comfort me!

The wood thinned yet more, and the pines grew yet larger, sending up huge stems, like columns eager to support the heavens. More trees of other kinds appeared; the forest was growing richer! The roses were now trees, and their flowers of astonishing splendour.

Suddenly I spied what seemed a great house or castle; but its forms were so strangely indistinct, that I could not be certain it was more than a chance combination of tree-shapes. As I drew nearer, its lines yet held together, but neither they nor the body of it grew at all more definite; and when at length I stood in front of it, I remained as doubtful of its nature as before. House or castle habitable, it certainly was not; it might be a ruin overgrown with ivy and roses! Yet of building hid in the foliage, not the poorest wall-remnant could I discern. Again and again I seemed to descry what must be building, but it always vanished before closer inspection. Could it be, I pondered, that the ivy had embraced a huge edifice and consumed it, and its interlaced branches retained the shapes of the walls it had assimilated? – I could be sure of nothing concerning the appearance.

Before me was a rectangular vacancy – the ghost of a doorway without a door: I stepped through it, and found myself in an open space like a great hall, its floor covered with grass and flowers, its walls and roof of ivy and vine, mingled with roses.

There could be no better place in which to pass the night! I gathered a quantity of withered leaves, laid them in a corner, and threw myself upon them. A red sunset filled the hall, the night was warm, and my couch restful; I lay gazing up at the live ceiling, with its tracery of branches and twigs, its clouds of foliage, and peeping patches of loftier roof. My eyes went wading about as if tangled in it, until the sun was down, and the sky beginning to grow dark. Then the red roses turned black, and soon the yellow and white alone were visible. When they vanished, the stars came instead, hanging in the leaves like live topazes, throbbing and sparkling and flashing many colours: I was canopied with a tree from Aladdin's cave!

Then I discovered that it was full of nests, whence tiny heads, nearly indistinguishable, kept popping out with a chirp or two, and disappearing again. For a while there were rustlings and stirrings and little prayers; but as the darkness grew, the small heads became still, and at last every feathered mother had her brood quiet under her wings, the talk in the little beds was over, and God's bird-nursery at rest beneath the waves of sleep. Once more a few flutterings made me look up: an owl went sailing across. I had only a glimpse of him, but several times felt the cool wafture of his silent wings. The mother birds did not move again; they saw that he was looking for mice, not children.

About midnight I came wide awake, roused by a revelry, whose noises were yet not loud. Neither were they distant; they were close to me, but attenuate. My eyes were so dazzled, however, that for a while I could see nothing; at last they came to themselves.

I was lying on my withered leaves in the corner of a splendid hall. Before me was a crowd of gorgeously dressed men and gracefully robed women, none of whom seemed to see me. In dance after dance they vaguely embodied the story of life, its meetings, its passions, its partings. A student of Shakspere, I had learned something of every dance alluded to in his plays, and hence partially understood several of those I now saw – the minuet, the pavin, the hey, the coranto, the lavolta. The dancers were attired in fashion as ancient as their dances.

A moon had risen while I slept, and was shining through the countless-windowed roof; but her light was crossed by so many shadows that at first I could distinguish almost nothing of the faces of the multitude; I could not fail, however, to perceive that there was something odd about them: I sat up to see them better. – Heavens! could I call them faces? They were skull fronts! – hard, gleaming bone, bare jaws, truncated noses, lipless teeth which could no more take part in any smile! Of these, some flashed set and white and murderous; others were clouded with decay, broken and gapped, coloured of the earth in which they seemed so long to have lain! Fearfuller yet, the eye-sockets were not empty; in each was a lidless living eye! In those wrecks of faces, glowed or flashed or sparkled eyes of every colour, shape, and expression. The beautiful, proud eye, dark and lustrous, condescending to whatever it rested upon, was the more terrible; the lovely, languishing eye, the more repulsive; while the dim, sad eyes, less at variance with their setting, were sad exceedingly, and drew the heart in spite of the horror out of which they gazed.

I rose and went among the apparitions, eager to understand something of their being and belongings. Were they souls, or were they and their rhythmic motions but phantasms of what had been? By look nor by gesture, not by slightest break in the measure, did they show themselves aware of me; I was not present to them: how much were they in relation to each other? Surely they saw their companions as I saw them! Or was each only dreaming itself and the rest? Did they know each how they appeared to the others – a death with living eyes? Had they used their faces, not for communication, not to utter thought and feeling, not to share existence with their neighbours, but to appear what they wished to appear, and conceal what they were? and, having made their faces masks, were they therefore deprived of those masks, and condemned to go without faces until they repented?

'How long must they flaunt their facelessness in faceless eyes?' I wondered. 'How long will the frightful punition endure? Have they at length begun to love and be wise? Have they yet yielded to the shame that has found them?'

I heard not a word, saw not a movement of one naked mouth. Were they because of lying bereft of speech? With their eyes they spoke as if longing to be understood: was it truth or was it falsehood that spoke in their eyes? They seemed to know one another: did they see one skull beautiful, and another plain? Difference must be there, and they had had long study of skulls!

My body was to theirs no obstacle: was I a body, and were they but forms? or was I but a form, and were they bodies? The moment one of the dancers came close against me, that moment he or she was on the other side of me, and I could tell, without seeing, which, whether man or woman, had passed through my house.

On many of the skulls the hair held its place, and however dressed, or in itself however beautiful, to my eyes looked frightful on the bones of the forehead and temples. In such case, the outer ear often remained also, and at its tip, the jewel of the ear as Sidney calls it, would hang, glimmering, gleaming, or sparkling, pearl or opal or diamond – under the night of brown or of raven locks, the sunrise of golden ripples, or the moonshine of pale, interclouded, fluffy cirri – lichenous all on the ivory-white or damp-yellow naked bone. I looked down and saw the daintily domed instep; I looked up and saw the plump shoulders basing the spring of the round full neck – which withered at half-height to the fluted shaft of a gibbose cranium.

The music became wilder, the dance faster and faster; eyes flared and flashed, jewels twinkled and glittered, casting colour and fire on the pallid grins that glode through the hall, weaving a ghastly rhythmic woof in intricate maze of multitudinous motion, when sudden came a pause, and every eye turned to the same spot: – in the doorway stood a woman, perfect in form, in holding, and in hue, regarding the company as from the pedestal of a goddess, while the dancers stood 'like one forbid', frozen to a new death by the vision of a life that killed. 'Dead things, I live!' said her scornful glance. Then, at once, like leaves in which an instant wind awakes, they turned each to another, and broke afresh into melodious consorted motion, a new expression in their eyes, late solitary, now filled with the interchange of a common triumph. 'Thou also,' they seemed to say, 'wilt soon become weak as we! thou wilt soon become like unto us!' I turned mine again to the woman – and saw upon her side a small dark shadow.

She had seen the change in the dead stare; she looked down; she understood the talking eyes; she pressed both her lovely hands on the shadow, gave a smothered cry, and fled. The birds moved rustling in their nests, and a flash of joy lit up the eyes of the dancers, when suddenly a warm wind, growing in strength as it swept through the place, blew out every light. But the low moon yet glimmered on the horizon with 'sick assay' to shine, and a turbid radiance yet gleamed from so many eyes, that I saw well enough what followed. As if each shape had been but a snow-image, it began to fall to pieces, ruining in

A Tragedy of Bones

the warm wind. In papery flakes the flesh peeled from its bones, dropping like soiled snow from under its garments; these fell fluttering in rags and strips, and the whole white skeleton, emerging from garment and flesh together, stood bare and lank amid the decay that littered the floor. A faint rattling shiver went through the naked company; pair after pair the lamping eyes went out; and the darkness grew round me with the loneliness. For a moment the leaves were still swept fluttering all one way; then the wind ceased, and the owl floated silent through the silent night.

Not for a moment had I been afraid. It is true that whoever would cross the threshold of any world, must leave fear behind him; but, for myself, I could claim no part in its absence. No conscious courage was operant in me; simply, I was not afraid. I neither knew why I was not afraid, nor wherefore I might have been afraid. I feared not even fear – which of all dangers is the most dangerous.

I went out into the wood, at once to resume my journey. Another moon was rising, and I turned my face toward it.

I had not gone ten paces when I caught sight of a strange-looking object, and went nearer to know what it might be. I found it a mouldering carriage of ancient form, ruinous but still upright on its heavy wheels. On each side of the pole, still in its place, lay the skeleton of a horse; from their two grim white heads ascended the shrivelled reins to the hand of the skeleton-coachman seated on his tattered hammer-cloth; both doors had fallen away; within sat two skeletons, each leaning back in its corner.

Even as I looked, they started awake, and with a cracking rattle of bones, each leaped from the door next it. One fell and lay; the other stood a moment, its structure shaking perilously; then with difficulty, for its joints were stiff, crept, holding by the back of the carriage, to the opposite side, the thin leg-bones seeming hardly strong enough to carry its weight, where, kneeling by the other, it sought to raise it, almost falling itself again in the endeavour.

The prostrate one rose at length, as by a sudden effort, to the sitting posture. For a few moments it turned its yellowish skull to this side and that; then, heedless of its neighbour, got upon its feet by grasping the spokes of the hind wheel. Half erected thus, it stood with its back to the other, both hands holding one of its knee-joints. With little less difficulty and not a few contortions, the kneeling one rose next, and addressed its companion.

'Have you hurt yourself, my lord?' it said, in a voice that sounded far-off, and ill-articulated as if blown aside by some spectral wind.

'Yes, I have,' answered the other, in like but rougher tone. 'You would do nothing to help me, and this cursed knee is out!'

'I did my best, my lord.'

'No doubt, my lady, for it was bad! I thought I should never find my feet again! – But, bless my soul, madam! are you out in your bones?'

She cast a look at herself.

'I have nothing else to be out in,' she returned; '– and *you* at least cannot complain! But what on earth does it mean? Am I dreaming?'

'*You* may be dreaming, madam – I cannot tell; but this knee of mine forbids me the grateful illusion. – Ha! I too, I perceive, have nothing to walk in but bones! – Not so unbecoming to a man, however! I trust to goodness they are not *my* bones! every one aches worse than another, and this loose knee worst of all! The bed must have been damp – and I too drunk to know it!'

'Probably, my lord of Cokayne!'

'What! what! – You make me think I too am dreaming – aches and all! How do *you* know the title my roistering bullies give me? I don't remember you! – Anyhow, you have no right to take liberties! My name is – I am lord — tut, tut! What do you call me when I'm – I mean when you are sober? I cannot – at the moment, – Why, what *is* my name? – I must have been *very* drunk when I went to bed! I often am!'

'You come so seldom to mine, that I do not know, my lord; but I may take your word for *that!*'

'I hope so!'

'– if for nothing else!'

'Hoity toity! I never told you a lie in my life!'

'You never told me anything but lies.'

'Upon my honour! – Why, I never saw the woman before!'

'You knew me well enough to lie to, my lord!'

'I do seem to begin to dream I have met you before, but, upon my oath, there is nothing to know you by! Out of your clothes, who is to tell who you may not be? – One thing I *may* swear – that I never saw you so much undressed before! – By heaven, I have no recollection of you!'

'I am glad to hear it: my recollections of you are the less distasteful! – Good morning, my lord!'

She turned away, hobbled, clacking, a few paces, and stood again.

'You are just as heartless as – as – any other woman, madam! –

Where in this hell of a place shall I find my valet? – What was the cursed name I used to call the fool?'

He turned his bare noddle this way and that on its creaking pivot, still holding his knee with both hands.

'I will be your valet for once, my lord,' said the lady, turning once more to him. '– What can I do for you? It is not easy to tell!'

'Tie my leg on, of course, you fool! Can't you see it is all but off? Heigho, my dancing days!'

She looked about with her eyeless sockets and found a piece of fibrous grass, with which she proceeded to bind together the adjoining parts that had formed the knee. When she had done, he gave one or two carefully tentative stamps.

'You used to stamp rather differently, my lord!' she said, as she rose from her knees.

'Eh? what! – Now I look at you again, it seems to me I used to hate you! – Eh?'

'Naturally, my lord! You hated a good many people! – your wife, of course, among the rest!'

'Ah, I begin, I be-gin – But – I must have been a long time somewhere! – I really forget! – There! your damned, miserable bit of grass is breaking! – We used to get on *pretty* well together – eh?'

'Not that I remember, my lord. The only happy moments I had in your company were scattered over the first week of our marriage.'

'Was that the way of it? Ha! ha! – Well, it's over now, thank goodness!'

'I wish I could believe it! Why were we sitting there in that carriage together? It wakes apprehension!'

'I think we were divorced, my lady!'

'Hardly enough: we are still together!'

'A sad truth, but capable of remedy: the forest seems of some extent!'

'I doubt! I doubt!'

'I am sorry I cannot think of a compliment to pay you – without lying, that is. To judge by your figure and complexion you have lived hard since I saw you last! I cannot surely be *quite* so naked as your ladyship! – I beg your pardon, madam! I trust you will take it I am but jesting in a dream! It is of no consequence, however; dreaming or waking, all's one – all merest appearance! You can't be certain of anything, and that's as good as knowing there is nothing! Life may teach any fool that!'

'It has taught me the fool I was to love you!'

'You were not the only fool to do that! Women had a trick of falling in love with me: – I had forgotten that you were one of them!'

'I did love you, my lord – a little – at one time!'

'Ah, there was your mistake, my lady! You should have loved me much, loved me devotedly, loved me savagely – loved me eternally! Then I should have tired of you the sooner, and not hated you so much afterward! – But let bygones be bygones! – *Where* are we? Locality is the question! To be or not to be, is *not* the question!'

'We are in the other world, I presume!'

'Granted! – but in which or what sort of other world? This can't be hell!'

'It must: there's marriage in it! You and I are damned in each other.'

'Then I'm not like Othello, damned in a fair wife! – Oh, I remember my Shakspere, madam!'

She picked up a broken branch that had fallen into a bush, and steadying herself with it, walked away, tossing her little skull.

'Give that stick to me,' cried her late husband; 'I want it more than you.'

She returned him no answer.

'You mean to make me beg for it?'

'Not at all, my lord. I mean to keep it,' she replied, continuing her slow departure.

'Give it me at once; I mean to have it! I require it.'

'Unfortunately, I think I require it myself!' returned the lady, walking a little quicker, with a sharper cracking of her joints and clinking of her bones.

He started to follow her, but nearly fell: his knee-grass had burst, and with an oath he stopped, grasping his leg again.

'Come and tie it up properly!' he would have thundered, but he only piped and whistled!

She turned and looked at him.

'Come and tie it up instantly!' he repeated.

She walked a step or two farther from him.

'I swear I will not touch you!' he cried.

'Swear on, my lord! there is no one here to believe you. But, pray, do not lose your temper, or you will shake yourself to pieces, and where to find string enough to tie up all your crazy joints, is more than I can tell.'

A Tragedy of Bones

She came back, and knelt once more at his side – first, however, laying the stick in dispute beyond his reach and within her own.

The instant she had finished retying the joint, he made a grab at her, thinking, apparently, to seize her by the hair; but his hard fingers slipped on the smooth poll.

'Disgusting!' he muttered, and laid hold of her upper arm-bone.

'You will break it!' she said, looking up from her knees.

'I will, then!' he answered, and began to strain at it.

'I shall not tie your leg again the next time it comes loose!' she threatened.

He gave her arm a vicious twist, but happily her bones were in better condition than his. She stretched her other hand toward the broken branch.

'That's right: reach me the stick!' he grinned.

She brought it round with such a swing that one of the bones of the sounder leg snapped. He fell, choking with curses. The lady laughed.

'Now you will have to wear splints always!' she said; 'such dry bones never mend!'

'You devil!' he cried.

'At your service, my lord! Shall I fetch you a couple of wheel-spokes? Neat – but heavy, I fear!'

He turned his bone-face aside, and did not answer, but lay and groaned. I marvelled he had not gone to pieces when he fell. The lady rose and walked away – not all ungracefully, I thought.

'What can come of it?' I said to myself. 'These are too wretched for any world, and this cannot be hell, for the Little Ones are in it, and the sleepers too! What can it all mean? Can things ever come right for skeletons?'

'There are words too big for you and me: *all* is one of them, and *ever* is another,' said a voice near me which I knew.

I looked about, but could not see the speaker.

'You are not in hell,' it resumed. 'Neither am I in hell. But those skeletons are in hell!'

Ere he ended I caught sight of the raven on the bough of a beech, right over my head. The same moment he left it, and alighting on the ground, stood there, the thin old man of the library, with long nose and long coat.

'The male was never a gentleman,' he went on, 'and in the bony stage of retrogression, with his skeleton through his skin, and his character outside his manners, does not look like one. The female is less vulgar, and has a little heart. But, the restraints of society removed, you see them now just as they are and always were!'

'Tell me, Mr Raven, what will become of them,' I said.

'We shall see,' he replied. 'In their day they were the handsomest couple at court; and now, even in their dry bones, they seem to regard their former repute as an inalienable possession; to see their faces, however, may yet do something for them! They felt themselves rich too while they had pockets, but they have already begun to feel rather pinched! My lord used to regard my lady as a worthless encumbrance, for he was tired of her beauty and had spent her money; now he needs her to cobble his joints for him! These changes have roots of hope in them. Besides, they cannot now get far away from each other, and they see none else of their own kind: they must at last grow weary of their mutual repugnance, and begin to love one another! for love, not hate, is deepest in what Love "loved into being."'

'I saw many more of their kind an hour ago, in the hall close by!' I said.

'Of their kind, but not of their sort,' he answered. 'For many years these will see none such as you saw last night. Those are centuries in advance of these. You saw that those could even dress themselves a little! It is true they cannot yet retain their clothes so long as they would – only, at present, for a part of the night; but they are pretty steadily growing more capable, and will by and by develop faces; for every grain of truthfulness adds a fibre to the show of their humanity. Nothing but truth can appear; and whatever is must seem.'

'Are they upheld by this hope?' I asked.

'They are upheld by hope, but they do not in the least know their hope; to understand it, is yet immeasurably beyond them,' answered Mr Raven.

His unexpected appearance had caused me no astonishment. I was like a child, constantly wondering, and surprised at nothing.

'Did you come to find me, sir?' I asked.

'Not at all,' he replied. 'I have no anxiety about you. Such as you always come back to us.'

'Tell me, please, who am I such as?' I said.

'I cannot make my friend the subject of conversation,' he answered, with a smile.

'But when that friend is present!' I urged.

'I decline the more strongly,' he rejoined.

'But when that friend asks you!' I persisted.

'Then most positively I refuse,' he returned.

'Why?'

'Because he and I would be talking of two persons as if they were one and the same. Your consciousness of yourself and my knowledge of you are far apart!'

The lapels of his coat flew out, and the lappets lifted, and I thought the metamorphosis of *homo* to *corvus* was about to take place before my eyes. But the coat closed again in front of him, and he added, with seeming inconsequence,

'In this world never trust a person who has once deceived you. Above all, never do anything such a one may ask you to do.'

'I will try to remember,' I answered; '– but I may forget!'

'Then some evil that is good for you will follow.'

'And if I remember?'

'Some evil that is not good for you, will not follow.'

The old man seemed to sink to the ground, and immediately I saw the raven several yards from me, flying low and fast.

Part Two

THE GREEN LIFE

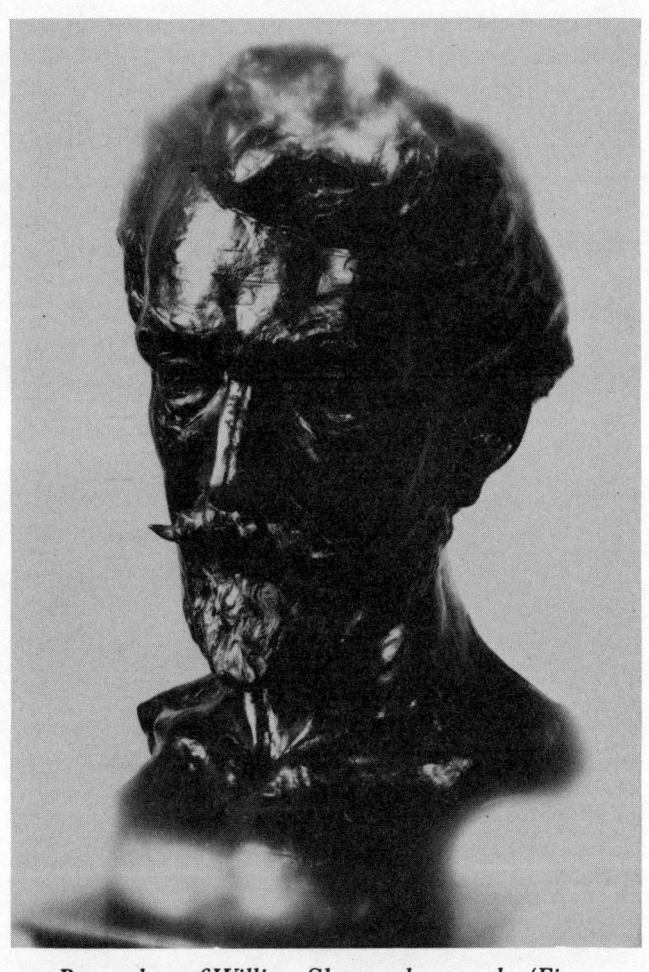

Bronze bust of William Sharp, who was also 'Fiona Macleod', by Alexander J. Stoddart; photographed by Leslie Forbes

Fiona Macleod

A seven-year-old boy knelt to drink from a spring by a sea-loch in Argyll, and, looking up, beheld a tall woman standing in a mist of wild hyacinths under three great sycamores. He watched wide-eyed, unafraid. She did not speak but she smiled, and because of the love and beauty in her eyes, he ran to her. 'She stooped and lifted blueness out of the flowers as one might lift foam out of a pool,' he later wrote, and it seemed to the child that she threw it over him.

'When I was found lying among the hyacinths dazed and, as was thought, ill, I asked eagerly after the lady in white, and with hair all shiny-gold like buttercups; but when I found I was laughed at, or at last, when I passionately persisted, was told I was sun-dazed and had been dreaming, I said no more – but I did not forget.'

That child was William Sharp, born, he believed, under a lucky star, who grew up to be a man of letters, whose prolific output included poems, short stories, novels, travel sketches, biographies of Dante Gabriel Rossetti, Shelley, Heine, Browning and Joseph Severn the friend of Keats (which are still cited by subsequent biographers of these men), art and literary criticism of a high quality, and some dozen edited anthologies of poetry and prose in the Canterbury and Camelot series produced by Ernest Rhys, who was responsible for the famous Everyman Library. In all, Sharp produced some fifty works in as little as thirty years before his untimely death in 1905. He was only fifty years old.

That child also became Fiona Macleod, mysterious, reclusive, whose personality did not fully emerge in Sharp's psyche until he was about forty, but was then to dominate the man and his writing and to gain celebrity as the literary conundrum of the day. Fiona retold old Celtic myths and legends with such power and originality that she was hailed as a star of the Celtic Renaissance of the 1890s, whose other lights included W. B. Yeats and George Russell (A.E.). That she refused to ally herself to the political aspirations of that movement, together with the fact that Sharp lied repeatedly to keep her identity private, largely contributed to her – and his – sad neglect or ridicule in the history of Scottish letters.

Most of what we know of William Sharp, his correspondence, fragments of diary and autobiography, are contained in the *Memoir* finely and affectionately written by his wife and first cousin, Elizabeth, a talented journalist, critic, and editor in her own right, and published in one volume in 1910 and in two volumes (with an extensive bibliography) in 1912. Apart from a critical biography, *William Sharp – 'Fiona Macleod'* by Professor Flavia Alaya of New York University and published by Harvard University Press in 1970; a handful of papers and articles; a well-produced biographical booklet with a selection of poems and prose, by Konrad Hopkins and Ronald van Roekel, leading authorities on Sharp whose Paisley publishing firm, Wilfion Books (from a combination of William's and Fiona's names), honours the man and the writer; and a reprint of Sharp's *Iona* by Floris Books (Edinburgh, 1982), there is little to commemorate what Alaya has called 'a phenomenon of genuine importance to literary history and no mere eccentricity of a strayed imagination'. That phenomenon was Fiona Macleod.

To find Fiona, it is necessary first to discover William Sharp.

He was born on 12 September 1855 at 4 Garthland Place, Paisley, the eldest child in a family of three sons and five daughters born to David Galbreath Sharp, a wealthy Scottish textile merchant whose family originated in Dunblane. From his mother, Katherine Brooks, who was of Swedish descent, he inherited his blond good looks and tall physique. He was, in the words of a friend, 'Viking in build, Scandinavian in cast of mind, a Celt in heart and spirit,' a description which would have pleased him, for he placed more importance on his racial origins than on his more immediate genetic inheritance.

Surprisingly few childhood episodes are recorded. Those that are seem to reflect the dual aspect of his nature from the earliest days. Elizabeth remembers first meeting Willie on the shores of Loch Long when he was 'a merry mischievous little boy in his eighth year with bright-brown curly hair, blue-gray eyes and a laughing face and dressed in a tweed kilt; eager, active in his endless invention of games and occupations and a veritable despot over his sisters at play. His chief delight was his punt in which he showed off a good deal to his London cousins' (Elizabeth, though a Scot with Paisley roots, was born in London).

Her next sight of him, at nineteen in Dunoon, made an equally vivid impression. 'I saw the tall, thin figure pass through our garden gate at sunset... and stride swiftly up the path. He was six feet one inch in height, very thin, with slightly sloping shoulders. He was good-looking, with a fair complexion and high colouring; gray-blue eyes, brown hair closely cut, a sensitive mouth and winning smile. He looked delicate but full of vitality. He spoke very rapidly, and when excited his words seemed to tumble one over the other, so that it was not always easy to understand him.'

In these portraits may be glimpsed the future student at Glasgow University who spent rapt evenings at the theatre and opera and most of the night devouring books on poetry, mysticism, occultism, mythology, philosophy and literature, yet never sat his degree. The Australian adventurer who explored the outback and studied the ways of the Aborigines but could not find work. The penniless poet who sat entranced at the feet of the middle-aged D. G. Rossetti in the midst of his Bohemian circle, absorbing the creed and conversation of the Pre-Raphaelites, and lost his job in a London bank. The compulsive writer whose output matched his energy, and whose persuasive manner once earned him, from a bewildered publisher, the advance of a hundred pounds on a novel not yet started and never to be written. The correspondent and conversationalist who counted among his friends and admirers members of the more advanced literary and artistic circles on the Continent and on both sides of the Atlantic, including Frédéric Mistral and Paul Bourget, Walt Whitman and Henry James, Oscar Wilde and William Butler Yeats, George Meredith and R. L. Stevenson. The restless traveller who summered when possible in the Highlands and wintered for his health in England, France and North Africa, but preferring Italy and Sicily, ever on the move from one house to another, one friend to another, one country to another (including four trips to America), continually working until, burned out mentally and physically, he died at Castello di Maniace in Sicily on 6 December 1905, a thousand miles from his birthplace.

The Victorian era, Scotland, Presbyterianism and parents who reflected that creed and generation were strong, if unacknowledged, influences in his life. David Sharp was 'genial, observant, humorous' and, Elizabeth tells us, 'a finished mimic' with a passion for the West Highlands. For three months every summer he rented a house in Arran or on the shores of some sea-loch where he taught his son to swim, row and fish, and together they sailed most of the beautiful coastal waters. From his mother, who was 'a serious reader', he inherited an early love of literature, but this was not a subject to be taken seriously by his people. Elizabeth writes that 'he met with no encouragement from either parent in his wish to throw himself into the study of science or literature as a profession, for such a course seemed to offer no prospects for his future.'

The Scots Kirk, with its strong moral and repressive ethos, was at least partly responsible for his nine years' courtship of Elizabeth, when they met secretly in parks and cemeteries for fear of what their families would think of such a near-incestuous relationship. As a young man, William was quick to reject what he saw as 'the sterilizing effect of Calvinism' and declare himself to be a pagan. Later, he was to bring out, edit and write under seven pseudonyms the entire contents of the first and only number of *The Pagan Review*.

Scotland, too, though always dear to him, he was to reject in favour of London and the milder south, in particular Sicily, which reminded him of the Highlands and whose mythology and Greek past were in harmony with his Celtic roots.

William, then, was a rebel against family, country, religion and the repressions of his age. The price he paid was guilt which acted as a goad urging him to prove to his family, the world at large and to himself, no doubt, that his chosen way of life – freedom – could be as successful in the worldly sense as managing a factory, fathering a family and sitting at the head of the Sharp pew on Sundays. Guilt was a hard taskmaster, forcing him to write compulsively, read and study relentlessly – he seldom allowed himself more than four hours of sleep at night – so that his health, never robust, continually broke down. His life was lived in feverish justification of his rejection of the ideals and expectations of his generation. Try as Elizabeth does in her *Memoir* to ignore the existence of his family by rarely mentioning them, try as William did in his snatches of autobiography to detach himself from his early influences, they were the mould that shaped the man.

But the mischievous lad who punted on Loch Long has another side to his nature. Elizabeth writes that 'the great heather-clad hills, peak behind peak, the deep waters of the winding lochs were a ceaseless delight to the boy'. Above all, he was attracted to a small pine grove above the house which seemed enchanted, away from the world of human beings, but peopled with playmates visible only to him. 'I went there very often,' he later wrote to Elizabeth. 'I thought that belt of firs had a personality as individual as that of any human being, a sanctity not to be disturbed by sport of play.' At the age of six, he was conscious of 'a Presence that was benign and beautiful'. He felt a great power behind the beauty, behind the wind, the sunshine, the silence and this 'awoke in him a desire to belong to it'. So much so that he built a little altar of stones and strewed it with white flowers.

That power, that presence – the Green Life, as he called it, experienced only in moments of ecstasy as 'a dazzle in the brain' – was to draw him, to haunt him for the rest of his life until finally on his death-bed he found it. 'Oh, the beautiful Green Life again!' he declared in joyful recognition. 'Ah, all is well.'

In this child may be glimpsed his *alter ego*, or, as he saw it, a secondary personality who was, much later, to emerge as the formidable Fiona Macleod.

The chief influences in 'Fiona's' childhood were, Elizabeth records, 'the wind, the woods and the sea', and Barbara, the family nurse, who nurtured 'her' on fairy tales, Gaelic songs and legends of the Celtic heroes and Viking rovers which later were to become the substance of Fiona's work.

This, too, was the sensitive sibling who, behind closed Victorian doors, was aware of his mother's seven subsequent confinements, and who may even have witnessed the mystery and pain of childbirth to the point of identification with the woman and rejection of the progenitor. As an adult, this child was to write 'Don't despise me when I say that I am in some things more a woman than a man.' Throughout his writing career he was to be obsessed with childbirth, extraordinarily sympathetic to the rights of women and, in the words of Professor Alaya, capable of writing on occasion with 'stinging insight into the potential tragedy of womanhood'.

This was the schoolchild who three times ran away from his boarding house not to the comforts of home, but to live out of doors in his beloved world of nature; this the adolescent who joined a gypsy encampment near Ardentinny and who travelled with them for three months as their star- and sun-brother; this the youngster who during a summer's convalescence from typhoid found the old Gael, Seumas Macleod, 'at sunrise looking seaward with his bonnet removed from his white locks', who told him 'every morning like this I take off my hat to the beauty of the world'. Seumas was more father than fisherman, more god than man to this child. He was Fiona's spiritual father whose surname 'she' was later to use.

Like William, Fiona, too, was a rebel against the shackles of background, convention and sex, but where William's restlessness could be seen as an escape, Fiona's journeying was more purposeful, a continual seeking after the Green Life. She was the true creative artist, who, in about 1893, broke free from the psyche of William Sharp in 'the person' of Fiona Macleod.

Introduced by William to the literary world as his cousin, she was soon to become eerily real not just to the outside world, but also to William and Elizabeth themselves. 'There is something of a strange excitement in the knowledge that two people are here: so intimate and yet so far-off,' William wrote to his wife from Arran. 'For it is with me as though Fiona was asleep in another room. I catch myself listening for her step sometimes, for the sudden opening of a door. It is unawaredly that she whispers to me.' She was awesome, sometimes terrifying, often scolding William for his faults. Konrad Hopkins, in his essay *Wilfion and the Green Life*, writes, 'She was his demon; he was possessed by her.'

At the same time, Fiona was also dear to him. In a letter written to Elizabeth in the year of his death, William says: 'Fiona Macleod has just been made an honorary member of a French League of writers ... we're glad, aren't we, you and I? She's our daughter, isn't she?'

The effort of keeping up her vast correspondence (Fiona even received a proposal of marriage) typewritten by William and signed by his sister, Mary; of continuing to write both as Fiona and William; of keeping her identity secret to all but a handful of close friends, was a strain that ultimately tore him apart.

This secrecy caused much speculation in the literary world, which was to lead to Sharp's firm denial in a note to the *Glasgow Evening Times* that 'Miss Fiona Macleod is not Mr William Sharp, Miss Fiona Macleod is not Mrs William Sharp, Miss Fiona Macleod is – Miss Fiona Macleod.' But readers were not satisfied. *The Highland News*, in an article entitled 'Mystery. Mystery. All in a Celtic Haze', hinted at a female James Macpherson, the perpetrator of the Ossian controversy.

But secrecy was necessary to William on several counts. At a superficial level, his fun-loving nature delighted in mysteries. Elizabeth had found this out in the days of their courtship. 'He delighted in the very fact of secrecy, of the mystery, and indeed, mystification, which I did not then realize was a marked characteristic of his nature.'

Then, too, his second self was female, which might have suggested to prurient Victorian minds unmentionable immoral practices. But Sharp was no transvestite (though Hopkins suggests a kind of 'psychic' transvestite, so to speak) or sexual deviant. Fiona existed not on the physical plane but on the spiritual and intellectual level only. As far as is known, and in spite of the fact that William and Elizabeth had no children, William's sexual life was that of a happily married man who may or may not (according to Professor Alaya) have had at least one brief but passionate extra-marital affair. Hopkins suggests, too, that it was because Fiona was endowed with 'psychic, visionary and magical faculties' that William was abnormally secretive about her identity. Certainly he asserted more than once that if the secret were revealed, Fiona would die. Realizing, however, how hurt his friends would be when they heard of the deception, he left a note to be sent to each one after his death:

> This will reach you after my death. You will think that I have wholly deceived you about Fiona Macleod. But, in an intimate sense this is not so: though and inevitably in certain details I have misled you. Only it is a mystery. I cannot explain. Perhaps you will intuitively understand or may come to understand. 'The rest is silence.'
> William Sharp
>
> It is only right, however, to add that I, and I only, was the author in the literal and literary sense − of all written under the name of 'Fiona Macleod'.

This was a generous gesture, for Sharp must have known the hurt that such a confession would do to his posthumous reputation. Eighty years on, the damage is not yet repaired.

And yet, in one sense, the denial was no lie. In a lecture to the Aberdeen Centre of the Franco-Scottish Society in 1907, W. B. Yeats, who was not privy to the secret until after Sharp's death, called him 'the most extraordinary psychic' he had ever encountered. '... Fiona Macleod was a secondary personality − as distinct a secondary personality as those one reads about in books of psychical research. At times (William Sharp) was really to all intents and purposes a different being.'

Elizabeth writes that 'the Fiona mood could not be commanded at will. Different influences awakened it, and its duration depended largely on environment. "W.S." would set himself to work normally, and was, so far, master of his mind. But for the expression of the "F.M." self, he had to wait upon mood, or seek conditions to induce it.'

As to how a man could subdivide his soul, not even Fiona could explain. Her answer was: 'I write, not because I know a mystery and would reveal it, but because I have known a mystery, and am today as a child before it, and can neither reveal nor interpret it.'

'That mystery,' Elizabeth explains, 'concerns the evolution of a human soul; and the part of it for which "the man" is consciously and personally responsible, is the method he used, the fiction he created and deliberately fostered – rightly or wrongly – for the protection of his inner compelling self.'

Where William found freedom and renewed health and vigour in the south and particularly in the rugged beauty of a Sicily steeped in mythology, Fiona's heart was firmly fixed in the Highlands, more specifically Iona, in Celtic folklore, and in Druidism. Of her fourteen works – novels, short stories, essays, poetry and plays – the majority were written between 1894 and 1897, a tremendous output considering the honed and finished quality of the writing, the poetic and evocative style of the prose.

Of the three novels, *Pharais* (a somewhat inaccurate rendering of the Gaelic 'Pàrras', meaning Paradise), *The Mountain Lovers* and *Green Fire*, the last is the most self-revealing. The story tells of Alan, who is torn between his love for the dark, earthy Ynys and her sister, the fair, free, pagan Annaik. Both have children by him who die, though later Ynys gives birth to a son who lives. His marriage to Ynys gives Alan an understanding of the fate and suffering of women, but it is his relationship with Annaik that leads him to 'a deeper conception of womanhood'. This is the theme underlying all three novels, which in *Green Fire* is extended to a belief in 'a woman saviour who would come near to all of us, because in her heart would be the blind tears of the child, and the bitter tears of the man, and the patient tears of the woman; who would be the Compassionate One, with no doctrine to teach, no way to show, but only deep, wonderful, beautiful, inalienable, unquenchable compassion.'

'For in truth,' Alan continues, 'there is the divine, eternal, feminine counterpart to the divine eternal male, and both are needed to explain the mystery of the dual spirit within us, the mystery of the Two in One.'

This mystery of the divine Two in One was reflected more humbly in the dual personality of William Sharp.

In the shorter pieces by Fiona Macleod, the best of which were collected into three volumes entitled *Spiritual Tales*, *Barbaric Tales*, and *Tragic Romances*, the underlying theme is innocent love in the land of the Green Life followed by separation and change before return to the original state on a higher plane.

There is a dream-like quality about these tales that is not of the known world. It is difficult to place them in any physical setting however remote and beautiful, and it is impossible to visualize the author as male or female, flesh and blood. Both tales and author belong, it would seem, to a world that lies on the fringe of the known earth, to be found where Sharp found it, 'beyond the beauty of nature', and yet, to the reader, it is recognizable. This is not alien landscape. If Fiona existed deep in William's psyche, these strange evocative stories appeal to us at that level and have the same reality as dreams. There can be no true sense of time or place, for the Celtic world created by Fiona is myth. The physical, historical reality of that world was harsh and cruel. In fact, there never was a golden age, nor probably ever will be. But myth, in a sense, is 'truer' than history, and there can be few who do not recognize Fiona's Green Life. Whether he or she finds it in music or in mountains, in poetry or in nature, in a loving human relationship or in God, the reader recognizes that other place. The genius of Fiona Macleod is that she opens the right doors.

George Meredith was also to call Fiona 'a woman of genius; the genius too, that is rarest, that drives deep thoughts before it'. Yeats insisted that she had 'rediscovered the art of the mythmaker ... It was minds like hers that created Aphrodite out of love and the foam of the sea, and Prometheus out of human thought and its likeness to leaping fire.' Hopkins says that 'she was both the mythmaker and the myth. An anomaly, she defied rational explanation. She did and did not exist.'

Not everyone saw Fiona's work in the same light. Some were to change their opinion with the passing of time. In 1900, Ernest Rhys called her writing 'vital and individual ... harmonious and natural', but thirty years later, in *Everyman Remembers*, he stated that Sharp's works 'do not stand the hard test, and in the end fall into that limbo in which are hidden so many lost books of verse, so many romances that once delighted sentimental readers, and so many novels which had a month's run before they dropped into the pit'. Arthur Waugh, in a piece for the *Spectator* in 1936, called Fiona Macleod a 'dilettante' and suggests that her books were the rejected works of William Sharp, produced under another name.

None the less, at the height of her fame, Fiona was a cult figure in both Britain and America, and her works inspired other creative artists, such as Neil Gunn whose first short stories, Roderick Watson suggests, were in the style of Fiona Macleod, and such as the American composers Charles T. Griffes and Edward MacDowell, and the English composers Arnold Bax and Rutland Boughton, the latter of whom turned her play *The Immortal Hour* into a successful opera of the same title. There may not yet be a full-scale revival of interest in or reassessment of Fiona's works, whose appeal will always be to a select audience, but this audience is aware of their existence and responds to their uncanny power to stimulate the imagination, which becomes flooded with Fiona's vision of the Green Life. To accomplish this not insignificant literary feat is the lasting achievement of Fiona Macleod – and of William Sharp.

To those who would accuse her work of being artificial and sentimental, Alaya points out that Fiona's tales were 'exercises in literary impressionism, a widespread late-nineteenth-century experiment colored by memory and association'. As such, they are as valid as those works written in any other literary form or style, including realism. Sentimentality today cloys too sweetly on sophisticated palates. We are only too aware that tears solve none of the problems of the world. But with Sharp and other Victorian writers, sentimentality was a genuine attempt to express compassion for the underprivileged, and William was a compassionate man.

Sharp was, however, more than the sum total of his two personalities. William, the boisterous boy, the rebel, the compulsive writer, the man of passionate friendships and enthusiasms, was the first to emerge while Fiona lay dormant. 'When she awoke,' Elizabeth writes, 'she becomes the deeper, the more impelling, the more essential factor.' Fiona, whose creed was 'to live in beauty – which is to put into four words all the dream and spiritual effort of the soul of man', threatened to dominate William, thus causing 'acute conflict', for he was concerned to keep up his hard-won reputation as the writer William Sharp.

Out of this conflict there arose yet another personality, 'Wilfion, as [Elizabeth] named the inner and third Self that lay behind that dual expression'. It was this personality that realized the need to control the two separated selves and 'bring them into some kind of conscious harmony'. Elizabeth continues: 'For though the difference between the two literary expressions was so marked, there was, nevertheless, a special characteristic of Wilfion that linked the dual nature together – the psychic quality of seership.'

Wilfion, then, was not only the link controlling William and Fiona but also the one who saw visions and experienced psychic phenomena. This was the aspect of Sharp of which Yeats was to say, 'Sharp had in many ways an extraordinarily primitive mind. He was fond of speaking of himself as the representative of the old bards and not like a man of this age at all.'

It was as Wilfion the seer that he experienced 'that dazzle in the brain' which took him over the border of the physical into the 'gardens of psychic consciousness, or, as he called it "the Green Life".'

It was as Wilfion the visionary that William was to write after Rossetti's death, 'I am borne down not with the sense of annihilation, but with the vastness of life and the imminence of things spiritual: I know from something beyond and out of myself that we are now but dying to live, that there is no death which is but as a child's dream in a weary night.'

It was as Wilfion the mystic that Fiona advised an unknown correspondent, 'do not speak of the spiritual life as "another life". There is no other life! What we mean by that is with us now. The great misconception of Death is that it is the only door to another world.'

If it is not too fanciful a conception, it could perhaps be said that Wilfion was the soul of Sharp, able to move out of the physical dimension with more ease than most. It is as Wilfion that Sharp would seem to influence those with psychic abilities today. It is no coincidence that Konrad Hopkins was guided to leave his native America and set up a publishing firm in Paisley, Scotland, where Sharp was born, and call it Wilfion Books. Nor is it so strange that the Kentish medium Margo Williams should have found herself in contact through automatic writing with William Sharp, who was previously unknown to her. Between 1976 and 1980, Margo received some ninety-two verses and a prose piece which she believes were dictated to her by William Sharp, and which were published as *The Wilfion Scripts* (Wilfion Books, 1980). It is perhaps conceivable that those who are able to perceive what William called 'the Green Life' while in the flesh, may as easily contact the physical life while in the spirit.

As a writer, William Sharp was not in the first league, although in his day he was readily accepted into the leading literary and artistic circles at home and abroad. He wrote too much, too quickly, diversified too readily, threw himself into too many projects, befriended too many people, travelled too often and too far to the detriment of his health and writing. But as Fiona Macleod, his work has a freshness and originality, a polished, sculpted quality that the following selection of tales indicates and that is recognized as literature by discerning readers and scholars today. It is surely time for literary historians to forget the controversy and forgive the deceit, if such it was. It is arguable, says Hopkins, that Fiona Macleod is William Sharp's 'greatest fictional creation, a "character" who dwelt vitally and luminously in his psyche and who has survived him in the books he assigned to her name'.

Sharp's chosen message to the world inscribed on the Celtic cross that crowns his Sicilian grave is two-fold as befits his two personalities:

Farewell to the known and exhausted
Welcome the unknown and illimitable
W.S.

Love is more great than we conceive, and Death
is the keeper of unknown redemptions.
F.M.

Frank Rinder, who, with his wife Edith, was for many years a close friend of Sharp, summed up the man.

I can but bear testimony to the ever-ready and eager sympathy, to the sunny winsomeness, to the nobility of the soul that has passed. William Sharp was one of the most lovable, one of the most remarkable men of our time.

E.S.

The Last Supper

> *. . . and there shall be*
> *Beautiful things made new . . .*
> F.M.

This 'spiritual morality' as Sharp called it was first published in *The Washer of the Ford*, and later included in Volume One of Macleod's collected stories, *Spiritual Tales*. Sharp himself believed it to be one of Fiona's finest works. In it 'in a sense my inner life of the spirit is concentrated . . . I shall never do anything better.'

T. A. Janvier agreed. 'Of all in the book, my strongest affection is for *The Last Supper*. It seems to me to the most purely beautiful, and the profoundest thing that you have done.'

It is no coincidence that the child's name is Art, who through his vision of Christ and the Twelve Weavers is initiated into an understanding of all that is most important to an artist and in life. Nor is it strange that Iosa tells Art, 'I go to my home in the heart of women.' This was one of Sharp's strongest beliefs that the true essence of Messiah was to be found in woman. Elizabeth Sharp wrote that *The Last Supper* was the work of Wilfion's psychic visionary power and was 'the result of direct vision.'

The Gaelic is spelt phonetically for easier reading and I have added, where necessary, a translation.

E.S.

The last time that the Fisher of Men was seen in Strath-Nair was not of Alasdair Macleod but of the little child, Art Macarthur, him that was born of the woman Mary Gilchrist, that had known the sorrow of women.

He was a little child, indeed, when, because of his loneliness and having lost his way, he lay sobbing among the bracken by the streamside in the Shadowy Glen.

When he was a man, and had reached the gloaming of his years, he was loved of men and women, for his songs are many and sweet, and his heart was true, and he was a good man and had no evil against any one.

It is he who saw the Fisher of Men when he was but a little lad: and some say that it was on the eve of the day that Alasdair Òg died, though of this I know nothing. And what he saw, and what he heard, was a moonbeam that fell into the dark sea of his mind, and sank therein, and filled it with light for all the days of his life. A moonlit mind was that of Art Macarthur: him that is known best as Ian Mòr, Ian Mòr of the Hills, though why he took the name of Ian Cameron is known to none now but one person, and that need not be for the telling here. He had music always in his mind. I asked him once why he heard what so few heard, but he smiled and said only: 'When the heart is full of love, cool dews of peace rise from it and fall upon the mind: and that is when the song of Joy is heard.'

It must have been because of this shining of his soul that some who loved him thought of him as one illumined. His mind was a shell that held the haunting echo of the deep seas: and to know him was to catch a breath of the infinite ocean of wonder and mystery and beauty of which he was the quiet oracle. He has peace now, where he lies under the heather upon a hillside far away: but the Fisher of Men will send him hitherward again, to put a light upon the wave and a gleam upon the brown earth.

I will tell this *sgeul* [tale] as Ian Mòr that was the little child Art Macarthur, told it to me.

Often and often it is to me all as a dream that comes unawares. Often and often have I striven to see into the green glens of the mind whence it comes, and whither, in a flash, in a rainbow gleam, it vanishes. When I seek to draw close to it, to know whether it is a winged glory out of the soul, or was indeed a thing that happened to me in my tender years, lo – it is a dawn drowned in day, a star lost in the sun, the falling of dew.

But I will not be forgetting: no, never: no, not till the silence of the grass is over my eyes: I will not be forgetting that gloaming.

Bitter tears are those that children have. All that we say with vain words is said by them in this welling spray of pain. I had the sorrow that day. Strange hostilities lurked in the familiar bracken. The soughing of the wind among the trees, the wash of the brown water by

The Last Supper

my side, that had been companionable, were voices of awe. The quiet light upon the grass flamed.

The fierce people that lurked in shadow had eyes for my helplessness. When the dark came I thought I should be dead, devoured of I knew not what wild creature. Would mother never come, never come with saving arms, with eyes like soft candles of home?

Then my sobs grew still, for I heard a step. With dread upon me, poor wee lad that I was, I looked to see who came out of the wilderness. It was a man, tall and thin and worn, with long hair hanging adown his face. Pale he was as a moonlit cot on the dark moor, and his voice was low and sweet. When I saw his eyes I had no fear upon me at all. I saw the mother-look in the grey shadow of them.

'And is that you, Art *lennavan mo* [my child]?' he said, as he stooped and lifted me.

I had no fear. The wet was out of my eyes.

'What is it you will be listening to now, my little lad?' he whispered, as he saw me lean, intent, to catch I know not what.

'Sure,' I said, 'I am not for knowing: but I thought I heard a music away down there in the wood.'

I heard it, for sure. It was a wondrous sweet air, as of one playing the feadan in a dream. Callum Dall, the piper, could give no rarer music than that was; and Callum was a seventh son, and was born in the moonshine.

'Will you come with me this night of the nights, little Art?' the man asked me, with his lips touching my brow and giving me rest.

'That I will indeed and indeed,' I said. And then I fell asleep.

When I awoke we were in the huntsman's booth, that is at the far end of the Shadowy Glen.

There was a long rough-hewn table in it, and I stared when I saw bowls and a great jug of milk and a plate heaped with oat-cakes, and beside it a brown loaf of rye-bread.

'Little Art,' said he who carried me, 'are you for knowing now who I am?'

'You are a prince, I'm thinking,' was the shy word that came to my mouth.

'Sure, *lennav-aghray* [my dear child], that is so. It is called the Prince of Peace I am.'

'And who is to be eating all this?' I asked.

'This is the last supper,' the prince said, so low that I could scarce hear; and it seemed to me that he whispered, 'For I die daily, and ever ere I die the Twelve break bread with me.'

It was then I saw that there were six bowls of porridge on the one side and six on the other.

'What is your name, O prince?'

'Iosa.'

'And will you have no other name than that?'

'I am called Iosa mac Dhe [Jesus, Son of God].'

'And is it living in this house you are?'

'Ay. But Art, my little lad, I will kiss your eyes, and you shall see who sup with me.'

And with that the prince that was called Iosa kissed me on the eyes, and I saw.

'You will never be quite blind again,' he whispered, and that is why all the long years of my years I have been glad in my soul.

What I saw was a thing strange and wonderful. Twelve men sat at that table, and all had eyes of love upon Iosa. But they were not like any men I had ever seen. Tall and fair and terrible they were, like morning in a desert place; all save one, who was dark, and had a shadow upon him and in his wild eyes.

It seemed to me that each was clad in radiant mist. The eyes of them were as stars through that mist.

And each, before he broke bread, or put spoon to the porridge that was in the bowl before him, laid down upon the table three shuttles.

Long I looked upon that company, but Iosa held me in his arms, and I had no fear.

'Who are these men?' he asked me.

'The Sons of God,' I said, I not knowing what I said, for it was but a child I was.

He smiled at that. 'Behold,' he spoke to the twelve men who sat at the table, 'behold the little one is wiser than the wisest of ye.' At that all smiled with the gladness and the joy, save one; him that was in the shadow. He looked at me, and I remembered two black lonely tarns upon the hillside, black with the terror because of the kelpie and the drowner.

'Who are these men?' I whispered, with the tremor on me that was come of the awe I had.

'They are the Twelve Weavers, Art, my little child.'

'And what is their weaving?'

'They weave for my Father, whose web I am.'

The Last Supper

At that I looked upon the prince, but I could see no web.

'Are you not Iosa the Prince?'

'I am the Web of Life, Art *lennavan-mo*.'

'And what are the three shuttles that are beside each Weaver?'

I know now that when I turned my child's-eyes upon these shuttles I saw that they were alive and wonderful, and never the same to the seeing.

'They are called *Beauty* and *Wonder* and *Mystery*.'

And with that Iosa mac Dhe sat down and talked with the Twelve. All were passing fair, save him who looked sidelong out of dark eyes. I thought each, as I looked at him, more beautiful than any of his fellows; but most I loved to look at the twain who sat on either side of Iosa.

'He will be a Dreamer among men,' said the prince; 'so tell him who ye are.'

Then he who was on the right turned his eyes upon me. I leaned to him, laughing low with the glad pleasure I had because of his eyes and shining hair, and the flame as of the blue sky that was his robe.

'I am the Weaver of Joy,' he said. And with that he took his three shuttles that were called Beauty and Wonder and Mystery, and he wove an immortal shape, and it went forth of the room and out into the green world, singing a rapturous sweet song.

Then he that was upon the left of Iosa the Life looked at me, and my heart leaped. He, too, had shining hair, but I could not tell the colour of his eyes for the glory that was in them. 'I am the Weaver of Love,' he said, 'and I sit next the heart of Iosa.' And with that he took his three shuttles that were called Beauty and Wonder and Mystery and he wove an immortal shape, and it went forth of the room and into the green world singing a rapturous sweet song.

Even then, child as I was, I wished to look on no other. None could be so passing fair, I thought, as the Weaver of Joy and the Weaver of Love.

But a wondrous sweet voice sang in my ears, and a cool, soft hand laid itself upon my head, and the beautiful lordly one who had spoken said, 'I am the Weaver of Death,' and the lovely whispering one who had lulled me with rest said, 'I am the Weaver of Sleep.' And each wove with the shuttles of Beauty and Wonder and Mystery, and I knew not which was the more fair, and Death seemed to me as Love, and in the eyes of Dream I saw Joy.

My gaze was still upon the fair wonderful shapes that went forth from these twain – from the Weaver of Sleep, an immortal shape of star-eyed Silence, and from the Weaver of Death a lovely Dusk with a heart of hidden flame – when I heard the voice of two others of the Twelve. They were like the laughter of the wind in the corn, and like the golden fire upon that corn. And the one said, 'I am the Weaver of Passion,' and when he spoke I thought that he was both Love and Joy, and Death and Life, and I put out my hands. 'It is Strength I give,' he said, and he took and kissed me. Then, while Iosa took me again upon his knee, I saw the Weaver of Passion turn to the white glory beside him, him that Iosa whispered to me was the secret of the world, and that was called 'The Weaver of Youth.' I know not whence nor how it came, but there was a singing of skiey birds when these twain took the shuttles of Beauty and Wonder and Mystery, and wove each an immortal shape, and bade it go forth out of the room into the green world, to sing there for ever and ever in the ears of man a rapturous sweet song.

'O Iosa,' I cried, 'Are these all thy brethren? for each is fair as thee, and all have lit their eyes at the white fire I see now in thy heart.'

But, before he spake, the room was filled with music. I trembled with the joy, and in my ears it has lingered ever, nor shall ever go. Then I saw that it was the breathing of the seventh and eighth, of the ninth and the tenth of those star-eyed ministers of Iosa whom he called the Twelve: and the names of them were the Weaver of Laughter, the Weaver of Tears, the Weaver of Prayer, and the Weaver of Peace. Each rose and kissed me there. 'We shall be with you to the end, little Art,' they said: and I took hold of the hand of one, and cried, 'O beautiful one, be likewise with the woman my mother,' and there came back to me the whisper of the Weaver of Tears: 'I will, unto the end.'

Then, wonderingly, I watched him likewise take the shuttles that were ever the same and yet never the same, and weave an immortal shape. And when this Soul of Tears went forth of the room, I thought it was my mother's voice singing that rapturous sweet song, and I cried out to it.

The fair immortal turned and waved to me. 'I shall never be far from thee, little Art,' it sighed, like summer rain falling on leaves: 'but I go now to my home in the heart of women.'

There were now but two out of the Twelve. Oh the gladness and the joy when I looked at him who had his eyes fixed on the face of Iosa that was the Life! He lifted the three shuttles of Beauty and Wonder and Mystery, and he wove a Mist of Rainbows in that room; and in the glory I saw that even the dark twelfth one lifted up his eyes and smiled.

'O what will the name of you be?' I cried, straining my arms to the beautiful lordly one. But he did not hear, for he wrought Rainbow after Rainbow out of the mist of glory that he made, and sent each out into the green world, to be for ever before the eyes of men.

'He is the Weaver of Hope,' whispered Iosa mac Dhe; 'and he is the soul of each that is here.'

Then I turned to the twelfth, and said 'Who art thou, O lordly one with the shadow in the eyes.'

But he answered not, and there was silence in the room. And all there, from the Weaver of Joy to the Weaver of Peace, looked down, and said nought. Only the Weaver of Hope wrought a rainbow, and it drifted into the heart of the lonely Weaver that was twelfth.

'And who will this man be, O Iosa mac Dhe?' I whispered.

'Answer the little child,' said Iosa, and his voice was sad.

Then the Weaver answered:

'I am the Weaver of Glory –,' he began, but Iosa looked at him, and he said no more.

'Art, little lad,' said the Prince of Peace, 'he is the one who betrayeth me for ever. He is Judas, the Weaver of Fear.'

And at that the sorrowful shadow-eyed man that was the twelfth took up the three shuttles that were before him.

'And what are these, O Judas?' I cried eagerly, for I saw that they were black.

When he answered not, one of the Twelve leaned forward and looked at him. It was the Weaver of Death who did this thing.

'The three shuttles of Judas the Fear-Weaver, O little Art,' said the Weaver of Death, 'are called Mystery, and Despair, and the Grave.'

And with that Judas rose and left the room. But the shape that he had woven went forth with him as his shadow: and each fared out into the dim world, and the Shadow entered into the minds and into the hearts of men, and betrayed Iosa that was the Prince of Peace.

Thereupon, Iosa rose and took me by the hand, and led me out of that room. When, once, I looked back I saw none of the Twelve save only the Weaver of Hope, and he sat singing a wild sweet song that he had learned of the Weaver of Joy, sat singing amid a mist of rainbows and weaving a radiant glory that was dazzling as the sun.

And at that I woke, and was against my mother's heart, and she with the tears upon me, and her lips moving in a prayer.

The Washer of the Ford

'... We are woven in one loom, and the Weaver thrids our being with the sweet influences, not only of the Pleides, but of the living world of which each is no more than a multi-coloured thread: as, in turn, He thrids the wandering wind with the inarticulate cry, the yearning, the passion, the pain, of that bitter clan, the Human.

'Truly we are all one. It is a common tongue we speak, though the wave has its own whisper, and the wind its own sigh, and the lip of man its word, and the heart of woman its silence.'

F.M.
(From the Prologue to *The Washer of the Ford*)

This powerful allegory is the titular story of the volume, *The Washer of the Ford*, which was first published in 1895. Interwoven with Celtic, Norse and Christian imagery, the story may be read as a journey through physical life and death into renewed life on the psychic plane. Water and blood, music and poetry, vision and blindness, peace and the sword, the fruit of knowledge, the child that leads, the river of death, these are all symbols at the heart of all mythology. 'Truly we are one.'

Sharp wrote to his wife, 'I think my most imaginative work will be found in the titular piece, *The Washer of the Ford*, which still, tho' written and revised some time ago, haunts me!'

E.S.

When Torcall the Harper heard of the death of his friend, Aodh-of-the-Songs, he made a vow to mourn for him for three seasons – a green time, an apple time, and a snow time.

There was sorrow upon him because of that death. True, Aodh was not of his kindred, but the singer had saved the harper's life when his friend was fallen in the Field of Spears.

Torcall was of the people of the north – of the men of Lochlin. His song was of the fjords and of strange gods, of the sword and the war-galley, of the red blood and the white breast, of Odin and Thor and Freya, of Balder and the Dream-God that sits in the rainbow, of the starry North, of the flames of pale blue and flushing rose that play around the Pole, of sudden death in battle, and of Valhalla.

Aodh was of the south isles, where these shake under the thunder of the western seas. His clan was of the isle that is now called Barra, and was then Aoidû; but his mother was a woman out of a royal rath in Banba, as men of old called Eiré or Eireann. She was so fair that a man died of his desire of her. He was named Ulad, and was a prince. 'The Melancholy of Ulad' was long sung in his land after his end in the dark swamp, where he heard a singing, and went laughing glad to his death. Another man was made a prince because of her. This was Aodh the Harper, out of the Hebrid Isles. He won the heart out of her, and it was his from the day she heard his music and felt his eyes flame upon her. Before the child was born, she said, 'He shall be the son of love. He shall be called Aodh. He shall be called Aodh-of-the-Songs.' And so it was.

Sweet were his songs. He loved, and he sang, and he died.

And when Torcall that was his friend knew this sorrow, he rose and made his vow, and went out for evermore from the place where he was.

Since the hour of the Field of Spears he had been blind. Torcall Dall he was upon men's lips thereafter. His harp had a moonshine wind upon it from that day, it was said: a beautiful strange harping when he went down through the glen, or out upon the sandy machar by the shore, and played what the wind sang, and the grass whispered, and the tree murmured, and the sea muttered or cried hollowly in the dark.

Because there was no sight to his eyes, men said he saw and he heard. What was it he heard and he saw that they saw not and heard not? It was in the voice that sighed in the strings of his harp, so the saying was.

When he rose and went away from his place, the Maormor asked him if he went north, as the blood sang; or south, as the heart cried; or west, as the dead go; or east, as the light comes.

'I go east,' answered Torcall Dall.

'And why so, Blind Harper?'

'For there is darkness always upon me, and I go where the light comes.'

The Washer of the Ford

On that night of the nights, a fair wind blowing out of the west, Torcall the Harper set forth in a galley. It splashed in the moonshine as it was rowed swiftly by nine men.

'Sing us a song, O Torcall Dall!' they cried.

'Sing us a song, Torcall of Lochlin,' said the man who steered. He and all his company were of the Gael: the Harper only was of the Northmen.

'What shall I sing?' he asked. 'Shall it be of war that you love, or of women that twine you like silk o' the kine; or shall it be of death that is your meed; or of your dread, the Spears of the North?'

A low sullen growl went from beard to beard.

'We are under *ceangal*, Blind Harper,' said the steersman, with downcast eyes because of his flaming wrath; 'we are under bond to take you safe to the mainland, but we have sworn no vow to sit still under the lash of your tongue. 'Twas a wind-fleet arrow that sliced the sight out of your eyes: have a care lest a sudden sword-wind sweep the breath out of your body.'

Torcall laughed a low, quiet laugh.

'Is it death I am fearing now – I who have washed my hands in blood, and had love, and known all that is given to man? But I will sing you a song, I will.'

And with that he took his harp, and struck the strings.

There is a lonely stream afar in a lone dim land:
It hath white dust for shore it has, white bones bestrew the strand:
The only thing that liveth there is a naked leaping sword;
But I, who a seer am, have seen the whirling hand
    Of the Washer of the Ford.

A shadowy shape of cloud and mist, of gloom and dusk, she stands,
    The Washer of the Ford:
She laughs, at times, and strews the dust through the hollow of her hands.
She counts the sins of all men there, and slays the red-stained horde –
The ghosts of all the sins of men must know the whirling sword
    Of the Washer of the Ford.

> She stoops and laughs when in the dust she sees a writhing limb:
> 'Go back into the ford,' she says, 'and hither and thither swim;
> Then I shall wash you white as snow, and shall take you by the hand,
> And slay you here in the silence with this my whirling brand,
> And trample you into the dust of this white windless sand' –
> > This is the laughing word
> > Of the Washer of the Ford
> > Along that silent strand.

There was silence for a time after Torcall Dall sang that song. The oars took up the moonshine and flung it hither and thither like loose shining crystals. The foam at the prow curled and leaped.

Suddenly one of the rowers broke into a long, low chant –

> *Yo, eily-a-ho, ayah-a-ho, eily-ayah-a-ho,*
> > Singeth the Sword
> *Eily-a-ho, ayah-a-ho, eily-ayah-a-ho,*
> > Of the Washer of the Ford!

And at that all ceased from rowing. Standing erect, they lifted up their oars against the stars, and the wild voices of them flew out upon the night –

> *Yo, eily-a-ho, ayah-a-ho, eily-ayah-a-ho,*
> > Singeth the Sword
> *Eily-a-ho, ayah-a-ho, eily-ayah-a-ho,*
> > Of the Washer of the Ford!

Torcall Dall laughed. Then he drew his sword from his side and plunged it into the sea. When he drew the blade out of the water and whirled it on high, all the white shining drops of it swirled about his head like a sleety rain.

And at that the steersman let go the steering-oar and drew his sword, and clove a flowing wave. But with the might of his blow the sword spun him round, and the sword sliced away the ear of the man who had the sternmost oar. Then there was blood in the eyes of all there. The man staggered, and felt for his knife, and it was in the heart of the steersman.

Then because these two men were leaders, and had had a

The Washer of the Ford

blood-feud, and because all there, save Torcall, were of one or the other side, swords and knives sang a song.

The rowers dropped their oars; and four men fought against three.

Torcall laughed, and lay back in his place. While out of the wandering wave the death of each man clambered into the hollow of the boat, and breathed its chill upon its man, Torcall the Blind took his harp. He sang this song, with the swirling spray against his face, and the smell of blood in his nostrils, and the feet of him dabbling in the red tide that rose there.

> Oh 'tis a good thing the red blood, by Odin his word!
> And a good thing it is to hear it bubbling deep.
> And when we hear the laughter of the Sword,
> Oh, the corbies croak, and the old wail, and the women weep!
>
> And busy will she be there where she stands,
> Washing the red out of the sins of all this slaying horde;
> And trampling the bones of them into white powdery sands,
>   And laughing low at the thrist of her thirsty sword –
>   The Washer of the Ford!

When he had sung that song there was only one man whose pulse still beat, and he was at the bow.

'A bitter black curse upon you, Torcall Dall!' he groaned out of the ooze of blood that was in his mouth.

'And who will you be?' said the Blind Harper.

'I am Fergus, the son of Art, the son of Fergus of the Dûns.'

'Well, it is a song for your death I will make, Fergus mac Art mhic Fheargus: and because you are the last.'

With that Torcall struck a wild sob out of his harp, and he sang –

> Oh, death of Fergus, that is lying in the boat here,
>   Betwixt the man of the red hair and him of the black beard,
> Rise now, and out of thy cold white eyes take out the fear,
>   And let Fergus mac Art mhic Fheargus see his weird!
>
> Sure, now, it's a blind man I am, but I'm thinking I see
>   The shadow of you crawling across the dead.
> Soon you will twine your arm around his shaking knee,
>   And be whispering your silence into his listless head.
>
> And that is why, O Fergus –

But here the man hurled his sword into the sea, and with a choking cry fell forward; and upon the white sands he was, beneath the trampling feet of the Washer of the Ford.

II

It was a fair wind that blew beneath the stars that night. At dawn the mountains of Skye were like turrets of a great Dûn against the east.

But Torcall the blind Harper did not see that thing. Sleep, too, was upon him. He smiled in that sleep, for in his mind he saw the dead men, that were of the alien people, his foes, draw near the stream that was in a far place. The shaking of them, poor tremulous frostbit leaves they were, thin and sere, made the only breath there was in that desert.

At the ford – this is what he saw in his vision – they fell down like stricken deer with the hounds upon them.

'What is this stream?' they cried in the thin voice of rain across the moors.

'The River of Blood,' said a voice.

'And who are you that are in the silence?'

'I am the Washer of the Ford.'

And with that each red soul was seized and thrown into the water of the ford; and when white as a sheep-bone on the hill, was taken in one hand by the Washer of the Ford and flung into the air, where no wind was and where sound was dead, and was then severed this way and that, in four whirling blows of the sword from the four quarters of the world. Then it was that the Washer of the Ford trampled upon what fell to the ground, till under the feet of her was only a white sand, white as powder, light as the dust of the yellow flowers that grow in the grass.

It was at that Torcall Dall smiled in his sleep. He did not hear the washing of the sea; no, nor any idle plashing of the unoared boat. Then he dreamed, and it was of the woman he had left, seven summer-sailings ago in Lochlin. He thought her hand was in his, and that her heart was against his.

'Ah, dear beautiful heart of woman,' he said, 'and what is the pain that has put a shadow upon you?'

It was a sweet voice that he heard coming out of sleep.

'Torcall, it is the weary love I have.'

'Ah, heart o' me, dear! sure 'tis a bitter pain I have had too, and I away from you all these years.'

'There's a man's pain, and there's a woman's pain.'

'By the blood of Balder, Hildyr, I would have both upon me to take it off the dear heart that is here.'

'Torcall!'

'Yes, white one.'

'We are not alone, we two in the dark.'

And when she had said that thing, Torcall felt two baby arms go round his neck, and two leaves of a wild-rose press cool and sweet against his lips.

'Ah! what is this?' he cried, with his heart beating, and the blood in his body singing a glad song.

A low voice crooned in his ear: a bitter-sweet song it was, passing-sweet, passing-bitter.

'Ah, white one, white one,' he moaned; 'ah, the wee fawn o' me! Baby o' foam, bonnie wee lass, put your sight upon me that I may see the blue eyes that are mine too and Hildyr's.'

But the child only nestled closer. Like a fledgling in a great nest she was. If God heard her song, He was a glad God that day. The blood that was in her body called to the blood that was in his body. He could say no word. The tears were in his blind eyes.

Then Hildyr leaned into the dark, and took his harp, and played upon it. It was of the fonnsheen he had learned, far, far away, where the isles are.

She sang: but he could not hear what she sang.

Then the little lips, that were like a cool wave upon the dry sand of his life, whispered into a low song: and the wavering of it was like this in his brain –

Where the winds gather
   The souls of the dead,
O Torcall, my father,
   My soul is led!

In Hildyr-mead
   I was thrown, I was sown:
Out of thy seed
   I am sprung, I am blown!

> But where is the way
>   For Hildyr and me,
> By the hill-moss grey
>   Or the grey sea?
>
> For a river is here,
>   And a whirling Sword —
> And a Woman washing
>   By a Ford!

With that, Torcall Dall gave a wild cry, and sheathed an arm about the wee white one, and put out a hand to the bosom that loved him. But there was no white breast there, and no white babe: and what was against his lips was his own hand red with blood.

'O Hildyr!' he cried.

But only the splashing of the waves did he hear.

'O white one!' he cried.

But only the scream of a sea-mew, as it hovered over that boat filled with dead men, made answer.

III

All day the Blind Harper steered the galley of the dead. There was a faint wind moving out of the west. The boat went before it, slow, and with a low, sighing wash.

Torcall saw the red gaping wounds of the dead, and the glassy eyes of the nine men.

'It is better not to be blind and to see the dead,' he muttered, 'than to be blind and to see the dead.'

The man who had been steersman leaned against him. He took him in his shuddering grip and thrust him into the sea.

But when, an hour later, he put his hand to the coolness of the water, he drew it back with a cry, for it was on the cold, stiff face of the dead man that it had fallen. The long hair had caught in a cleft in the leather where the withes had given.

For another hour Torcall sat with his chin in his right hand, and his unseeing eyes staring upon the dead. He heard no sound at all, save the lap of wave upon wave, and the *suss* of spray against spray, and a bubbling beneath the boat, and the low, steady swish of the body that trailed alongside the steering oar.

The Washer of the Ford

At the second hour before sundown he lifted his head. The sound he heard was the sound of waves beating upon rocks.

At the hour before sundown he moved the oar rapidly to and fro, and cut away the body that trailed behind the boat. The noise of the waves upon the rocks was now a loud song.

When the last sunfire burned upon his neck, and made the long hair upon his shoulders ashine, he smelt the green smell of grass. Then it was too that he heard the muffled fall of the sea, in a quiet haven, where shelves of sand were.

He followed that sound, and while he strained to hear any voice the boat grided upon the sand, and drifted to one side. Taking his harp, Torcall drove an oar into the sand, and leaped on to the shore. When he was there, he listened. There was silence. Far, far away he heard the falling of a mountain-torrent, and the thin, faint cry of an eagle, where the sun-flame dyed its eyrie as with streaming blood.

So he lifted his harp, and, harping low, with a strange, wild song on his lips, moved away from that place, and gave no more thought to the dead.

It was deep gloaming when he came to a wood. He felt the cold green breath of it.

'Come,' said a voice, low and sweet.

'And who will *you* be?' asked Torcall the Harper, trembling because of the sudden voice in the stillness.

'I am a child, and here is my hand, and I will lead you, Torcall of Lochlin.'

The blind man had fear upon him.

'Who are you that in a strange place are for knowing who I am?'

'Come.'

'Ay, sure, it is coming I am, white one; but tell me who you are, and whence you came, and whither we go.'

Then a voice that he knew sang:

O where the winds gather
   The souls of the dead,
O Torcall, my father,
   My soul is led!

But a river is here,
   And a whirling Sword –
And a Woman washing
   By a Ford!

Torcall Dall was as the last leaf on a tree at that.

'Were you on the boat?' he whispered hoarsely.

But it seemed to him that another voice answered: *'Yea, even so.'*

'Tell me, for I have blindness: Is it peace?'

'It is peace.'

'Are you man, or child, or of the Hidden People?'

'I am a shepherd.'

'A shepherd? Then, sure, you will guide me through this wood? And what will be beyond this wood?'

'A river.'

'And what river will that be?'

'Deep and terrible. It runs through the Valley of the Shadow.'

'And is there no ford there?'

'Ay, there is a ford.'

'And who will guide me across that ford?'

'She.'

'Who?'

'The Washer of the Ford.'

But hereat Torcall Dall gave a sore cry and snatched his hand away, and fled sidelong into an alley of the wood.

It was moonshine when he lay down, weary. The sound of flowing water filled his ears.

'Come,' said a voice.

So he rose and went. When the cold breath of the water was upon his face, the guide that led him put a fruit into his hand.

'Eat, Torcall Dall!'

He ate. He was no more Torcall Dall. His sight was upon him again. Out of the blackness shadows came; out of the shadows, the great boughs of trees; from the boughs, dark branches and dark clusters of leaves; above the branches, white stars; below the branches, white flowers; and beyond these, the moonshine on the grass and the moonfire on the flowing of a river dark and deep.

'Take your harp, O Harper, and sing the song of what you see.'

Torcall heard the voice, but saw no one. No shadow moved. Then he walked out upon the moonlit grass; and at the ford he saw a woman stooping and washing shroud after shroud of woven moonbeams: washing them there in the flowing water, and singing low a song that he did not hear. He did not see her face. But she was young, and with long black hair that fell like the shadow of night over a white rock.

The Washer of the Ford

So Torcall took his harp, and he sang:

    Glory to the great Gods, it is no Sword I am seeing;
    Nor do I see aught but the flowing of a river.
    And I see shadows on the flow that are ever fleeing,
    And I see a woman washing shrouds for ever and ever.

Then he ceased, for he heard the woman sing:

    Glory to God on high, and to Mary, Mother of Jesus,
    Here am I washing away the sins of the shriven,
    O Torcall of Lochlin, throw off the red sins that ye cherish
    And I will be giving you the washen shroud that they wear in
        Heaven.

Filled with a great awe, Torcall bowed his head. Then once more he took his harp, and he sang:

    O well it is I am seeing, Woman of the Shrouds,
    That you have not for me any whirling of the Sword;
    I have lost my gods, O woman, so what will the name be
    Of thee and thy gods, O woman that art Washer of the Ford?

But the woman did not look up from the dark water, nor did she cease from washing the shrouds made of the woven moonbeams. The Harper heard this song above the sighing of the water:

    It is Mary Magdalene my name is, and I loved Christ.
    And Christ is the Son of God, and Mary the Mother of Heaven.
    And this river is the river of death, and the shadows
    Are the fleeing souls that are lost if they be not shriven.

Then Torcall drew nigher unto the stream. A melancholy wind was upon it.
    'Where are all the dead of the world?' he said.
    But the woman answered not.
    'And what is the end, you that are called Mary?'
    Then the woman rose.
    'Would you cross the Ford, O Torcall the Harper?'

He made no word upon that. But he listened. He heard a woman singing faint and low, far away in the dark. He drew more near.

'Would you cross the Ford, O Torcall?'

He made no word upon that; but once more he listened. He heard a little child crying in the night.

'Ah, lonely heart of the white one,' he sighed, and his tears fell.

Mary Magdalene turned and looked upon him.

It was the face of Sorrow she had. She stooped and took up the tears.

'They are bells of joy,' she said. And he heard a faint, sweet ringing in his ears.

A prayer came out of his heart. A blind prayer it was, but God gave it wings. It flew to Mary, who took and kissed it, and gave it song.

'It is the Song of Peace,' she said. And Torcall had peace.

'What is best, O Torcall?' she asked, – rustling-sweet as rain among the trees her voice was. 'What is best? The sword, or peace?'

'Peace,' he answered; and he was white now, and was old.

'Take your harp,' Mary said, 'and go in unto the Ford. But, lo, now I clothe you with a white shroud. And if you fear the drowning flood, follow the bells that were your tears; and if the dark affright you, follow the song of the prayer that came out of your heart.'

So Torcall the Harper moved into the whelming flood, and he played a wild, strange air like the laughing of a child.

Deep silence there was. The moonshine lay upon the obscure wood, and the darkling river flowed sighing through the soundless gloom.

The Washer of the Ford stooped once more. Low and sweet, as of yore and for ever, over the drowning souls she sang her immemorial song.

Silk o' the Kine

Silk o' the Kine, one of the poetic 'secret' names of conquered Erin, was in ancient days, there and in the Scottish Isles, a designation for a woman of rare beauty. The name Eilidh (pronounced Eil-ih, with a long accent on the first syllable) is also ancient, but lingers in the Isles still, and indeed throughout the Western Highlands, as also, I understand, in Connaught and Connemara. Somhairle (Somerled) is pronounced So-irl'u.

F.M.

This story was first published in *The Sin Eater* while its sequel, *Ula and Urla*, appeared in *The Washer of the Ford*. They would seem better placed together for the Isla and Eilidh of the court of King Somhairle became the Ula and Urla in the rath of Coll mac Torcall. The theme of these two stories is one close to Macleod's heart, the indestructibility of love either by separation or death. In love with death, the lovers, doomed to die, are, after a sea-change, reunited as Ula and Urla, and after a death-change, become Isla and Eilidh once again. On earth both live on in the life of their child. Beyond death, both exist for ever with the Celtic gods in the Green Life.

E.S.

'What I shall now be telling you,' said Ian Mòr to me once – and indeed, I should remember the time of it well: for it was in the last year of his life, when rarely any other than myself saw aught of Ian of the Hills – 'What I shall now be telling you is an ancient forgotten tale of a man and woman of the old heroic days. The name of the man was Isla, and the name of the woman was Eilidh.'

'Ah, yes, for sure,' Ian added, as I interrupted him; 'I knew you would be saying that: but it is not of Eilidh that loved Cormac that I am now speaking. Nor am I taking the hidden way with Isla, that was my friend, nor with Eilidh that is my name-child, whom you know. Let the Birdeen be, bless her bonnie heart! No, what I am for telling you is all as new to you as the green grass to a lambkin: and no one has heard it from these tired lips o' mine since I was a boy, and learned it off the mouth of old Barabal MacAodh that was my foster-mother.'

Of all the many tales of the olden time that Ian Mòr told me, and are to be found in no book, this was the last. That is why I give it here, where I have spoken much of him.

Ian told me this thing one winter night, while we sat before the peats, where the ingle was full of warm shadows. We were in the croft of the small hill-farm of Glenivore, which was held by my cousin, Silis Macfarlane. But we were alone then, for Silis was over at the far end of the Strath, because of the baffling against death of her dearest friend, Giorsal MacDiarmid.

It was warm there, before the peats, with a thick wedge of spruce driven into the heart of them. The resin crackled and sent blue sparks of flame up through the red and yellow tongues that licked the sooty chimney-slopes, in which, as in a shell, we could hear an endless soughing of the wind.

Outside, the snow lay deep. It was so hard on the surface that the white hares, leaping across it, went soundless as shadows, and as trackless.

In the far-off days, when Somhairle was Maormor of the Isles, the most beautiful woman of her time was named Eilidh.

The king had sworn that whosoever was his best man in battle, when next the Fomorian pirates out of the north came down upon the isles, should have Eilidh to wife.

Eilidh, who, because of her soft, white beauty, for all the burning brown of her by the sun and wind, was also called Silk o' the Kine, laughed low when she heard this. For she loved the one man in all the world for her, and that was Isla, the son of Isla Mòr the blind chief of Islay. He, too, loved her even as she loved him. He was a poet as well as a warrior, and scarce she knew whether she loved best the fire in his eyes when, girt with his gleaming weapons and with his fair hair unbound, he went forth to battle: or the shine in his eyes when, harp in hand, he chanted of the great deeds of old, or made a sweet song to her, Eilidh, his queen of women: or the flame in his eyes when, meeting her at the setting of the sun, he stood speechless, wrought to silence because of his worshipping love of her.

One day she bade him go to the Isle of the Swans to fetch her

Silk o' the Kine

enough of the breast-down of the wild cygnets for her to make a white cloak of. While he was still absent – and the going there, and the faring thereupon, and the returning, took three days – the Fomorians came down upon the Long Island.

It was a hard fight that was fought, but at last the Norlanders were driven back with slaughter. Somhairle, the Maormor, was all but slain in that fight, and the corbies would have had his eyes had it not been for Osra mac Osra, who, with his javelin, slew the spearman who had waylaid the king while he slipped in the Fomorian blood he had spilt.

While the ale was being drunk out of the great horns that night, Somhairle called for Eilidh.

The girl came to the rath where the king and his warriors feasted; white and beautiful as moonlight among turbulent black waves.

A murmur went up from many bearded lips. The king scowled. Then there was silence.

'I am here, O King,' said Eilidh. The sweet voice of her was like soft rain in the woods at the time of the greening.

Somhairle looked at her. Sure, she was fair to see. No wonder men called her Silk o' the Kine. His pulse beat against the stormy tide in his veins. Then, suddenly, his gaze fell upon Osra. The heart of his kinsman that had saved him was his own: and he smiled, and lusted after Eilidh no more.

'Eilidh, that art called Silk o' the Kine, dost thou see this man here before me?'

'I see the man.'

'Let the name of him then be upon your lips.'

'It is Osra mac Osra.'

'It is this Osra and no other man that is to wind thee, fair Silk o' the Kine. And by the same token, I have sworn to him that he shall lie breast to breast with thee this night. So go hence to where Osra has his sleeping-place, and await him there upon the deer-skins. From this hour thou art his wife. It is said.'

Then a silence fell again upon all there, when, after a loud surf of babbling laughter and talk, they saw that Eilidh stood where she was, heedless of the king's word.

Somhairle gloomed. The great black eyes under his cloudy mass of hair flamed upon her.

'Is it dumb you are, Eilidh,' he said at last, in a cold, hard voice; 'or do you wait for Osra to take you hence?'

'I am listening,' she answered; and that whisper was heard by all there. It was as the wind in the heather, low and sweet.

Then all listened.

The playing of a harp was heard. None played like that, save Isla mac Isla Mòr.

Then the deer-skins were drawn aside, and Isla came among those who feasted there.

'Welcome, O thou who wast afar off when the foe came,' began Somhairle, with bitter mocking.

But Isla took no note of that. He went forward till he was nigh upon the Maormor. Then he waited.

'Well, Isla that is called Isla-Aluinn, Isla fair-to-see, what is the thing you want of me, that you stand there, close-kin to death I am warning you?'

'I want Eilidh that is called Silk o' the Kine.'

'Eilidh is the wife of another man.'

'There is no other man, O King.'

'A brave word that! And who says it, O Isla, my over-lord?'

'I say it.'

Somhairle, the great Maormor, laughed, and his laugh was like a black bird of omen let loose against a night of storm.

'And what of Eilidh?'

'Let her speak.'

With that the Maormor turned to the girl, who did not quail.

'Speak, Silk o' the Kine!'

'There is no other man, O King.'

'Fool, I have this moment wedded you and Osra mac Osra.'

'I am wife to Isla-Aluinn.'

'Thou canst not be wife to two men.'

'That may be, O King. I know not. But I am wife to Isla-Aluinn.'

The king scowled darkly. None at the board whispered even. Osra shifted uneasily, clasping his sword-hilt. Isla stood, his eyes ashine as they rested on Eilidh. He knew nothing in life or death could come between them.

'Art thou not still a maid, Eilidh?' Somhairle asked at last.

'No.'

'Shame to thee, wanton.'

The girl smiled; but in her eyes, darkened now, there shone a flame.

'Is Isla-Aluinn the man?'

Silk o' the Kine

'He is the man.'

With that the king laughed a bitter laugh.

'Seize him!' he cried.

But Isla made no movement. So those who were about to bind him stood by, ready with naked swords.

'Take up your harp,' said Somhairle.

Isla stooped, and lifted the harp.

'Play now the wedding song of Osra mac Osra and Eilidh Silk o' the Kine.'

Isla smiled; but it was a grim smile that, and only Eilidh understood. Then he struck the harp, and he sang thus far this song out of his heart to the woman he loved better than life.

Eilidh, Eilidh, heart of my life, my pulse, my flame,
There are two men loving thee and two who are calling thee wife:

But only one husband to thee, Eilidh, that art my wife, and my joy;
Ay, sure, thy womb knows me, and the child thou bearest is mine.

Thou to me, I to thee, there is nought else in the world, Eilidh Silk o' the Kine;
Nought else in the world, no, no other man for thee, no woman for me!

But with that Somhairle rose, and dashed the hilt of his great spear upon the ground.

'Let the twain go,' he shouted.

Then all stood or leaned back as Isla and Eilidh slowly moved through their midst, hand in hand. Not one there but knew they went to their death.

'This night shall be theirs,' cried the king with mocking wrath; 'then, Osra, you can have your will of Silk o' the Kine, that is your wife; and have Isla-Aluinn to be your slave; and this for the rising and setting of three moons from tonight. Then they shall each be blinded and made dumb, and that for the same space of time; and at the end of that time they shall be thrown upon the snow to the wolves.'

Nevertheless, Osra groaned in his heart because of that night of Isla with Eilidh. Not all the years of the years could give him a joy like unto that.

In the silence in the mid-dark he went stealthily to where the twain lay.

It was there he was found in the morning, where he had died soundlessly, with Eilidh's dagger up to the hilt in his heart.

But none saw them go save one, and that was Sorch, the brother of Isla – Sorch who, in later days, was called Sorch Mouth o' Honey because of his sweet songs. Of all songs that he sang none was so sweet against the ears as that of the love of Eilidh and Isla. Two lovers these that loved as few love: and deathless, too, because of that great love.

And what Sorch saw was this. Just before the rising of the sun, Isla and Eilidh came hand in hand from out of the rath, where they had lain awake all night because of their deep joy.

Silently, but unhasting, fearless still as of yore, they moved across the low dunes that withheld the sea from the land.

The waves were just frothed, so low were they. The loud glad singing of them filled the morning. Eilidh and Isla stopped when the first waves met their feet. They cast their raiment from them. Eilidh flung the gold fillet of her dusky hair far into the sea. Isla broke his sword, and saw the two halves shelve through the moving greenness. Then they turned and kissed each other upon the lips.

And the end of the song of Sorch is this: that neither he nor any man knows whether they went to life or to death; but that Isla and Eilidh swam out together against the sun, and were seen never again by any of their kin or race. Two strong swimmers were these who swam out together into the sunlight – Eilidh and Isla.

Ula and Urla

Ula and Urla were under vow to meet by the Stone of Sorrow. But Ula, dying first, stumbled blindfold when he passed the Shadowy Gate; and, till Urla's hour was upon her, she remembered not.

These were the names that had been given to them in the north isles, when the birlinn that ran down the war-galley of the Vikings brought them before the Maormor.

No word had they spoken that day, and no name. They were of the Gael, though Ula's hair was yellow, and though his eyes were blue as the heart of a wave. They would ask nothing, for both were in love with death. The Maormor of Siol Tormaid looked at Urla, and his desire gnawed at his heart. But he knew what was in her mind, because he saw into it through her eyes, and he feared the sudden slaying in the dark.

Nevertheless, he brooded night and day upon her beauty. Her skin was more white than the foam of the moon: her eyes were as a star-lit dewy dusk. When she moved, he saw her like a doe in the fern: when she stooped, it was as the fall of wind-swayed water. In his eyes there was a shimmer as of the sun-flood in a calm sea. In that dazzle he was led astray.

'Go,' he said to Ula, on a day of the days. 'Go: the men of Siol Torquil will take you to the south isles, and so you can hale to your own place, be it Eirèann or Manannan, or wherever the south wind puts its hand upon your home.'

It was on that day Ula spoke for the first time.

'I will go, Coll mac Torcall; but I go not alone. Urla that I love goes whither I go.'

'She is my spoil. But, man out of Eirèann – for so I know you to be, because of the manner of your speech – tell me this: Of what clan and what place are you, and whence is Urla come; and by what shore was it that the men of Lochlin whom we slew took you and her out of the sea, as you swam against the sun, with waving swords upon the strand when the Viking-boat carried you away?'

'How know you these things?' asked Ula, that had been Isla, son of the king of Islay.

'One of the sea-rovers spake before he died.'

'Then let the Viking speak again. I have nought to say.'

With that the Maormor frowned, but said no more. That eve Ula was seized, as he walked in the dusk by the sea, singing low to himself an ancient song.

'Is it death?' he said, remembering another day when he and Eilidh, that they called Urla, had the same asking upon their lips.

'It is death.'

Ula frowned, but spake no word for a time. Then he spake.

'Let me say one word with Urla.'

'No word canst thou have. She, too, must die.'

Ula laughed low at that.

'I am ready,' he said. And they slew him with a spear.

When they told Urla, she rose from the deerskins and went down to the shore. She said no word then. But she stooped, and she put her lips upon his cold lips, and she whispered in his unhearing ear.

That night Coll mac Torcall went secretly to where Urla was. When he entered, a groan came to his lips and there was froth there: and that was because the spear that had slain Ula was thrust betwixt his shoulders by one who stood in the shadow. He lay there till the dawn. When they found Coll the Maormor he was like a seal speared upon a rock, for he had his hands out, and his head was between them, and his face was downward.

'Eat dust, slain wolf,' was all that Eilidh, whom they called Urla, said, ere she moved away from that place in the darkness of the night.

When the sun rose, Urla was in a glen among the hills. A man who shepherded there took her to his mate. They gave her milk, and because of her beauty and the frozen silence of her eyes, bade her stay with them and be at peace.

They knew in time that she wished death. But first, there was the birthing of the child.

'It was Isla's will,' she said to the woman. Ula was but the shadow of a bird's wing: an idle name. And she, too, was Eilidh once more.

'It was death he gave you when he gave you the child,' said the woman once.

'It was life,' answered Eilidh, with her eyes filled with the shadow of dream. And yet another day the woman said to her that it would be well to bear the child and let it die: for beauty was like sunlight on a day of clouds, and if she were to go forth young and alone and so wondrous fair, she would have love, and love is best.

'Truly, love is best,' Eilidh answered. 'And because Isla loved me, I would that another Isla came into the world and sang his songs – the songs that were so sweet, and the songs that he never sang, because I gave him death when I gave him life. But now he shall live again, and he and I shall be in one body, in him that I carry now.'

At that the woman understood, and said no more. And so the days grew out of the nights, and the dust of the feet of one month was in the eyes of that which followed after; and this until Eilidh's time was come.

Dusk after dusk, Ula that was Isla the Singer, waited by the Stone of Sorrow. Then a great weariness came upon him. He made a song there, where he lay in the narrow place; the last song that he made, for after that he heard no trampling of the hours.

> The swift years slip and slide adown the steep;
>   The slow years pass; neither will come again.
> Yon huddled years have weary eyes that weep,
>   These laugh, these moan, these silent frown, these plain,
>   These have their lips acurl with proud disdain.
>
> O years with tears, and tears through weary years,
>   How weary I who in your arms have lain:
> Now, I am tired: the sound of slipping spears
>   Moves soft, and tears fall in a bloody rain,
>   And the chill footless years go over me who am slain.
>
> I hear, as in a wood, dim with old light, the rain,
>   Slow falling; old, old, weary, human tears:
> And in the deepening dark my comfort is my Pain,
>   Sole comfort left of all my hopes and fears,
>   Pain that alone survives, gaunt hound of the shadowy years.

But, at the last, after many days, he stirred. There was a song in his ears.

He listened. It was like soft rain in a wood in June. It was like the wind laughing among the leaves.

Then his heart leaped. Sure, it was the voice of Eilidh!

'*Eilidh! Eilidh! Eilidh!*' he cried. But a great weariness came upon him again. He fell asleep, knowing not the little hand that was in his, and the small, flower-sweet body that was warm against his side.

Then the child that was his looked into the singer's heart, and saw there a mist of rainbows, and midway in that mist was the face of Eilidh, his mother.

Thereafter, the little one looked into his brain that was so still, and he saw the music that was there: and it was the voice of Eilidh his mother.

And, again, the birdeen, that had the blue of Isla's eyes and the dream of Eilidh's, looked into Ula's sleeping soul: and he saw that it was not Isla nor yet Eilidh, but that it was like unto himself, who was made of Eilidh and Isla.

For a long time the child dreamed. Then he put his ear to Isla's brow, and listened. Ah, the sweet songs that he heard. Ah, bittersweet moonseed of song! Into his life they passed, echo after echo, strain after strain, wild air after wild sweet air.

'Isla shall never die,' whispered the child, 'for Eilidh loved him. And I am Isla and Eilidh.'

Then the little one put his hands above Isla's heart. There was a flame there, that the Grave quenched not.

'O flame of love!' sighed the child, and he clasped it to his breast: and it was a moonshine glory about the two hearts that he had, the heart of Isla and the heart of Eilidh, that were thenceforth one.

At dawn he was no longer there. Already the sunrise was warm upon him where he lay, new-born, upon the breast of Eilidh.

'It is the end,' murmured Isla when he waked. 'She has never come. For sure, now, the darkness and the silence.'

Then he remembered the words of Maol the Druid, he that was a seer, and had told him of Orchil, the dim goddess who is under the brown earth, in a vast cavern, where she weaves at two looms. With one hand she weaves life upward through the grass; with the other she weaves death downward through the mould; and the sound of the weaving is Eternity, and the name of it in the green world is Time. And, through all, Orchil weaves the weft of Eternal Beauty, that passeth not, though its soul is Change.

And these were the words of Orchil, on the lips of Maol the Druid, that was old, and knew the mystery of the Grave.

When thou journeyest towards the Shadowy Gate take neither Fear with thee nor Hope, for both are abashed hounds of silence in that place; but take only the purple nightshade for sleep, and a vial of tears and wine, tears that shall be known unto thee and old wine of love. So shalt thou have thy silent festival, ere the end.

So therewith Isla, having, in his weariness, the nightshade of sleep, and in his mind the slow dripping rain of familiar tears, and deep in his heart the old wine of love, bowed his head.

It was well to have lived, since life was Eilidh. It was well to cease to live, since Eilidh came no more.

Then suddenly he raised his head. There was music in the green world above. A sunray opened the earth about him: staring upward he beheld Angus Ogue.

'Ah, fair face of the god of youth,' he sighed. Then he saw the white birds that fly about the head of Angus Ogue, and he heard the music that his breath made upon the harp of the wind.

'Arise,' said Angus; and, when he smiled the white birds flashed their wings and made a mist of rainbows.

'Arise,' said Angus Ogue again, and, when he spoke, the spires of the grass quivered to a wild, sweet haunting air.

So Isla arose, and the sun shone upon him, and his shadow passed into the earth. Orchil wove it into her web of death.

'Why dost thou wait here by the Stone of Sorrow, Isla that was called Ula at the end?'

'I wait for Eilidh, who cometh not.'

At that the wind-listening god stooped and laid his head upon the grass.

'I hear the coming of a woman's feet,' he said, and he rose.

'Eilidh! Eilidh!' cried Isla, and the sorrow of his cry was a moan in the web of Orchil.

Angus Ogue took a branch, and put the cool greenness against his cheek.

'I hear the beating of a heart,' he said.

'Eilidh! Eilidh! Eilidh!' Isla cried, and the tears that were in his voice were turned by Angus into dim dews of remembrance in the babe-brain that was the brain of Isla and Eilidh.

'I hear a word,' said Angus Ogue, 'and that word is a flame of joy.'

Isla listened. He heard a singing of birds. Then, suddenly, a glory came into the shine of the sun.

'I have come, Isla my king!'

It was the voice of Eilidh. He bowed his head, and swayed; for it was his own life that came to him.

'*Eilidh!*' he whispered.

And so, at the last, Isla came into his kingdom.

But are they gone, these twain, who loved with deathless love? Or is this a dream that I have dreamed?

Afar in an island-sanctuary that I shall not see again, where the wind chants the blind oblivious rune of Time, I have heard the grasses whisper: *Time never was, Time is not.*

Mircath

The Mire-chath was the name given to the war-frenzy that often preceded and accompanied battle.

F.M.

One of the four Viking *seanachas* (traditional lore) of Ian Mòr Cameron, *Mircath* was first published in *The Washer of the Ford*. Essentially masculine, this short and savage saga seems to reflect Sharp's exultant love of the sea and sailing, his knowledge of Scottish West Coast waters and above all, his own part-Celtic part-Scandinavian background of which he was supremely proud. As Fiona Macleod, Sharp records that Ian Mòr recited his seanachas before a peat-fire at a hill-sheiling. 'Sometimes, indeed, these brief tales were like waves: one saw them rise, congregate, and expand in a dark billow – and the next moment there was a vanishing puff of spray, and the billow lapsed.'

E.S.

When Haco the Laugher saw the islanders coming out of the west in their birlinns, he called to his Vikings, 'Now of a truth we shall hear the Song of the Sword!'

The ten galleys of the summer-sailors spread out into two lines of five boats, each boat an arrow-flight from those on either side.

The birlinns came on against the noon. In the sun-dazzle they loomed black as a shoal of pollack. There were fifteen in all, and from the largest, midway among them, flew a banner. On this banner was a disc of gold.

'It is the Banner of the Sunbeam!' shouted Olaf the Red, who with Torquil the One-Armed was hero-man to Haco. 'I know it well. The Gael who fight under that are warriors indeed.'

'Is there a saga-man here?' cried Haco. At that a great shout went up from the Vikings: 'Harald the Smith!'

A man rose among the bow-men in Olaf's boat. It was Harald. He took a small square harp, and he struck the strings. This was the song he sang:

> Let loose the hounds of war,
>   The whirling swords!
> Send them leaping afar,
> Red in their thirst for war;
> Odin laughs in his car
>   At the screaming of the swords!
>
> Far let the white ones fly,
>   The whirling swords!
> Afar off the ravens spy
> Death-shadows cloud the sky.
> Let the wolves of the Gael die
>   'Neath the screaming swords!
>
> The Shining Ones yonder
>   High in Valhalla
> Shout now, with thunder,
> *Drive the Gaels under,*
> *Cleave them asunder,* –
>   *Swords of Valhalla!*

A shiver passed over every Viking. Strong men shook as a child when lightning plays. Then the trembling passed. The mircath, the war-frenzy came on them. Loud laughter went from boat to boat. Many tossed the great oars, and swung them down upon the sea, splashing the sun-dazzle into a yeast of foam. Others sprang up and whirled their javelins on high, catching them with bloody mouths: others made sword-play, and stammered thick words through a surf of froth upon their lips. Olaf the Red towered high on the steering-plank of the *Calling Raven*, swirling round and round a mighty battleaxe: on the *Sea-Wolf*, Torquil One-Arm shaded his eyes, and screamed hoarsely wild words that no one knew the meaning of. Only Haco was still for a time. Then he, too, knew the mircath; and he stood up in the *Red-Dragon* and laughed loud and long. And when Haco the Laugher laughed, there was ever blood and to spare.

The birlinns of the islanders drave on apace. They swayed out into a curve, a black crescent there in the gold-sprent blue meads of the sea. From the great birlinn that carried the Sunbeam came a chanting voice:

> O, 'tis a good song the sea makes when blood is on the wave,
> And a good song the wave makes when its crest of foam is red!
> For the rovers out of Lochlin the sea is a good grave,
> And the bards will sing tonight to the sea-moan of the dead!
>   Yo-ho-a-h'eily-a-yo, eily, ayah, a yo!
>   Sword and Spear and Battle-axe sing the Song of Woe!
>   Ayah, eily, a yo!
>   Eily, ayah, a yo!

Then there was a swirling and dashing of foam. Clouds of spray filled the air from the thresh of the oars.

No man knew aught of the last moments ere the birlinns bore down upon the Viking-galleys. Crash and roar and scream, and a wild surging; the slashing of swords, the whistle of arrows, the fierce hiss of whirled spears, the rending crash of battle-axe and splintering of the javelins; wild cries, oaths, screams, shouts of victors, and yells of the dying; shrill taunts from the spillers of life, and savage choking cries from those drowning in the bloody yeast that bubbled and foamed in the maelstrom where the war-boats swung and reeled this way and that; and, over all, the loud death-music of Haco the Laugher.

Olaf the Red went into the sea, red indeed, for the blood streamed from head and shoulders, and fell about him as a scarlet robe. Torquil One-Arm fought, blind and arrow-sprent, till a spear went through his neck, and he sank among the dead. Louder and louder grew the fierce shouts of the Gael; fewer the savage screaming cries of the Vikings. Thus it was till two galleys only held living men. The *Calling Raven* turned and fled, with the nine men who were not wounded to the death. But, on the *Red-Dragon*, Haco the Laugher still laughed. Seven men were about him. These fought in silence.

Then Toscar mac Aonghas, that was leader of the Gael, took his bow. None was arrow-better than Toscar of the Nine Battles. He laid down his sword and took his bow, and an arrow went through the right eye of Haco the Laugher. He laughed no more. The seven died in silence. Swaran Swiftfoot was the last. When he fell, he wiped away the blood that streamed over his face.

'*Skoal!*' he cried to the hero of the Gael, and with that he whirled his battle-axe at Toscar mac Aonghas; and the soul of Toscar met his, in the dark mist, and upon the ears of both fell at one and the same time the glad laughter of the gods in Valhalla.

The Laughter of Scathach the Queen

Scathach (pronounced Sca-ya or Sky-ya) was an Amazonian Queen of the Island of Skye, and is supposed to have given her name to that island.

F.M.

This savage tale, originally published in *The Washer of the Ford*, is based on the Celtic legend that records how the god-hero Cuchullin spent a year and a day at the court of the warrior Queen Scathach to learn two daring feats; how to leap over the dangerous gorge that led to Scathach's dun and how to thrust the *Gae Bolg*, or Belly Spear, which was thrown by the foot. Fiona Macleod, writing to W. B. Yeats in 1899, says, 'From the standpoint of literary art *per se* I think [my] best work is that wherein the barbaric [the old Gaelic or Celto-Scandinavian] note occurs.' *The Laughter of Scathach the Queen* is one of the three stories she mentions.

E.S.

In the year when Cuchullin left the Isle of Skye, where Scathach the warrior-queen ruled with the shadow of death in the palm of her sword-hand, there was sorrow because of his beauty. He had fared back to Eiré, at the summons of Concobar mac Nessa, Ard-Righ of Ulster. For the Clan of the Red Branch was wading in blood, and there were seers who beheld that bitter tide rising and spreading.

Cuchullin was only a youth in years; but he had come to Skye a boy, and he had left it a man. None fairer had ever been seen of Scathach or of any woman. He was tall and lithe as a young pine; his skin was as white as a woman's breast; his eyes were of a fierce bright blue, with a white light in them as of the sun. When bent, and with arrow half-way drawn, he stood on the heather, listening against the belling of the deer; or when he leaned against a tree, dreaming not of eagle-chase or wolf-hunt, but of the woman whom he had never met; or, when by the dûn, he played at sword-whirl or spear-thrust, or raced the war-chariot across the machar – then, and ever there were eyes upon his beauty, and there were some who held him to be Angus Ogue himself. For there was a light about him, such as the hills have in the sun-glow an hour before set. His hair was the hair of Angus and of the fair gods, earth-brown shot with gold next his head, ruddy as flame midway, and, where it sprayed into a golden mist of fire, yellow as windy sunshine.

But Cuchullin loved no woman upon Skye, and none dared openly to love Cuchullin, for Scathach's heart yearned for him, and to cross the Queen was to put the shroud upon oneself. Scathach kept an open face for the son of Lerg. There was no dark frown above the storm in her eyes when she looked at his sunbright face. Gladly she slew a woman because Cuchullin had lightly reproved the maid for some idle thing; and once, when the youth looked in grave silence at three Viking captives whom she had spared because of their comely manhood, she put her sword through the heart of each, and sent him the blade, dripping red, as the flower of love.

But Cuchullin was a dreamer, and he loved what he dreamed of, and that woman was not Scathach, nor any of her warrior-women who made the Isle of Mist a place of terror for those cast upon the wild shores, or stranded there in the ebb of inglorious battle.

Scathach brooded deep upon her vain desire. Once, in a windless, shadowy gloaming, she asked him if he loved any woman.

'Yes,' he said. 'Etáin.'

Her breath came quick and hard. It was for pleasure to her then to think of Cuchullin lying white at her feet, with the red blood spilling from the whiteness of his breast. But she bit her under lip, and said quietly –

'Who is Etáin?'

'She is the wife of Mídir.'

And with that the youth turned and moved haughtily away. She did not know that the Etáin of whom Cuchullin dreamed was no woman that he had seen in Eiré, but the wife of Mídir, the King of Faerie, who was so passing fair that Mac Greine*, the beautiful god, had made for her a grianan all of shining glass, where she lives in a dream, and in that sun-bower is fed at dawn upon the bloom of flowers and at dusk upon their fragrance. *O ogham mhic Gréine, tha e boidheach,* † she

---

* 'Angus, Celtic god of love and beauty – E.S.
† 'O beauty of my love the Sun-lord' (*lit.* 'O youth, son of the Sun, how fair he is!') – F.M.

sighs for ever in her sleep; and that sigh is in all sighs of love for ever and ever.

Scathach watched him till he was lost behind the flare of the camp fires of the rath. For long she stood there, brooding deep, till the sickle of the new moon, which had been like a blown feather over the sun as it sank, stood out in silver-shine against the blue-black sky, now like a wake in the sea because of the star-dazzle that was there. And what the Queen brooded upon was this: Whether to send emissaries to Eirèann, under bond to seek in that land till they found Mídir and Etáin, and to slay Mídir and bring to her the corpse, for a gift from her to lay before Cuchullin; or to bring Etáin to Skye, where the Queen might see her lose her beauty and wane into death. Neither way might win the heart of Cuchullin. The dark tarn of the woman's mind grew blacker with the shadow of that thought.

Slowly she moved dûn-ward through the night.

'As the moon sometimes is seen rising out of the east,' she muttered, 'and sometimes, as now, is first seen in the west, so is the heart of love. And if I go west, lo, the moon may rise along the sunway; and if I go east, lo, the moon may be a white light over the setting sun. And who that knoweth the heart of man or woman can tell when the moon of love is to appear full-orbed in the east, or sickle-wise in the west?'

It was on the day following that tidings came out of Eirèann. An Ultonian [Ulsterman] brought a sword to Cuchullin from Concobar the Ard-Righ.

'The sword has ill upon it, and will die unless you save it, Cuchulain, son of Lerg,' said the man.

'And what is that ill, Ultonian?' asked the youth.

'It is thirst.'

Then Cuchullin understood.

On the night of his going none looked at Scathach. She had a flame in her eyes.

At moonrise she came back into the rath. No one meeting her looked in her face. Death lay there, like the levin behind a cloud. But Maev, her chief captain, sought her, for she had glad news.

'I would slay you for that glad news, Maev,' said the Dark Queen to the warrior-woman, 'for there is no glad news unless it be that Cuchullin is come again; only, I spare, for you saved my life that day the summer-sailors burned my rath in the south.'

Nevertheless Scathach had gladness because of the tidings. Three

Viking galleys had been driven into Loch Scavaig, and been dashed to death there by the whirling wind and the narrow, furious seas. Of the ninety men who had sailed in them, only a score had reached the rocks, and these were now lying bound at the dûn, awaiting death.

'Call out my warriors,' said Scathach, 'and bid all meet at the oak near the Ancient Stones. And bring thither the twenty men that lie bound in the dûn.'

There was a scattering of fire and a clashing of swords and spears when the word went from Maev. Soon all were at the Stones beneath the great oak.

'Cut the bonds from the feet of the sea-rovers, and let them stand.' Thus commanded the Queen.

The tall, fair men out of Lochlin stood with their hands bound behind them. In their eyes burned wrath and shame, because that they were the sport of women. A bitter death theirs, with no sword-song for music. 'Take each by his long yellow hair,' said Scathach, 'and tie the hair of each to a down-caught bough of the oak.'

In silence this thing was done. A shadow was in the paleness of each Viking face.

'Let the boughs go,' said Scathach.

The five score warrior women who held the great boughs downward sprang back. Up swept the branches, and from each swung a living man, swaying in the wind by his long yellow hair.

Great men they were, strong warriors; but stronger was the yellow hair of each, and stronger than the hair the bough wherefrom each swung, and stronger than the boughs the wind that swayed them idly like drooping fruit, with the stars silvering their hair and the torch-flares reddening the white soles of their dancing feet.

Then Scathach the Queen laughed loud and long. There was no other sound at all there, for none ever uttered sound when Scathach laughed that laugh, for then her madness was upon her.

But at the last, Maev strode forward and struck a small clarsach that she carried, and to the wild notes of it sang the death-song of the Vikings –

O arone a-ree, eily arone, arone!
'Tis a good thing to be sailing across the sea!
How the women smile and the children are laughing glad
When the galleys go out into the blue sea – arone!
    O eily arone, arone!

But the children may laugh less when the wolves come,
And the women may smile less in the winter-cold;
For the Summer-sailors will not come again, arone!
    O arone a-ree, eily arone, arone!

I am thinking they will not sail back again, O no!
The yellow-haired men that came sailing across the sea:
For 'tis wild apples they would be, and swing on green branches,
And sway in the wind for the corbies to preen their eyne.
    O eily arone, eily a-ree!

And it is pleasure for Scathach the Queen to see this:
To see the good fruit that grows upon the Tree of the Stones.
Long, speckled fruit it is, wind-swayed by its yellow roots,
And like men they are with their feet dancing in the void air!
    O, O, arone, aree, eily arone!

When she ceased, all there swung swords and spears, and flung flaring torches into the night, and cried out –

O arone a-ree, eily arone, arone,
O, O, arone, a-ree, eily arone!

Scathach laughed no more. She was weary now. Of what avail any joy of death against the pain she had in her heart, the pain that was called Cuchullin?

Soon all was dark in the rath. Flame after flame died out. Then there was but one red glare in the night, the watch-fire by the dûn. Deep peace was upon all. Not a heifer lowed, not a dog bayed against the moon. The wind fell into a breath, scarce enough to lift the fragrance from flower to flower. Upon the branches of a great oak swung motionless a strange fruit, limp and grey as the hemlock that hangs from ancient pines.

The Festival of the Birds

> A few places in the world are to be held holy, because of the love which consecrates them and the faith which enshrines them. Their names are themselves talismans of spiritual beauty.
>
> F.M.
> (From *Iona*)

The Three Marvels of Iona, of which *The Festival of the Birds* is the first legend, was originally included in *The Washer of the Ford*. A beautiful tale, it is redolent of that blending of 'paganism and romance and spiritual beauty' which is the hallmark of all Macleod's work. It also highlights another of Sharp's favourite themes, the reversal of Christian mission whereby the Druid has much to teach the Priest. Sharp, in spite of his professed paganism, did not condemn Catholicism, for he had found during his visits to the Western Isles that those which had remained true to the old faith at the time of the Reformation retained more of their Celtic customs and beliefs. He went so far as to identify Macleod as a Catholic. To Sharp in the role of Macleod, Iona was 'in spiritual geography, the Mecca of the Gael'. He saw it as 'the little Syrian Bethlehem' from whence would come 'the Daughter of God, now as the Divine Spirit embodies through mortal birth in a Woman, as once through mortal birth in a Man, the coming of a new Presence and Power ... the Shepherdess [who] shall call us home'.

E.S.

Before dawn, on the morning of the hundredth Sabbath after Colum the White had made glory to God in Hy, that was therefore called Ioua and thereafter I-shona and is now Iona, the Saint beheld his own Sheep in a vision.

Much fasting and long pondering over the missals, with their golden and azure and sea-green initials and earth-brown branching

The Festival of the Birds

letters, had made Colum weary. He had brooded much of late upon the mystery of the living world that was not man's world.

On the eve of that hundredth Sabbath, which was to be a holy festival in Iona, he had talked long with an ancient greybeard out of a remote isle in the north, the wild Isle of the Mountains, where Scathach the Queen hanged the men of Lochlin by their yellow hair.

This man's name was Ardan, and he was of the ancient people. He had come to Hy because of two things. Maolmòr, the King of the northern Picts, had sent him to learn of Colum what was this god-teaching he had brought out of Eiré: and for himself he had come, with his age upon him, to see what manner of man this Colum was, who had made Ioua, that was 'Innis-nan-Dhruidhneach' – the Isle of the Druids – into a place of new worship.

For three hours Ardan and Colum had walked by the sea-shore. Each learned of the other. Ardan bowed his head before the wisdom. Colum knew in his heart that the Druid saw mysteries.

In the first hour they talked of God. Colum spake, and Ardan smiled in his shadowy eyes. 'It is for the knowing,' he said, when Colum ceased.

'Ay, sure,' said the Saint: 'and now, O Ardan the wise, is my God thy God?'

But at that Ardan smiled not. He turned the grave, sad eyes of him to the west. With his right hand he pointed to the Sun that was like a great golden flower. 'Truly, He is thy God and my God.' Colum was silent. Then he said: 'Thee and thine, O Ardan, from Maolmòr the Pictish king to the least of thy slaves, shall have a long weariness in Hell. That fiery globe yonder is but the Lamp of the World: and sad is the case of the man who knows not the torch from the torch-bearer.'

And in the second hour they talked of Man. Ardan spake, and Colum smiled in his deep, grey eyes.

'It is for laughter that,' he said, when Ardan ceased.

'And why will that be, O Colum of Eiré?' said Ardan. Then the smile went out of Colum's grey eyes, and he turned and looked about him.

He beheld, near, a crow, a horse and a hound.

'These are thy brethren,' he said scornfully.

But Ardan answered quietly, 'Even so.'

The third hour they talked about the beasts of the earth and the fowls of the air.

At the last Ardan said: 'The ancient wisdom hath it that these are the souls of men and women that have been, or are to be.'

Whereat Colum answered: 'The new wisdom, that is old as eternity, declareth that God created all things in love. Therefore are we at one, O Ardan, though we sail to the Isle of Truth from the West and the East. Let there be peace between us.'

'Peace,' said Ardan.

That eve, Ardan of the Picts sat with the monks of Iona. Colum blessed him and said a saying. Oran of the Songs sang a hymn of beauty. Ardan rose, and put the wine of guests to his lips, and chanted this rune:

O Colum and monks of Christ,
It is peace we are having this night:
Sure, peace is a good thing,
And I am glad with the gladness.

We worship one God,
Though ye call him Dè –
And I say not, *O Dia!*
But cry *Bea'uil!*

For it is one faith for man,
And one for the living world,
And no man is wiser than another –
And none knoweth much.

None knoweth a better thing than this:
The Sword, Love, Song, Honour, Sleep.
None knoweth a surer thing than this:
Birth, Sorrow, Pain, Weariness, Death.

Sure, peace is a good thing;
Let us be glad of Peace:
We are not men of the Sword,
But of the Rune and the Wisdom.

I have learned a truth of Colum,
He hath learned of me:
All ye on the morrow shall see
A wonder of the wonders.

The Festival of the Birds

> The thought is on you, that the Cross
> Is known only of you:
> Lo, I tell you the birds know it
> That are marked with the Sorrow.
>
> Listen to the Birds of Sorrow,
> They shall tell you a great Joy:
> It is Peace you will be having,
> With the Birds.

No more would Ardan say after that, though all besought him.

Many pondered long that night. Oran made a song of mystery. Colum brooded through the dark; but before dawn he slept upon the fern that strewed his cell. At dawn, with waking eyes, and weary, he saw his Sleep in a vision.

It stood grey and wan beside him.

'What art thou, O Spirit?' he said.

'I am thy Sleep, Colum.'

'And is it peace?'

'It is peace.'

'What wouldest thou?'

'I have wisdom. Thy heart and thy brain were closed. I could not give you what I brought. I brought wisdom.'

'Give it.'

'Behold!'

And Colum, sitting upon the strewed fern that was his bed, rubbed his eyes that were heavy with weariness and fasting and long prayer. He could not see his Sleep now. It was gone as smoke that is licked up by the wind.

But on the ledge of the hole that was in the eastern wall of his cell he saw a bird. He leaned his elbow upon the *leabhar-aifrionn* that was by his side.* Then he spoke.

'Is there song upon thee, O *Bru-dhearg*?'

Then the Red-breast sang, and the singing was so sweet that tears came into the eyes of Colum, and he thought the sunlight that was streaming from the east was melted into that lilting sweet song. It was a hymn that the Bru-dhearg sang, and it was this:

---

* The '*leabhar-aifrionn*' (pron. lyo-ur eff-runn) is a missal: literally a massbook, or chapel-book. *Bru-dhearg* is literally red-breast.

Holy, Holy, Holy,
    Christ upon the Cross:
My little nest was near,
    Hidden in the moss.

Holy, Holy, Holy,
    Christ was pale and wan:
His eyes beheld me singing
    Bron, Bron, mo Bron!*

Holy, Holy, Holy,
    'Come near, O wee brown bird!'
Christ spake: and lo, I lighted
    Upon the Living Word.

Holy, Holy, Holy,
    I heard the mocking scorn!
But *Holy, Holy, Holy*
    I sang against a thorn!

Holy, Holy, Holy,
    Ah, his brow was bloody:
Holy, Holy, Holy,
    All my breast was ruddy.

Holy, Holy, Holy,
    Christ's-Bird shalt thou be:
Thus said Mary Virgin
    There on Calvary.

Holy, Holy, Holy,
    A wee brown bird am I:
But my breast is ruddy
    For I saw Christ die.

Holy, Holy, Holy,
    By this ruddy feather,
Colum, call thy monks, and
    All the birds together.

---

* 'O my Grief, my Grief.'

And at that Colum rose. Awe was upon him, and joy.

He went out and told all to the monks. Then he said Mass out on the green sward. The yellow sunshine was warm upon his grey hair. The love of God was warm in his heart.

'Come, all ye birds!' he cried.

And lo, all the birds of the air flew nigh. The golden eagle soared from the Cuchullins in far-off Skye, and the osprey from the wild lochs of Mull; the gannet from above the clouds, and the fulmar and petrel from the green wave: the cormorant and the skua from the weedy rock, and the plover and the kestrel from the machar: the corbie and the raven from the moor, and the snipe and the bittern and the heron: the cuckoo and cushat from the woodland: the crane from the swamp, the lark from the sky, and the mavis and the merle from the green bushes: the yellowyite, the shilfa, and the lintie, the gyalvonn and the wren and the redbreast, one and all, every creature of the wings, they came at the bidding.

'Peace!' cried Colum.

'Peace!' cried all the Birds, and even the Eagle, the Kestrel, the Corbie, and the Raven cried *Peace, Peace!*

'I will say the Mass,' said Colum the White.

And with that he said the Mass. And he blessed the birds.

When the last chant was sung, only the Bru-dhearg remained.

'Come, O Ruddy-Breast,' said Colum, 'and sing to us of the Christ.'

Through a golden hour thereafter the Redbreast sang. Sweet was the joy of it.

At the end Colum said, 'Peace! In the name of the Father, the Son, and the Holy Ghost.'

Thereat Ardan the Pict bowed his head, and in a loud voice repeated –

'*Sìth* (shee)! *An ainm an Athar, 's an mhic, 's an Spioraid Naoimh!*'

And to this day the song of the Birds of Colum, as they are called in Hy, is *Sìth – Sìth – Sìth – an – ainm – Chriosd –*

'Peace – Peace – Peace – in the name of Christ!'

Cathal of the Woods

The English equivalent of *Annir-Choille*, as the following tale originally was named, would be the Wood-nymph. The word *Annir* is an ancient compound Gaelic word for a maiden.

F.M.

The Annir-Choille first appeared in *The Washer of the Ford*, and was later included under its new title in *Barbaric Tales*. Reflective of Sharp's childhood experience of nature, of his attitude to Christianity and of his concept of God, this deeply compassionate story was considered by W. B. Yeats to be 'one of the most vital things' Fiona Macleod had written. T. A. Janvier who knew of Fiona's identity commented, 'nor would a woman have written *The Annir-Choille*, I think, as it is written here. Fiona has shown her double sex in this story more completely, it seems to me, than in any other. It is written with a man's sense of decency and a woman's sense of delicacy – and the love of both man and woman is in it to a very extraordinary degree!'

Sharp's creed is best summed up in the following lines which he wrote in a Christmas card to his wife in 1894:

> The universe is eternally, omnipresently and continuously filled with the breath of God.
>
> Every breath of God creates a new convolution in the brain of Nature: and with every moment of change in the brain of Nature, new loveliness is wrought upon the earth.
>
> Every breath of God creates a new convolution in the brain of the Human Spirit, and with every moment of change in the brain of the Human Spirit, new hopes, aspirations, dreams, are wrought within the Soul of the Living.
>
> And there is no Evil anywhere in the Light of this creative Breath: but only, everywhere, a redeeming from Evil, a winning towards Good.

Cathal of the Woods which blends the mystery of Celtic paganism with, ultimately, the spirit of Christianity is deeply reflective of this creed.

E.S.

When Cathal mac Art, that was called Cathal Gille-Mhoire, Cathal the Servant of Mary, walked by the sea, one night of the nights in a green May, there was trouble in his heart.

It was not long since he had left Iona. The good St Colum, in sending the youth to the Isle of Â-rinn, as it was then called, gave him a writing for St Molios, the holy man who lived in the sea-cave of the small Isle of the Peak, that is in the eastward hollow at the south end of Arran. A sorrow it was to him to leave the fair isle in the west. He had known glad years there – since, in one of the remote isles to the north, he had seen his father slain by a man of Lochlin, and his mother carried away in a galley oared by fierce yellow-haired men. No kith or kin had he but the old priest, that was the brother of his father, Cathal Gille-Chriosd, Cathal the Servant of Christ.

On Iona he had learned the way of Christ. He had a white robe; and could, with a shaven stick and a thin tuft of seal-fur, or with the feather-quill of a wild swan or a solander, write the holy words upon strained lambskin or parchment, and fill the big letters, that were here and there, with earth-brown and sky-blue and shining green, with scarlet of blood and gold of sun-warm sands. He could sing the long holy hymns, too, that Colum loved to hear; and it was his voice that had the sweetest clear-call of any on the island. He was in the nineteenth year of his years when a Frankish prince, who had come to Iona for the blessing of the Saint, wanted him to go back with him to the Southlands. He promised many things because of that voice. Cathal dreamed often, in the hot drowsy afternoons of the month that followed, of the long white sword that would slay so well; and of the white money that might be his to buy fair apparel with, and a great black stallion accoutred with trappings wrought with gold, and a bed of down; and of white hands, and white breasts, and the white song of youth.

He had not gone with the Frankish prince, nor wished to go. But he dreamed often. It was on a day of dream that he lay on his back in the hot grass upon a dune, near where the cells of the monks were. The sunglow bathed the isle in a golden haze. The strait was a shimmering dazzle, and the blue wavelets that made curves in the soft white sand seemed to spill gold flakes and change them straightway into little jets of foam or bubbles of rainbow-spray. Cathal had made a song for his delight. His pain was less when he had made it. Now, lying there, and dreaming at times of the words of the Frankish prince, and remembering at times the stranger words of the old pagan helot, Neis, who had come with him out of the north, he felt fire burn in his veins; and he sang:

> O where in the north, or where in the south, or where in the east or west
> Is she who hath the flower-white hands and the swandown breast?
> O, if she be west, or east she be, or in the north or south,
> A sword will leap, a horse will prance, ere I win to Honey-Mouth.
>
> She has great eyes, like the doe on the hill, and warm and sweet she is,
> O, come to me, Honey-Mouth, bend to me, Honey-Mouth, give me thy kiss!
>
> *White Hands* her name is, where she reigns amid the princes fair:
> White hands she moves like swimming swans athrough her dusk-wave hair:
> White hands she puts about my heart, white hands fan up my breath:
> White hands take out the heart of me, and grant me life or death!
>
> White hands make better songs than hymns, white hands are young and sweet:
> O, a sword for me, O Honey-Mouth, and a war-horse fleet!
> O wild sweet eyes! O glad wild eyes! O mouth, how sweet it is!
> O, come to me, Honey-Mouth! bend to me, Honey-Mouth! give me thy kiss!

When he had ceased he saw a shadow fall upon the white sand beyond the dune. He looked up, and beheld Colum the Saint.

'Who taught you that song?' said the white holy one, in a voice hard and stern.

'No one, O Colum.'

'Then the Evil One is indeed here. Cathal, I promised that you would be having a holy name soon, but that name I will not be giving you now. You must come to me in sackcloth and with dust upon your head, with pain upon you, and with deep grief in your heart. Then only shall I bless you before the brothers and call you Cathal Gille-Mhoire, Cathal the Servant of Mary.'

A bitter, sad waiting it was for him who had fire in his young blood and was told to weave frost there, and to put silence upon the welling song in his heart. But at the end of the week Cathal was a holy monk again, and sang the hymns that Colum had taught him.

It was on the eve of the day when Colum blessed him before the brethren, and called him Gille-Mhoire, that he walked alone, brooding upon the evil of women and the curse they brought, and praying to Mary to save him from the sins of which he scarce knew the meaning. On his way back to his cell he passed old Neis, the helot, who said to him mockingly:

'It is a good thing that sorrow, Cathal mac Art, – and yet, sure, it is true that but for the hot love the slain man your father had for Foam that was your mother, you would not be here to praise your God or serve the woman whom the Arch-Druid yonder says is the Mother of God.'

Cathal bade the man eat silence, or it would go ill with him. But the words rankled. That night in his cell he woke, with on his lips his own sinful words:

White hands make better songs than hymns, white hands are
   young and sweet;
O, a sword for me, O Honey-Mouth, and a war-horse fleet!

On the morrow he went to Colum and told him that the Evil One would not give him peace. That night the Saint bade him make ready to go east to the Isle of Arran – the sole isle, then, where the Pictish folk would let the white robes of the Culdees go scatheless. To the holy Molios he was to go, him that dwelled in the sea-cave of the Isle of the Peak, that men already called the Holy Isle because of the preaching and the miracles of Molios.

'He is a wise man,' said Colum to himself, 'and he was a pagan Cruithne once, and a prince at that, and he knows the sweetness of sin, and will keep Cathal away from the snares that are set. With fasting, and much peril by day and weariness by night, the blood of the youth will forget the songs the Evil One has put into his mind and it will sing holy hymns. Great will be the glory. Cathal Gille-Mhoire will be a holy man while he has yet his youth upon him; and he will be a martyr to the flesh by day and by night and by night and by day, till the heathen put him to death because of the faith that is his.'

Thus it was that Cathal was blessed by Colum, and sent east among the wild Picts.

It was with joy that he served Molios. For four months he gave him all he had to give. The old saint passed word to Colum that Cathal was a saint and was assured of the crown of martyrdom, and lovingly he urged that the youth should be sent to the Isle of Mist in the north, the great isle that was ruled by Scathach the Queen. There, at the last Summer-sailing, the pagans had flayed a monk alive. A fair happy end: and Cathal was now worthy – and withal might triumph, and might even convert the heathen queen. 'She is wondrous fair to see,' he added, 'and Cathal is a comely youth.'

But Colum had answered that the young monk was to bide where he was, and to seek to win souls in the pagan Isle of Arran, where the Cross was still feared.

But with the coming of May and golden weather, the blood of Cathal grew warm. At times, even, he dreamed of the Frankish prince and the evil sweet words he had said.

Then a day of the days came. Molios and Cathal went to a hill-dûn where the Pict chieftain lived, and converted him and all the people in the dûn and all in the rath that was beyond the dûn. That eve the daughter of the warrior came upon Cathal walking in a solitary place, among the green pines beyond the rath. She was most sweet to look upon: tall and fair, with eyes like the sea in a cloudless noon, and hair like westward wheat turned back upon itself.

'What is the name men call you by, young Druid?' she said. 'I am Ardanna, the daughter of Ecta.'

'Your beauty is sweet to look upon, Ardanna. I am Cathal the son of Art the son of Aodh of the race of Alpein, from the isles of the sea. But I am not a Druid. I am a priest of Christ, a servant of Mary the Mother of God, and a son of God.'

Ardanna looked at him. A flush came into his face. In his eyes the same light flamed that was there when the Frankish prince told him of the delights of the world.

'Is it true, O Cathal, that the Druids – that the priests of Christ and the two other gods, the white-robed men whom we call Culdees, and of whom you are one, is it true that they will have nought to do with women?'

Cathal looked upon the woman no more, but on the ground at his feet.

'It is true, Ardanna.'

The girl laughed. It was a low, sweet, mocking laugh, but it went along Cathal's blood like cloud-fire along the sky. It was to him as though somewhat he had not seen was revealed.

'And is it a true thing that you holy men look at women askance, and as snares of peril and evil?'

'It is true, Ardanna; but not so upon those who are sisters of Christ, and whose eyes are upon heavenly things.'

'But what of those who are not sisters of your god, and are only women, fair to look upon, fair to woo, fair to love?'

Cathal again flushed. His eyes were still upon the ground. He made no answer.

Ardanna laughed low.

'Cathal!'

'Yes, fair daughter of Ecta?'

'Is it never longing for love you are?'

'There is but one love for us who have taken the vows of chastity.'

'What is chastity?'

Cathal raised his eyes and glanced at Ardanna. Her dark-blue eyes looked at him pure and sweet, though a smile was upon her mouth. He sighed.

'It is the sanctity of the body, Ardanna.'

'I do not understand,' she said simply. 'But tell me this, poor Cathal –'

'Why do you call me poor Cathal?'

'Because you have put your manhood from you – and you so young, and strong, and comely – and are not a warrior, and care neither for the sword, nor the chase, nor the harp, nor for women.'

Cathal was troubled. He looked again and again at Ardanna. The sunset light was in her yellow hair, which was about her as a glory. He had seen the moon as wondrous pale as her beautiful face. Like lilies her white hands were. He had dreamed of that flamelight in the eyes.

'I care,' he said.

She drew nearer, and leaned a little forward, and looked at him.

'You are good to look upon, Cathal – the comeliest youth I have ever seen.'

The monk flushed. This was the devil-tongue of which Colum had warned him. But how sweet the words were: like a harp that low voice. Sure, sweeter is a waking dream than a dream in sleep.

'I care,' he repeated dully.

'Look, Cathal.'

Slowly he raised his eyes. As his gaze moved upward it rested on the white breast which was like sea-foam swelling out of brown sea-weed, for she had a tanned fawn-skin belted and gold-claspt over the white robe she wore, and that had disparted for the warm air to play upon her bosom.

It troubled him. He let his eyes fall again. The red was on his face.

'Cathal!'

'Yes, Ardanna.'

'And you will never put your kiss upon a woman's lips? Never put your heart upon a woman's heart? Is it of cold sea water you are made – for even the running water in the streams is warmed by the sun? Tell me, Cathal, would you leave Molios the Culdee, – if –'

The monk of Christ suddenly flashed his eyes upon the woman.

'If what, Ardanna?' he asked abruptly; 'if what, Ardanna that is so witching fair?'

'If *I* loved you, Cathal? If I, the daughter of Ecta the chief, loved you, and took you to be my man, and you took me to be your woman, would you be content so?'

He stared at her as one in a dream. Then suddenly all the foolish madness that had been put upon him by Colum fell away. What did these old men, Colum and Molios, know? It is only the young who know what life is. They were old, and their blood was gelid.

He put up his arms, as though in prayer. Then he smiled. Ardanna saw a light in his eyes that sprang into her heart and sang a song there that whirled in her ears and dazzled her eyes and made her feel as though she had fallen over a great height and were still falling.

Cathal was no longer pale. A red flame burned in either cheek. The sunset-light behind him filled his hair with fire. His eyes were beacons.

'Cathal, Cathal!'

'Come, Ardanna!'

That was all. What need to say more. She was in his arm, and her heart throbbing against his that leapt in his body like a wolf fallen in a snare.

He stooped and kissed her. She lifted her eyes, and his brain swung. She kissed him, and he kissed her till she gave a low cry and gently thrust him back. He laughed.

'Why do you laugh, Cathal?'

'I? It is I who laugh now. The old men put a spell upon me. I am no more Cathal Gille-Mhoire, but Cathal mac Art. Nay, I am Cathal Gille-Ardanna.'

With that he plucked the branch of a rowan that grew near. He stripped it of its leaves, and threw them from him north, south, east, and west.

'Why do you that, Cathal-aluinn?' Ardanna asked, looking at him with eyes of love, and she like a summer morning there, because of the sunshine in her hair, and the wild roses on her face, and the hill-tarn blue of her eyes.

'These are all the hymns that Colum taught me. I give them back. I am knowing them no more. They are idle, foolish songs.'

Then the monk took the branch and broke it, and threw the pieces upon the ground and trampled upon them.

'Why do you that, Cathal-aluinn?' asked Ardanna, wondering at him with her home-call eyes.

'That is the branch of all the wisdom Colum taught me. Old Neis, the helot, was wise. It is a madness, all that. See, it is gone; it is beneath my feet. I am a man now.'

'But O Cathal, Cathal! this very day of the days, Ecta, my father, has become a man of the Christ-faith, him and his; and he would do what Molios asked now. And Molios would ask your death.'

'Death is a dream.'

With that Cathal leaned forward and kissed Ardanna upon the lips twice. 'A kiss for life that,' he said; 'and that a kiss for death.'

Ardanna laughed a low laugh. 'The monk can kiss,' she whispered; 'can the monk love?'

He put his arm about her, and they went into the dim dark greenness.

The moon rose slowly, a globe of pale golden fire which spilled unceasingly a yellow flame upon the suspended billows of the forest. Star after star emerged. Deep silence was in the woods, save for the strange passionate churring of a night-jar, where he leaned low from a pine branch and called to his mate, whose heart throbbed a flight-away amid the dewy shadows.

The wind was still. The white rays of the stars wandered over the moveless, over the shadowless and breathless green lawns of the tree-tops.

'What is that sound?' said Ardanna, a dim shape in the darkness, where she lay in the arms of Cathal.

'I know not,' said the youth; for the fevered blood in his veins sang a song against his ears.

'Listen!'

Cathal listened. He heard nothing. His eyes dreamed again into the silence.

'What is that sound?' she whispered against his heart once again. 'It is not from the sea, nor is it of the woods.'

'It is the moan of Heaven,' answered Cathal wearily; '*acaina' Pharrais*.'

II

They found them there in the twilight of the dawn. For long Ecta looked at them and pondered. Then he glanced at Molios. There were tears in the heart of the holy man, but in his eyes a deep anger.

'Bind him,' said Ecta.

Cathal woke with the thongs. His gaze fell upon Molios. He made no sign, and spake never a word; but he smiled.

'What now, O Molios?' asked Ecta.

'Take the woman away. Do with her as you will – spare or slay. It matters not. She is but a woman, and she hath wrought evil upon this man. To slay were well.'

'She is my daughter.'

'Spare, then, if you will; but take her away. Give her to a man. She shall never see this renegade again.'

With that, two men led Ardanna away. She gave a glance at Cathal, who smiled. No tears were in her eyes; but a proud fire was there, and she brooked no man's hand upon her, and walked free.

When she was gone, Molios spake.

'Cathal, that was called Cathal Gille-Mhoire, why have you done this thing?'

'Because I was weary of vain imaginings, and I am young; and Ardanna is fair, and we loved.'

'Such love is death.'

'So be it, Molios. Such death is sweet as love.'

Cathal of the Woods

'No ordinary death shalt thou have, blasphemer. Yet even now I would be merciful if I could. Dost thou call upon God?'

'I call upon the gods of my fathers.'

'Fool, they shall not save you.'

'Nevertheless, I call. I have nought to do with thy three gods, O Christian.'

'Hast thou no fear of hell?'

'I am a warrior, and the son of my father, and of a race of heroes. Why should I fear?'

Molios brooded a while.

'Take him,' he said at last, 'and bury him alive where his gods perchance will hear his cries and come and save him! Find me a hollow tree.'

'There is a great oak near here,' said Ecta, wondering, 'a great hollow oak whose belly would hold five men, each standing upon the other.'

With that he led them to an ancient tree.

'Dost thou repent, Cathal?' Molios asked.

'Ay,' the young man answered grimly; 'I repent. I repent that I wasted the good days serving you and your three false gods.'

'Blaspheme no more. Thou knowest that these three are one God.'

Cathal laughed mockingly.

'Hearken to him, Ecta,' he cried; 'this old Druid would have you believe that two men and a woman make one person! Believe that if you will! As for me, I laugh.'

But with that, at a sign from Molios, they lifted and slung him amid the branches of the oak, and let him slide feet foremost into the deep hollow heart of the tree.

When the law was done, Molios bade all near kneel in a circle round the oak. Then he prayed for the soul of the doomed man. As he ended this prayer, a laugh flew up among the high wind-swayed leaves. It was as though an invisible bird were there, mocking like a jay.

One by one, with bowed heads, Molios and Ecta and those with him withdrew, all save two young men who were bidden to stay. Upon these was bond laid, that they would not stir from that place for three days. They were to let none draw nigh: and no food was to be given to the victim: and if he cried to them, they were to take no heed, – nay, not though he called upon God or the Mother of God or upon the White Christ.

All that day there was no sound from the hollow tree. At the setting of the sun a blackbird lit upon a small branch that drooped over the aperture, and sang a brave lilt. Then the dark came, and the moon rose, and the stars glimmered through the dew.

At midnight the moon was overhead. A flood of pale gold rays lit up the branches of the oak, and turned the leaves into a lustrous bronze. The watchers heard a voice singing in the silence of the night – a voice muffled and obscure, as from one in a pit, or as that of a shepherd straying in a narrow corrie. Words they caught, though not all; and this was what they heard:

> O yellow lamp of Ioua* that is having a cold pale flame there,
> Put thy honey-sheen upon me who am close-caverned with Death:
> Sure it is nought I see now who have seen too much and too little:
> O moon, thy breast is softer and whiter than hers who burneth the day.
>
> Put thy white light on the grave where the dead man my father is,
>   And waken him, waken him, wake!
> And put thy soft shining on the breast of the woman my mother,
> So that she stir in her sleep and say to the Viking beside her,
> 'Take up thy sword, and let it lap blood, for it thirsts with long thirst.'
>
> And O Ioua, be as the sea-calm upon the hot heart of Ardanna, the girl:
> Tell her that Cathal loves her, and that memory is sweeter than life.
> I list her heart beating here in the dark and the silence,
> And it is not lonely I am, because of that, and remembrance.
>
> O yellow flame of Ioua, be a spilling of blood out of the heart of Ecta,
> So that he fall dead, inglorious, slain from within, as a greybeard;
> And light a fire in the brain of Molios, so that he shall go moonstruck,
> And men will jeer at him, and he will die at the last, idly laughing.

*Ioua was one of the early Celtic names of the moon. The allusion (in the fourth line) to the sun, in the feminine, is in accordance with ancient usage.

> For lo, I worship thee, Ioua; and if you can give my message to
>   Neis, –
> Neis the helot out of Aoidû, who is in Iona, bondman to Colum, –
> Tell him I hail you as Bandia, as god-queen and mighty,
> And that he had the wisdom and I was a fool with trickling ears of
>   moss.
>
> But grant me this, O goddess, a bitter moon-drinking for Colum!
> May he have the moonsong in his brain, and in his heart the
>   moonfire:
> Flame burn him in heart of flame, and may he wane as wax at the
>   furnace,
> And his soul drown in tears, and his body be a nothingness upon
>   the sands!

The watchers looked at each other, but said no word. On the pale face of each was fear and awe. What if this new god-teaching were false, and if Cathal was right, and the old gods were the lords of life and death? The moonlight fell upon them, and they saw doubt in the eyes of each other. Neither looked at the white fire. Out of the radiance, cold eyes might stare upon them: when at that, sure they would leap to the woods, laughing wild, and be as the beasts of the forest.

While it was still dark, an hour before the dawn, one of the twain awoke from a brief slumber. His gaze wandered from vague tree to tree. Thrice he thought he saw dim shapes glide from bole to bole or from thicket to thicket. Suddenly he discerned a tall figure, silent as a shadow, standing at the verge of the glade.

His low cry aroused his companion.

'What is it, Mûrta?' the young man asked in a whisper.

'A woman.'

When they looked again she was gone.

'It was one of the Hidden People,' said Mûrta, with restless eyes roaming from dusk to dusk.

'How are you for knowing that, Mûrta?'

'She was all in green, just like a green shadow she was, and I saw the green fire in her eyes.'

'Have you not thought of one that it might be?'

'Who?'

'Ardanna.'

With that the young man rose and ran swiftly to the place where he had seen the figure. But he could see no one. Looking at the ground he was troubled: for in the moonshine-dew he descried the imprint of small feet.

Thereafter they saw or heard nought, save the sights and sounds of the woodland.

At sunrise the two youths rose. Mûrta lifted up his arms, then sank upon his knees with bowed head.

'Why do you do that forbidden thing?' said Diarmid, that was his companion. 'Have you forgotten Cathal the monk that is up there alone with death? If Molios the holy one saw you worshipping the Light he would do unto you as he has done unto Cathal.'

But before Mûrta answered they heard the voice of Cathal once more – hoarse and dry it was, but scarce weaker than when it thrilled them at the rising of the moon.

This was what he chanted in his muffled voice out of his grave there in the hollow oak:

O hot yellow fire that streams out of the sky, sword-white and
   golden,
Be a flame upon the monks who are praying in their cells in Ioua!
Be a fire in the veins of Colum, and the hell that he preacheth be
   his,
And be a torch to the men of Lochlin that they discover the isle
   and destroy it!

For I see this thing, that the old gods are the gods that die not:
All else is a seeming, a dream, a madness, a tide ever ebbing.
Glory to thee, O Grian, lord of life, first of the gods Allfather,
Swords and spears are thy beams, thy breath a fire that
   consumeth.

And upon this isle of Â-rinn send sorrow and death and disaster,
Upon one and all save Ardanna, who gave me her bosom,
Upon one and all send death, the curse of a death slow and
   swordless,
From Molios of the Cave to Mûrta and Diarmid my doomsmen!

At that Mûrta moved close to the oak.
   'Hail, O Cathal!' he cried. There was silence.

'Art thou a living man still, or is it the death of thee that is singing there in the hollow oak?'

'My limbs perish, but I die not yet,' answered the muffled voice that had greeted the sun.

'I am Mûrta mac Mûrta mac Neisa, and my heart is sore for thee, Cathal!'

There was no word to this. A thrush upon a branch overhead lifted its wings, sang a wild sweet note, and swooped arrowly through the greengloom of the leaves.

'Cathal, that wert a monk, which is the true thing? Is it Christ, or the gods of our fathers?'

Silence. Three oaks away a woodpecker thrust its beak into the soft bark, tap-tapping, tap-tapping.

'Cathal, is it death you are having, there in the dark and the silence?'

Mûrta strained his ears, but he could hear no sound. Over the woodlands a voice floated, drowsy-warm and breast-white – the voice of a cuckoo calling a love-note from cool green shadow to shadow across a league of windless blaze.

Then Mûrta that was a singer, went to where the bulrushes grew by a little tarn that was in the moss an arrow-flight away. He plucked a last-year reed, straight and brown, and with his knife cut seven holes in it. With a thinner reed he scooped the hollow clean.

Thereupon he returned to the oak. Diarmid, who had begun to eat of the food that had been left with them, sat still, with his eyes upon him.

Mûrta put his hollow reed to his lips, and he played. It was a forlorn, sweet air that he had heard from a shepherding woman upon the hills. Then he played a burying-song of the islanders, wherein the wash of the sea and the rippling of the waves upon the shore was heard. Then played the song of love, and the beating of hearts was heard, and sighs, and a voice like a distant bird-song rose and fell.

When he ceased, a voice came out of the hollow oak –

'Play me a death-song, Mûrta mac Mûrta mac Neisa.'

Mûrta smiled, and he played again the song of love.

After that there was silence for a brief while. Then Mûrta played upon his reed for the time it takes a heron to mount her seventh spiral. Then he ceased, and threw away the reed, and stood erect, staring into the greenness. In his eyes was a strange shine. He sang:

Out of the wild hills I am hearing a voice, O Cathal!
And I am thinking it is the voice of a bleeding sword.
Whose is that sword? I know it well: it is the sword of the Slayer –
Him that is called Death, and the song that it sings I know:–
O where is Cathal macArt, that is the cup for the thirst of my lips?

Out of the cold greyness of the sea I am hearing, O Cathal,
I am hearing a wave-muffled voice, as of one who drowns in the depths:
Whose is that voice? I know it well: it is the voice of the Shadow –
Her that is called the Grave, and the song that she sings I know:–
O where is Cathal macArt, he has warmth for the chill that I have?

Out of the hot greenness of the wood I am hearing, O Cathal,
I am hearing a rustling step, as of one stumbling blind.
Whose is that rustling step? I know it well: the rustling walk of the Blind One –
She that is called Silence, and the song that she sings I know:–
O where is Cathal macArt, that has tears to water my stillness?

After that there was silence. Mûrta moved away. When he sat by Diarmid and ate, there was no word spoken. Diarmid did not look at him, for he had sung a song of death, and the shadow was upon him. He kept his gaze upon the moss: if he raised his eyes might he not see the Slayer, or the Shadow, or the Blind One?

Noon came. None drew nigh: not a face was seen shadowily afar off. Sometimes the hoofs of the deer rustled among the bracken. The snarling of young foxes in an oak-root hollow was like a red pulse in the heat. At times, in the sheer abyss of blue sky to the north, a hawk suspended: in the white-blaze southerly a blotch like swirled foam appeared for a moment at long intervals, as a gannet swung from invisible pinnacles of air to the invisible sea.

The afternoon drowsed through the sun-flood. The green leaves grew golden, saturated with light. At sundown a flight of wild doves rose out of the pines, wheeled against the shine of the west and flashed out of sight, flames of purple and rose, of foam-white and pink.

The gloaming came, silverly. The dew glistened on the fronds of the ferns, in the cups of the moss. From glade to glade the cuckoos called. The stars emerged delicately, as the eyes of fawns shining through the greengloom of the forest. Once more the moon snowed the easter frondage of the pines and oaks.

No one came nigh. Not a sound had sighed from the oak since Mûrta had sung at the goldening of the day. At sunset Mûrta had risen, to lean, intent, against the vast bole. His keen ears caught the jar of a beetle burrowing beneath the bark. There was no other sound.

At the fall of the dark the watchers heard the confused far noise of a festival. It waned as a lost wind. Dim veils of cloud obscured the moon; a low rainy darkness suspended over the earth.

Thus went the second day and the second night.

When, after the weary vigil of the hours, dawn came at last, Mûrta rose and struck the oak with a stone.

'Cathal!' he cried, 'Cathal!'

There was no sound: not a stir, not a sigh.

'Cathal! Cathal!'

Mûrta looked at Diarmid. Then, seeing his own thought in the eyes of his friend he returned to his side.

'The Blind One has been here,' said Diarmid in a low voice.

At noon there was thunder, and great heat. The noise of rustling wings filled the underwood.

Diarmid fell into a deep sleep. When the thunder had travelled into the hills, and a soft rain fell, Mûrta climbed into the branches of the oak. He stared down into the hollow, but could see nothing save a green dusk that became brown shadow, and brown shadow that grew into a blackness.

'*Cathal!*' he whispered.

Not a breath of sound ascended like smoke.

'Cathal! Cathal!'

The slow drip of the rain slipped and pattered among the leaves. The cry of a sea-bird flying inland came mournfully across the woods. A distant clang, as of a stricken anvil, iterated from the barren mountain beyond the forest.

'Cathal! Cathal!'

Mûrta broke a straight branch, stripped it of the leaves, and, forcing the thicker end downward, let it fall sheer.

It struck with a dull, soft thud. He listened: there was not a sound.

'A quiet sleep to you, monk,' he whispered, and slipped through the boughs, and was beside Diarmid again.

At dusk the rain ceased. A cool green freshness came into the air.

The stars were as wind-whirled fruit blown upward from the treetops. The moon, full-orbed and with a pulse of flame, led a tide of soft light across the brown shores of the world.

The vigils of the watchers were over. Mûrta and Diarmid rose. Without a word they moved across the glade: the faint rustle of their feet stirred the bracken: then they left the undergrowth, and were among the pines. Their shadows lapsed into the obscure wilderness. A doe, heavy with fawn, lay down among the dewy fern, and was at peace there.

III

At midnight, when the whole isle lay in the full flood of the moon, Cathal stirred.

For three days and three nights he had been in that dark hollow, erect, wedged as a spear imbedded in the jaws of a dead beast. He had died thrice: with hunger, with thirst, with weariness. Then when hunger was slain in its own pain, and thirst perished of its own agony, and weariness could no more endure, he stirred with the death-throe.

'I die,' he moaned.

'Die not, O white one,' came a floating whisper, he knew not whence, though it was to him as though the crushing walls of oak breathed the sound.

'I die,' he gasped, and the froth bubbled upon his nether lip. With that his last strength went. No more could he hold his head above his shoulder, nor would his feet sustain him. Like a stricken deer he sank. So thin was he, so worn, that he slipt into a narrow crevice where dead leaves had been, and lay there, drowning in the dark.

Was that death, or a cold air about his feet, he wondered? With a dull pain he moved them: they came against no tree-wood – the coolness about them was of dewy moss. A wild hope flashed into his mind. With feeble hands he strove to sink farther into the crevice.

'I die,' he gasped, 'I die now, at the last.'

'Die not, O white one,' breathed the same low sweet whisper, like leaves stirred by a nesting bird.

'Save, O save,' muttered the monk, hoarse with the death-dew.

Then a blackness came down upon him from a great height, and he swung in that blank gulf as a feather swirled this way and that in the void of an abyss.

When the darkness lifted again, Cathal was on his back, and breathing slow, but without pain. A sweet wonderful coolness and ease, that he knew now! Where was he? he wondered. Was he in that Pàrras that Colum and Molios had spoken of? Was he in Hy Bràsil, of which he had heard Aodh the Harper sing? Was he in Tir-nan-Òg, where all men and women are young for evermore, and there is joy in the heart and peace in the mind and delight by day and by night?

Why was his mouth so cool, that had burned dry as ash? Why were his lips moist, with a bitter-sweet flavour, as though the juice of fruit was there still?

He pondered, with closed eyes. At last he opened them, and stared upward. The profound black-blue dome of the sky held group after group of stars that he knew: was not that sword and belt yonder the sword-gear of Fionn? Yon shimmering cluster, were they not the dust of the feet of Alldai? That leaping green and blue planet, what could it be but the harp of Brigidh, where she sang to the gods?

A shadow crossed his vision. The next moment a cool hand was upon his eyes. It brought rest, and healing. He felt the blood move in his veins: his heart beat: a throbbing was in his throat.

Then he knew that he had strength to rise. With a great effort he put his weariness from off him, and staggered to his feet.

Cathal gave a low sob. A fair beautiful woman stood by him.

'Ardanna!' he cried, though even as the word leaped from his lips he knew that he looked upon no Pictish woman.

She smiled. All his heart was glad because of that. The light in her eyes was like the fire of the moon, bright and wonderful. The delicate body of her was pale green, and luminous as a leaf, with soft earth-brown hair falling down her shoulders and over the swelling breast; even as the small green mounds over the dead the two breasts were. She was clad only in her own loveliness, though the moonshine was about her as a garment.

'Like a green leaf: like a green leaf,' Cathal muttered over and over below his breath.

'Are you a dream?' he asked simply, having no words for his wonder.

'No, Cathal, I am no dream. I am a woman.'

'A woman? But . . . but . . . you have no body as other women have and I see the moonbeam that is on your breast shining upon the moss behind you!'

'Is it thinking you are, poor Cathal, that there are no women and no men in the world except those who are in thick flesh, and move about in the suntide?'

Cathal stared wonderingly.

'I am of the green people, Cathal. We are of the woods. I am a woman of the woods.'

'Hast thou a name, fair woman?'

'I am called Deòin.'*

'That is well. Truly "Green Breath" is a good name for thee. Are there others of thy kin in this place?'

'Look!' and at that she stopped, lifted the dew of a white flower in the moonshine, and put it upon his eyes.

Cathal looked about him. Everywhere he saw tall, fair pale-green lives moving to and fro: some passing out of trees, swift and silent as rain out of a cloud; some passing into trees, silent and swift as shadows. All were fair to look upon: tall, lithe, graceful, moving this way and that in the moonshine, pale green as the leaves of the lime, soft shining, with radiant eyes, and delicate earth-brown hair.

'Who are these, Deòin?' Cathal asked in a low whisper of awe.

'They are my people: the folk of the woods: the green people.'

'But they come out of trees: they come and they go like bees in and out of a hive.'

'Trees? That is your name for us of the woods. *We* are the trees.'

'*You* the trees, Deòin! How can that be?'

'There is life in your body. Where does it go when the body sleeps, or when the sap rises no more to heart or brain, and there is chill in the blood, and it is like frozen water? Is there a life in your body?'

'Ay, so. I know it.'

'The flesh is *your* body; the tree is *my* body.'

'Then you are the green life of a tree?'

'I am the green life of a tree.'

'And these?'

'They are as I am.'

'I see those that are men and those that are women and their offspring too I see.'

'They are as I am.'

'And some are crowned with pale flowers.'

'They love.'

'And hast thou no crown, Deòin, who art so fair?'

**Deo-uaine.*

'Neither hast thou, Cathal, though thy face is fair. Thy body I cannot see, because thou hast a husk about thee.'

With a low laugh Cathal removed his raiment from him. The whiteness of his body was like a flower there in the moonshine.

'That shall not be against me,' he said. 'Truly, I am a man no longer, if thee and thine will have me as one of the wood-folk.'

At that Deòin called. Many green phantoms glided out of the trees, and others, hand-in-hand, flower-crowned, crossed the glade.

'Look, green lives,' Deòin cried in her sweet leaf-whisper, rising now like a wind-song among birchen boughs; 'look, here is a human. His life is mine, for I saved him. I have put the moonshine dew upon his eyes. He sees as we see. He would be one of us, for all that he has no tree for his body, but flesh, white over red.'

One who had moved thitherward out of an ancient oak looked at Cathal.

'Wouldst thou be of the wood-folk, man?'

'Ay, fain am I; for sure, for sure, O Druid of the trees.'

'Wilt thou learn and abide by our laws, the first of which is that none may stir from his tree until the dusk has come, nor linger away from it when the dawn opens grey lips and drinks up the shadows?'

'I have no law now but the law of green life.'

'Good. Thou shalt live with us. Thy home shall be the hollow oak where thy kin left thee to die. Why did they do that evil deed?'

'Because I did not believe in the new gods.'

'Who are thy gods, man whom this green one here calls Cathal?'

'They are the Sun, and the Moon, and the Wind, and others that I will tell you of.'

'Hast thou heard of Keithoir?'

'No.'

'He is the god of the green world. He dreams, and his dreams are Springtide and Summertide and Appletide. When he sleeps without dream there is winter.'

'Have you no other god but this earth-god?'

'Keithoir is our god. We know no other.'

'If he is thy god, he is my god.'

'I see in the eyes of Deòin that she loves thee, Cathal the human. Wilt thou have her love?'

Cathal looked at the girl. His heart swam in light.

'Ay, if Deòin will give me her love, my love shall be hers.'

The Annir-Choille moved forward and brushed softly against him as a green branch.

He put his arms around her. She had a cool, sweet body to feel. He was glad she was no moonshine phantom. The beating of her heart against his made a music that filled his ears.

Deòin stooped and plucked white, dewy flowers. Of these she wove a wreath for Cathal. He, likewise, plucked the white blooms, and made a coronal of foam for the brown wave of her hair.

Then, hand in hand, they fared slowly forth across the moonlit glade. None crossed their path, though everywhere delicate green lives flitted from tree to tree. They heard a wonderful sweet singing, aerial, with a ripple as of leaves lipping a windy shore of light. A green glamour was in the eyes of Cathal. The green fire of life flamed in his veins.

IV

Molios, the saint of Christ, that lived in the sea-cave of the Isle of the Peak, so that even in his own day it was called the Holy Isle, endured to a great age.

Some say of him that before his hair was bleached white as the bog-cotton, he was slain by the heathen Picts, or by the fierce summer-sailors out of Lochlin. But that is an idle tale. His end was not thus. A Culdee, who had the soul of a bat, feared the truth, though that gave glory to God, and wrote both in ogham and lambskin the truthless tale that Molios went forth with the cross and was slain in a north isle.

On a day of the days every year, Molios fared to the Hollow Oak that was in the hill-forest beyond the rath of Ecta MacEcta. There he spake long upon the youth that had been his friend, and upon how the Evil One had prevailed with Cathal, and how the islander had been done to death there in the oak. Then he and all his company sang the hymns of peace, and great joy there was over the doom of Cathal the monk, and many would have cleft the great tree or burned it, so that the dust of the sinner might be scattered to the four winds: only this was banned by Molios.

It was well for Cathal, who slept there through the hours of light! Deep slumber was his, for never once did he hear the noontide voices, nor ever in his ears was the long rise and fall of the holy hymns.

But when, in the twentieth year after Cathal had been thrust into the hollow oak, Molios came at sundown, being weary with the heat, the saint heard a low, faint laughter issuing from the tree, like fragrance from a flower.

None other heard it. He saw that with gladness. Quietly he went with the islanders.

When the moon was over the pines, and all in the rath slept, Molios arose and went silently back into the forest.

When he came to the Doom-Tree he listened long, with his ear against the bark. There was no sound.

His voice was old and quavering, but fresh and young in the courts of heaven, when it reached there like a fluttering bird tired from long flight. He sang a holy hymn.

He listened. There was no laughter. He was glad at that. All had been a dream, for sure.

Then it was that he heard once again the low, mocking laughter. He started back, trembling.

'Cathal!' he cried, with his voice like a wuthering wind.

'I am here, O Molios,' said a voice behind him.

The old Culdee turned, as though arrow-nipped. Before him, white in the moonshine, stood a man, naked.

At first, Molios knew him not. He was so tall and strong, so fair and wonderful. Long locks of ruddy hair hung upon his white shoulders: his eyes were lustrous, and had the lovely, soft light of the deer. When he moved, it was swiftly and silently. No stag upon the hills was more fair to see.

Then, slowly, Cathal the monk swam into Cathal of the Woods. Molios saw him whom he knew of old, as a blue flame is visible within the flame of yellow.

'I am here, O Molios.'

Strange was the voice: faint and far the tone of it: yet it was that of a living man.

'Is it a spirit you are, Cathal?'

'I am no spirit. I am Cathal the monk that was, Cathal the man now.'

'How came you out of hell, you that are dead, and the dust of whose crumbling bones is in the hollow of this oak?'

'There is no hell, Culdee.'

'No hell!' Molios the Saint stared at the woodman in blank amaze.

'No hell,' he said again; 'and is there no heaven?'

'A hell there is, and a heaven there is: but not what Colum taught, and you taught.'

'Doth Christ live?'

'I know not.'

'And Mary?'

'I know not.'

'And God the Father?'

'I know not.'

'It is a lie that you have upon your lips. Sure, Cathal, you shall be dead indeed soon, to the glory of God. For I shall have thy dust scattered to the four winds, and thy bones consumed in flame, and a stake be driven through the place where thou wast.'

Once more Cathal laughed.

'Go back to thy sea-cave, Molios. Thou hast much to learn. Brood there upon the ways of thy God before thou judgest if He knoweth no more than thou dost. And see, I will show you a wonder. Only, first, tell me this one thing. What of Ardanna whom I loved?'

'She was accursed. She would not believe. When Ecta took the child from her, that was born in sin, to have the water put upon it with the sign of the Cross, she went north beyond the Hill of the Pinnacles. There she saw the young king of the Picts of Argyll, and he loved her, and she went to his dùn. He took her to his rath in the north, and she was his queen. He, and she, and the two sons she bore to him are all under the hill-moss now: and their souls are in hell.'

Cathal laughed, low and mocking.

'It is a good hell that, I am thinking, Molios. But come . . . I will show you a wonder.'

With that he stooped, and took the moonshine dew out of a white flower, and put it upon the eyes of the old man.

Then Molios saw.

And what he saw was a strangeness and a terror to him. For everywhere were green lives, fair and comely, gentle-eyed, lovely, of a soft shining. From tree to tree they flitted, or passed to and fro from the tree-boles, as wild bees from their hives.

Beside Cathal stood a woman. Beautiful she was, with eyes like stars in the gloaming. All of green flame she seemed, though the old monk saw her breast rise and fall, and the light lift of her earth-brown hair by a wind-breath eddying there, and the hand of her clasped in that of Cathal. Beyond her were fair and beautiful beings, lovely shapes like unto men and women, but soulless, though loving life and

Cathal of the Woods

hating death, which, of a truth, is all that the vain human clan does.

'Who is this woman, Cathal?' asked the saint, trembling.

'It is Deòin, whom I love, and who has given me life.'

'And these . . . that are neither green phantoms out of trees, nor yet men as we are?'

'These are the offspring of our love.'

Molios drew back in horror.

But Cathal threw up his arms, and with glad eyes cried:

'O green flame of life, pulse of the world! O Love! O youth! O Dream of Dreams!'

'O bitter grief,' Molios cried, 'O bitter grief that I did not slay thee utterly on that day of the days! Flame to thy flesh, and a stake through thy belly – that is the doom thou shouldst have had! My ban upon thee, Cathal, that was a monk, and now art a wild man of the woods: upon thee, and thy Annir-Choille, and all thy brood, I put the ban of fear and dread and sorrow, a curse by day and a curse by night!'

But with that a great dizziness swam into the brain of the saint, and he fell forward, and lay his length upon the moss, and there was no sight to his eyes, or hearing to his ears, or knowledge upon him at all until the rising of the sun.

When the yellow light was upon his face he rose. There was no face to see anywhere. Looking in the dew for the myriad feet that had been there, he saw none.

The old man knelt and prayed.

At the first praying God filled his heart with peace. At the second praying God filled his heart with wonder. At the third praying God whispered mysteriously, and he knew. Humble in his new knowledge, he rose. The tears were in his old eyes. He went up to the Hollow Oak, and blessed it, and the wild man that slept within it, and the Annir-Choille that Cathal loved, and the offspring of their love. He took the curse away, and he blessed all that God had made.

All the long weary way to the shore he went as one in a dream. Wonder and mystery were in his eyes.

At the shore he entered the little coracle that brought him daily from the Holy Isle, a triple arrow-flight seaward.

A child sat in it, playing with pebbles. It was Ardan, the son of Ardanna.

'Ardan mac Cathal,' began the saint, weary now, but glad with a strange new gladness.

'Who is Cathal?' said the boy.

'He that was thy father. Tell me, Ardan, hast thou ever seen aught moving in the woods – green lives out of the trees?'

'I have seen a green shine come out of the trees.'

Molios bowed his head.

'Thou shalt be as my son, Ardan; and when thou art a man thou shalt choose thy own way, and let no man hinder thee.'

That night Molios could not sleep. Hearing the loud wash of the sea, he went to the mouth of the cave. For a long while he watched the seals splashing in the silver radiance of the moonshine. Then he called them.

'O seals of the sea, come hither!'

At that all the furred swimmers drew near.

'Is it for the curse you give us every year of the years, O holy Molios?' moaned a great black seal.

'O Ron dubh, it is no curse I have for thee or thine, but a blessing, and peace. I have learned a wonder of God, because of an Annir-Coille in the forest that is upon the hill. But now I will be telling you the white story of Christ.'

So there, in the moonshine, with the flowing tide stealing from his feet to his knees, the old saint preached the gospel of love. The seals crouched upon the rocks, with their great brown eyes filled with glad tears.

When Molios ceased, each slipped again into the shadowy sea. All that night, while he brooded upon the mystery of Cathal and the Annir-Choille, with deep knowledge of hidden things, and a heart filled with the wonder and mystery of the world, he heard them splashing to and fro in the moon-dazzle, and calling, one to the other, 'We, too, are the sons of God.'

At dawn a shadow came into the cave. A white frost grew upon the face of Molios. Still was he, and cold, when Ardan, the child, awoke. Only the white lips moved. A ray of the sun slanted across the sea, from the great disc of whirling golden flame new risen. It fell softly upon the moving lips. They were still then, and Ardan kissed them because of the smile that was there.

The Anointed Man

This story is one of the Achanna series (see the *Dàn-nan-Ròn* and *Green Branches* in *Tragic Romances*) . . .

The forename Alison is properly a woman's name, but is occasionally given to a male child – whence, no doubt, the not infrequent occurrence of 'Alison' as a surname.

The surname Achanna is that familiar in the South as Hannay. As to my use of the forename Gloom, I should explain that the designation is, of course, not a real name. At the same time, I have actual warrant for its use for I knew a Uist man who, in the bitterness of his sorrow, after his wife's death in childbirth, named his son Mulad (i.e. the gloom of sorrow: grief).

F.M.

Although the other two stories in the Achanna series are redolent with Celtic fatalism, crime and retribution, prophecy and fulfilment, guilt, murder and death, *The Anointed Man* shines with spiritual beauty and is full of glimpses of the Green Life.

E.S.

Of the seven Achannas – sons of Robert Achanna of Achanna in Galloway, self-exiled in the far north because of a bitter feud with his kindred – who lived upon Eilanmore in the Summer Isles, there was not one who was not, in more or less degree, or at some time or other, fëy.

Doubtless I shall have occasion to allude to one and all again, and certainly to the eldest and youngest: for they were the strangest folk I have known or met anywhere in the Celtic lands, from the sea-pastures of the Solway to the kelp-strewn beaches of Lewis. Upon James, the seventh son, the doom of his people fell last and most heavily. Some day I may tell the full story of his strange life and tragic undoing, and of his piteous end. As it happened, I knew best the eldest and youngest of the brothers, Alison and James. Of the others,

Robert, Allan, William, Marcus, and Gloom, none save the last-named survives, if peradventure *he* does, or has been seen of man for many years past. Of Gloom (strange and unaccountable name, which used to terrify me – the more so as, by the savagery of fate, it was the name of all names suitable for Robert Achanna's sixth son) I know nothing beyond the fact that, ten years or more ago, he was a Jesuit priest in Rome, a bird of passage, whence come and whither bound no inquiries of mine could discover. Two years ago a relative told me that Gloom was dead; that he had been slain by some Mexican noble in an old city of Hispaniola, beyond the seas. Doubtless the news was founded on truth, though I have ever a vague unrest when I think of Gloom; as though he were travelling hitherward, as though his feet, on some urgent errand, were already white with the dust of the road that leads to my house.

But now I wish to speak only of Alison Achanna. He was a friend whom I loved, though he was a man of close on forty and I a girl less than half his years. We had much in common, and I never knew anyone more companionable, for all that he was called 'Silent Ally.' He was tall, gaunt, loosely-built. His eyes were of that misty blue which smoke takes when it rises in the woods. I used to think them like the tarns that lay amid the canna and gale-surrounded swamps in Uist, where I was wont to dream as a child.

I had often noticed the light on his face when he smiled – a light of such serene joy as young mothers have sometimes over the cradles of their firstborn. But for some reason I had never wondered about it, not even when I heard and dimly understood the half-contemptuous, half-reverent mockery with which, not only Alison's brothers, but even his father, at times used towards him. Once, I remember, I was puzzled when, on a bleak day in a stormy August, I overheard Gloom say, angrily and scoffingly, 'There goes the Anointed Man!' I looked, but all I could see was that, despite the dreary cold, despite the ruined harvest, despite the rotting potato-crop, Alison walked slowly onward, smiling, and with glad eyes brooding upon the grey lands around and beyond him.

It was nearly a year thereafter – I remember the date, because it was that of my last visit to Eilanmore – that I understood more fully. I was walking westward with Alison towards sundown. The light was upon his face as though it came from within; and when I looked again, half in awe, I saw that there was no glamour out of the west, for the evening was dull and threatening rain. He was in sorrow. Three months before, his brothers Allan and William had been drowned; a month later, his brother Robert had sickened, and now sat in the ingle from morning till the covering of the peats, a skeleton almost, shivering, and morosely silent, with large staring eyes. On the large bed in the room above the kitchen old Robert Achanna lay, stricken with paralysis. It would have been unendurable for me but for Alison and James, and, above all, for my loved girl-friend, Anne Gillespie, Achanna's niece, and the sunshine of his gloomy household.

As I walked with Alison I was conscious of a well-nigh intolerable depression. The house we had left was so mournful; the bleak sodden pastures were so mournful; so mournful was the stony place we were crossing, silent but for the thin crying of the curlews; and, above all, so mournful was the sound of the ocean as, unseen, it moved sobbingly round the isle: so beyond words distressing was all this to me, that I stopped abruptly, meaning to go no farther, but to return to the house, where at least there was warmth, and where Anne would sing for me as she spun.

But when I looked up into my companion's face I saw in truth the light that shone from within. His eyes were upon a forbidding stretch of ground, where the blighted potatoes rotted among a wilderness of round skull-white stones. I remember them still, these strange far-blue eyes, lamps of quiet joy, lamps of peace they seemed to me.

'Are you looking at Achnacarn?' (as the tract was called), I asked, in what I am sure was a whisper.

'Yes,' replied Alison slowly; 'I am looking. It is beautiful – beautiful. O God, how beautiful is this lovely world!'

I know not what made me act so, but I threw myself on a heathery ridge close by, and broke out into convulsive sobbings.

Alison stooped, lifted me in his strong arms, and soothed me with soft, caressing touches and quieting words.

'Tell me, my fawn, what is it? What is the trouble?' he asked again and again.

'It is *you* – it is *you*, Alison,' I managed to say coherently at last. 'It terrifies me to hear you speak as you did a little ago. You must be fey. Why – why do you call that hateful, hideous field beautiful on this dreary day – and – and after all that has happened, – O Alison?'

At this, I remember, he took his plaid and put it upon the wet heather, and then drew me thither, and seated himself and me beside him.

'Is it not beautiful, my fawn?' he asked, with tears in his eyes. Then, without waiting for my answer, he said quietly, 'Listen, dear, and I will tell you.'

He was strangely still – breathless, he seemed to me – for a minute or more. Then he spoke.

'I was little more than a child – a boy just in my teens – when something happened, something that came down the Rainbow-Arches of Cathair-Sìth.' He paused here, perhaps to see if I followed, which I did, familiar as I was with all fairy-lore. 'I was out upon the heather, in the time when the honey oozes in the bells and cups. I had always loved the island and the sea. Perhaps I was foolish, but I was so glad with my joy that golden day that I threw myself on the ground and kissed the hot, sweet ling, and put my hands and arms into it, sobbing the while with my vague, strange yearning. At last I lay still, nerveless, with my eyes closed. Suddenly I was aware that two tiny hands had come up through the spires of the heather, and were pressing something soft and fragrant upon my eyelids. When I opened them, I could see nothing unfamiliar. No one was visible. But I heard a whisper: 'Arise and go away from this place at once; and this night do not venture out, lest evil befall you.' So I rose, trembling, and went home. Thereafter I was the same, and yet not the same. Never could I see as they saw, what my father and brothers or the isle-folk looked upon as ugly or dreary. My father was wroth me many times, and called me a fool. Whenever my eyes fell upon those waste and desolated spots, they seemed to me passing fair, radiant with lovely light. At last my father grew so bitter that, mocking me the while, he bade me go to the towns and see there the squalor and sordid hideousness wherein men dwelled. But thus it was with me: in the places they call slums, and among the smoke of factories and the grime of destitution, I could see all that other men saw, only as vanishing shadows. What I saw was lovely, beautiful with strange glory, and the faces of men and women were sweet and pure, and their souls were white. So, weary and bewildered with my unwilling quest, I came back to Eilanmore. And on the day of my home-coming, Morag was there – Morag of the Falls. She turned to my father and called him blind and foolish. "He has the white light upon his brows," she said of me; "I can see it, like the flicker-light in a wave when the wind's from the south in thunder-weather. He has been touched with the Fairy Ointment. The Guid Folk know him. It will be thus with him till the day of his death, if a *duinshee** can die, being

* male fairy – E.S.

already a man dead yet born anew. He upon whom the Fairy Ointment has been laid must see all that is ugly and hideous and dreary and bitter through a glamour of beauty. Thus it hath been since the Mhic-Alpine ruled from sea to sea, and thus is it with the man Alison your son."

'That is all, my fawn; and that is why my brothers, when they are angry, sometimes call me the Anointed Man.'

'That is all.' Yes, perhaps. But oh, Alison Achanna, how often have I thought of that most precious treasure you found in the heather, when the bells were sweet with honey-ooze! Did the wild bees know of it? Would that I could hear the soft hum of their gauzy wings.

Who of us would not barter the best of all our possessions – and some there are who would surrender all – to have one touch laid upon the eyelids – one touch of the Fairy Ointment? But the place is far, and the hour is hidden. No man may seek that for which there can be no quest.

Only the wild bees know of it; but I think they must be the bees of Magh-Mell*. And there no man that liveth may wayfare – *yet*.

---

* The 'Happy Plain': a name for the Celtic Elysium – E.S.

Bibliography

THE GOLD KEY

HEIN, ROLLAND, *The Harmony Within* (Christian University Press, Michigan, 1982)
LEWIS, C. S., *The Great Divorce* (Macmillan, 1952)
LEWIS, C. S., *Surprised by Joy: The Shape of my Early Life* (Geoffrey Bles, 1955)
LEWIS, C. S., *George MacDonald: An Anthology* (Fount Paperbacks, 1983)
MACDONALD, GEORGE, *David Elginbrod* (Hurst and Blackett, 1863)
MACDONALD, GEORGE, *Adela Cathcart* (Hurst and Blackett, 1864)
MACDONALD, GEORGE, *The Portent* (Smith, Elder, 1864)
MACDONALD, GEORGE, *Dealings with the Fairies* (Strahan and Co., 1867)
MACDONALD, GEORGE, *The Seaboard Parish* (Tinsley, 1868)
MACDONALD, GEORGE, *Works of Fancy and Imagination*, 10 Vols (Strahan and Co., 1871)
MACDONALD, GEORGE, *The Princess and Curdie* (Chatto and Windus, 1883)
MACDONALD, GEORGE, *Castle Warlock, A Homely Romance* (Kegan Paul, 1883)
MACDONALD, GEORGE, *At the Back of the North Wind* (Blackie and Sons, 1886)
MACDONALD, GEORGE, *The Princess and the Goblin* (Blackie and Sons, 1886)
MACDONALD, GEORGE, *Poetical Works*, 2 Vols (Chatto and Windus, 1893)
MACDONALD, GEORGE, *Heather and Snow* (Chatto and Windus, 1893)
MACDONALD, GEORGE, *The Lost Princess or The Wise Woman* (Wells, Gardner, 1895)
MACDONALD, GEORGE, *Lilith, A Romance* (Chatto and Windus, 1895)
MACDONALD, GEORGE, *Salted with Fire* (Hurst and Blackett, 1897)
MACDONALD, GEORGE, *The Golden Key*, Afterword by W. H. Auden (The Bodley Head, 1967)

MACDONALD, GEORGE, *Phantastes*, Introduced by David Holbrook (J. M. Dent, 1983)
MACDONALD, GREVILLE, *George MacDonald and his Wife* (Allen and Unwin, 1924)
MAURICE, F. D., *The Kingdom of Christ*, Edited by A. Vidler (SCM Press, 1958)
TRIGGS, KATHY, *The Seeking Heart* (A Pickering Paperback, 1984)
TRIGGS, KATHY, (Ed.) *North Wind*, Journal of the George MacDonald Society, No. 4, The George MacDonald Society (The Library, King's College, 1985)
WOLFF, ROBERT LEE, *The Golden Key*, A Study of the Fiction of George MacDonald (Yale University Press, 1961)

THE GREEN LIFE

ALAYA, FLAVIA, *William Sharp – 'Fiona Macleod', 1855–1905* (Harvard University Press, 1970)

BOLD, ALAN, *The Sensual Scot* (Paul Harris Publishing, 1982)

DILLON, M., and CHADWICK, N., *The Celtic Realms* (Cardinal, 1977)

HOPKINS, KONRAD, 'Wilfion and the Green Life: A Study of William Sharp and Fiona Macleod,' *Twenty-seven to One*, edited by Bradford B. Broughton (The Ryan Press, 1970), pp. 26–44
HOPKINS, KONRAD, and VAN ROEKEL, RONALD, *William Sharp/Fiona Macleod*, Renfrewshire Men of Letters Series No. 2 (Renfrew District Libraries, 1977)
HOPKINS, KONRAD, and VAN ROEKEL, R., (Ed.) *The Wilfion Scripts* transmitted through the mediumship of Margo Williams (Wilfion Books, Publishers, 1980)

MACLEOD, FIONA, *Pharais* (Frank Murray, 1894)
MACLEOD, FIONA, *Reissue of the Shorter Stories of Fiona Macleod*, Vol. I Spiritual Tales, Vol. II Barbaric Tales, Vol. III Tragic Romances (Patrick Geddes and Colleagues, 1895)
MACLEOD, FIONA, *The Dominion of Dreams* (Constable, 1899)
MACLEOD, FIONA, *The Works of Fiona Macleod*, 7 Vols. Selected and Arranged by Mrs William Sharp (William Heinemann, 1910–12)
MACLEOD, FIONA, *Iona* (Floris Books, 1982)

MILLER, KARL, *Doubles* (Oxford University Press, 1985)

ROLLESTON, T. W., *Myths and Legends of the Celtic Race* (Constable, 1985)

SHARP, ELIZABETH A., *William Sharp (Fiona Macleod): A Memoir*, 2 Vols (Heinemann, 1912)

SHARP, WILLIAM, *The Human Inheritance, The New Hope, Motherhood* (Elliot Stock, 1882)

SHARP, WILLIAM, (ed.) *The Poems of Ossian*, translated by James Macpherson, (Patrick Geddes and Colleagues, 1896)

SHARP, WILLIAM, *Selected Writings of William Sharp*, 5 Vols, Selected and arranged by Mrs William Sharp (William Heinemann, 1912)

SQUIRE, CHARLES, *Celtic Myths and Legends* (Newcastle Publishing Co. Inc., 1975)

WATSON, RODERICK, *The Literature of Scotland* (Macmillan, 1984) pp. 312–13